WILLMAKER®

BY ATTORNEYS

BARBARA KATE REPA

STEPHEN ELIAS

RALPH WARNER

NOLO PRESS • BERKELEY

WILLMAKER

YOUR RESPONSIBILITY WHEN USING SELF-HELP LAW BOOKS & SOFTWARE

We've done our best to give you useful and accurate information in this software manual. But laws and procedures change frequently and are subject to differing interpretations. If you want legal advice backed by a guarantee, see a lawyer. If you use this software, it's your responsibility to make sure that the facts and general advice contained in it apply to your situation.

KEEPING UP TO DATE

To keep its books and software up to date, Nolo Press issues new printings and new editions periodically. New printings reflect minor legal changes and technical corrections. New editions contain major legal changes, major text additions or major reorganizations. To find out if a later printing or edition of any Nolo book is available, call Nolo Press at 510-549-1976 or check the catalog in the *Nolo News,* our quarterly newspaper.

To stay current, follow the Update service in the *Nolo News.* You can get a free two-year subscription by sending us the registration card included in your WillMaker package. In another effort to help you use Nolo's latest materials, we offer a 25% discount off the purchase of the new edition of your Nolo book when you turn in the cover of an earlier edition. (See the "Recycle Offer" in the back of the book.)

This manual was last revised in: **March 1996.**

Sixth Edition   MARCH 1996

Book design	Jackie Mancuso
Box design	Toni Ihara
Illustrations	Mari Stein
Proofreading	Robert Wells
Printing	Delta Lithograph

ISBN   Macintosh 0-87337-315-4

Library of Congress Card Catalog No. 84-63151

 Printed on 100% recycled paper with 25-35% post consumer waste.

For information on bulk purchases or corporate premium sales, please contact the Special Sales Department. For academic sales or textbook adoptions, ask for Academic Sales. Call 800-955-4775 or write to Nolo Press, Inc., 950 Parker Street, Berkeley, CA 94710.

WILLMAKER

ACKNOWLEDGMENTS

WillMaker originated as a joint effort by Nolo Press and Legisoft to bring self-help law into the computer age. In 1992, Nolo and Legisoft parted ways, and Legisoft is no longer involved with this product. However, Nolo acknowledges the important and original contributions of Legisoft's Jeff Scargle and Bob Bergstrom.

WillMaker 6 is the result of much labor and many laborers. We extend heartfelt thanks to the following folks.

For programming: Michael Sexton and Gloria Sadowski.

For designing, writing, editing and rewriting: Albin Renauer, Steve Elias, Barbara Kate Repa, Mary Randolph and Jake Warner.

For copious document-checking: Patti Gima.

For researching: Shae Irving.

For usability testing: Ann Heron, John O'Donnell, Eric Duong and Kevin Arndt.

For getting WillMaker into the public eye: Dayna Macy and Jennifer Spoerri.

For getting WillMaker into your local computer store: Ann Heron, Kevin Arndt and Eric Duong.

For proofreading: Robert Wells.

And a special thanks to the patient souls in Technical Support— Mark Stuhr, Gil Wilkelman and Bob Cosby.

WILLMAKER LICENSE

This is a software license agreement between Nolo Press and you as purchaser, for the use of the WillMaker program and accompanying manual. By using this program and manual, you indicate that you accept all terms of this agreement. If you do not agree to all the terms and conditions of this agreement, do not use the WillMaker program or manual, but return both to Nolo Press for a full refund.

Grant of License

In consideration of payment of the license fee, which is part of the price you paid for WillMaker, Nolo Press as licensor grants to you the right to use the enclosed program to produce wills for yourself and your immediate family, subject to the terms and restrictions set forth in this license agreement.

Copy, Use and Transfer Restrictions

The WillMaker manual and the program and its documentation are copyrighted. You may not give, sell or otherwise distribute copies of the program to third parties, except as provided in the U.S. Copyright Act. Under this license agreement, you may not use the program to prepare wills for commercial or nonprofit purposes, or use the program to prepare wills for people outside your immediate family.

Commercial Use of This Product

For information regarding commercial licensing of this product, including use by educational institutions and nonprofit organizations, call Nolo Press at (510) 549-1976.

Disclaimer of Warranty and Limited Warranty

This program and accompanying manual are sold "AS IS," without any implied or express warranty as to their performance or to the results that may be obtained by using the program.

As to the original purchaser only, Nolo Press warrants that the magnetic disk on which the program is recorded shall be free from defects in material and workmanship in normal use and service. If a defect in this disk occurs, the disk may be returned to Nolo Press. We will replace the disk free of charge. In the event of a defect, your exclusive remedy is expressly limited to replacement of the disk as described above.

Your Responsibilities for Your Documents

Although best efforts were devoted to making this material useful, accurate and up-to-date, please be aware that state laws and procedures change and may be interpreted differently. Also, we have no control over whether you carefully follow our instructions or properly understand the information in the WillMaker disk or manual.

Of necessity, therefore, Nolo Press does not make any guarantees about the use to which the software or manual are put, or the results of that use.

Any documents you make using WillMaker are yours and it is your responsibility to be sure they reflect your intentions. Have your WillMaker documents reviewed by an attorney in your state who specializes in wills and estate planning if you want a legal opinion about the effect of the documents or their legal interpretation.

Term

The license is in effect until terminated. You may terminate it at any time by destroying the program together with all copies and modifications in any form.

Entire Agreement

By using the WillMaker program, you agree that this license is the complete and exclusive statement of the agreement between you and Nolo Press regarding WillMaker.

WILLMAKER

ABOUT NOLO PRESS

The leading publisher of self-help law books and software since 1971

Nolo Press was founded in 1971 to show people how to do their own routine legal tasks and avoid costly lawyer fees. Early on, bar associations thundered against self-help law, claiming that lawyers were essential to help with even simple legal procedures. But Nolo persisted, sure that informed people armed with top-quality self-help information did not have to depend on lawyers. Over the years, more than three million customers have proven us right. Today, Nolo publishes over 70 self-help law books, audio tapes, videos and software packages—and is more committed than ever to making the law accessible.

ABOUT THE AUTHORS

Barbara Kate Repa, a Nolo author and editor, is president of the Bay Area Funeral Society and public member on the California Board of Funeral Directors and Embalmers. An advocate for the elderly, she maintains a small but tasteful shrine to Claude Pepper in her San Francisco home.

Stephen Elias practiced law in California, New York and Vermont until publishing his first Nolo book in 1982. Since then, he has written and edited more than 25 Nolo products. His hobbies include reading just about any type of book, playing tennis and taking long walks around the Sonoma County town where he lives.

Ralph Warner, who began his legal career as a legal aid attorney, is co-founder and publisher of Nolo Press. Since launching Nolo—and the self-help law movement—in 1971, Ralph has written, edited and vetted innumerable books and projects for Nolo Press. He lives bravely in Berkeley, in a house perched atop the San Andreas Fault.

ABOUT THE ILLUSTRATOR

Mari Stein is a freelance illustrator and writer who has illustrated many books for Nolo Press. She now enjoys the life of a writer/illustrator/yoga teacher/spinner in Ashland, Oregon.

WILLMAKER®

6

USERS' GUIDE

BY ELY NEWMAN & ALBIN RENAUER

PART 5

Creating Documents: The WillMaker Interviews

PART 6

Displaying and Printing Your Completed Documents

PART 7

Problems Running WillMaker

Appendix

PART 1

Introduction

Welcome to WillMaker 6 for Macintosh.

Using this program you can create three kinds of documents:

- a will
- healthcare directives in case of a terminal illness or permanent coma (also known as a "living will"), and
- a document setting out your final arrangements.

These three documents provide necessary legal instructions for family, friends and others in case of your death or permanent incapacitation.

This product is the work of a team of lawyers dedicated to making the law accessible to everyone. We've made every effort to make the program and manual thorough, accurate and easy-to-use. It has been refined through hundreds of hours of testing and use by non-lawyers to ensure you don't need a law degree to understand the information presented here.

A. About This Program

With WillMaker, you and the members of your immediate family can create these three legal documents yourselves. Although you have the option of making all three documents, you do not have to—you can easily create just the documents you want. Each kind of document serves a different purpose and is valid by itself. The table below (Section 1) describes what each kind of document is used for, and provides references to the legal section of this manual (which follows this Users' Guide) for more information.

Using WillMaker you can produce these documents in one evening, but we encourage you to relax and take your time. Remember, WillMaker doesn't charge by the hour. These are important decisions you are making. Be sure to consult the Legal Guide section of this manual and the online help that accompanies every screen if you have any questions about the law, or how to use this program. You can stop work at any time and pick up again where you left off.

1. What You're About to Do

After you install the program and start it up, you'll receive a brief orientation on how to use the program. Then you'll be asked to enter your name. This creates your first WillMaker "portfolio"—the computer file that stores your three documents.

DOCUMENTS IN YOUR WILLMAKER PORTFOLIO

Document	What It Can Do

Will

Legal Guide Chapters 1 through 12

- Leave property to family, friends and organizations
- Name alternate beneficiaries
- Name a guardian to care for your minor children
- Arrange for management of property you leave to minors
- Designate a personal representative (executor)
- Cancel debts others owe you
- Specify how debts and taxes you owe are to be paid

Healthcare Directives

Legal Guide Chapter 13

- Instruct healthcare providers as to what life-prolonging treatments you want if you are:
  — close to death from a terminal condition
  — in a permanent coma
  — pregnant when in a terminal condition or in a coma
- Name a trusted person to see that your wishes are carried out

Final Arrangements

Legal Guide Chapter 14

- Describe any organ or body donations you have made
- State your preferences about body burial or cremation
- Specify any ceremonies you want held
- Name a trusted person to see that your wishes are carried out

IF YOU MADE A WILL USING A PREVIOUS VERSION OF WILLMAKER

WillMaker 6 can convert portfolio files created with WillMaker 5, but can only convert the data from your healthcare directives and final arrangements documents. It cannot convert any data you entered to make your will.

The will in WillMaker 6 contains several new options not found in the WillMaker 5 will. These enhancements, unfortunately, make it impossible to convert the data from wills created with WillMaker 5. This means that in order to use the new features in the WillMaker 6 will, you must make a new will and enter this data again.

We believe that benefits of the new options in WillMaker 6 outweigh the inconvenience of reentering your will data. Take the time to check out the new options available in the WillMaker 6 will, and see if you don't agree.

Note Converting a WillMaker 5 portfolio file to WillMaker 6 format does not destroy the original file. The converted portfolio is saved as a new file, leaving the original file intact. If you are not yet ready to remake your will, or if you only want to make minor revisions to your existing will, be sure to keep a copy of the WillMaker 5 application on your hard disk so that you can edit your version 5 portfolio file.

For more information on converting WillMaker 5 portfolio files to version 6 files, read Part 3, Section C.

Once your portfolio is created, you come to a screen where you choose which of the three documents that make up your portfolio you want to work on.

Making your documents with WillMaker is like being interviewed. Each document has its own set of interview questions, and the answers you give determine what questions you'll be asked next. You can start or stop an interview any time you like, go back to prior questions, or switch over to another document interview at any time. In each case, when you return to a document interview, you pick up exactly where you left off.

When an interview is complete, your answers are combined with the appropriate legal language to create your document. You can then display this document on the screen and print it. You can also revisit any part of any interview to review or revise your answers.

Other members of your immediate family can make their own WillMaker portfolios and produce their own documents. However, remember that the WillMaker license restricts the use of this product to you and members of your immediate family.

2. What's New in WillMaker 6 for Macintosh

We've updated the program to take into account changes in the law in all states. The will interview has been revised to offer more options, especially for families. In addition, we've added many features that make WillMaker 6 even more comprehensive, flexible and easy-to-use.

Will

- You are offered new options that let you tailor your will to meet the needs of your particular family situation (whether you're married, how many children you have, their ages), including setting up a "pot trust." (See Legal Guide, Chapter 6.)

- You can print a letter of instruction to your personal representative (executor) describing his or her responsibilities. (See Legal Guide, Chapter 7.)

- You have more flexibility in naming alternate beneficiaries, trustees and property guardians for minors, and personal representatives (executors). (See Legal Guide, Chapters 6 and 7.)

Healthcare Directives

- You can specify special instructions that should be followed if you become terminally ill or comatose while pregnant. (See Legal Guide, Chapter 13, Section L.)

Program Features

- Legal help and program help have been revised, making it easier to get the kind of help you need. (See Users' Guide, Part 4.)
- An online version of this manual gives you point-and-click access to the information you'll need, when you need it. (See Users' Guide, Part 4.)
- A personal information feature lets you:
  — keep track of important information about the people you name in your will (see Users' Guide, Part 5, Section D)
  — re-enter previously used names without retyping them (see Users' Guide, Part 5, Section D).
- Optional password protection lets you restrict access to your personal portfolio. (See Users' Guide, Part 3, Section A4.)
- A "where am I?" feature tells you where you are in the interview process, what you've done, and what remains to be done. (See Users' Guide, Part 5, Section B3.)

B. About This Manual

The manual is divided into two main parts.

The first part, the Users' Guide, explains how to use the WillMaker computer program.

The second part, the Legal Guide, contains legal information. It explains:

- how to write your will and plan your estate
- the different purposes and effects of your will, healthcare directives and final arrangements document
- the peculiarities of your state's laws, and
- when you should consult a lawyer.

Ideally, you should read and understand the Legal Guide before you begin using the WillMaker computer program. If you have questions while running WillMaker on how to operate the program or on legal issues you need to consider while creating these documents, you can refer to the program's online Help system. (For more on using WillMaker's Help system, see Part 4.)

If you have a problem operating WillMaker that you can't solve after consulting both online help and the Users' Guide, take a short break from the keyboard and read Part 7, Section A.

If the problem continues, you can call Nolo Technical Support. (See Part 7, Section B.)

Typeface Conventions

This manual provides instructions on menus to select, buttons to click and keys to press. To make these instructions easier to follow, we use the following typeface conventions:

- KEYS that you are supposed to press are in SMALL CAPS.
- Key combinations are written COMMAND-O, which means "hold down the COMMAND key while pressing the O key."
- Names of **buttons** are in **bold** type, such as **OK** and **Continue**.

- The first letter on names of Menus and Menu Commands are capitalized, such as the New command from the File menu.
- Names of specific WillMaker screens are in quotation marks, such as the "Documents in Your Portfolio" screen.

C. System Requirements

To run WillMaker 6 for Macintosh, you need the following:

- 4 megabytes (MB) of RAM (Random Access Memory)
- a hard disk with at least 6 MB free space
- System 7 or higher
- a printer (to print out your final documents), and
- one high density floppy disk drive (for installation).

D. WillMaker 6 for Macintosh Package Contents

Your WillMaker 6 for Macintosh package should contain:

- two 3 1/2" installation disks
- this WillMaker manual
- a registration card, and
- envelopes in which to store your documents.

E. Register Your Copy

Registered owners of Nolo products receive a variety of free services and benefits.

But to provide these services, we need to know who you are. Please take the time now to complete and mail the registration card. You'll find it in the package this product came in.

No postage is necessary; just complete the card and mail it in. We also would appreciate any comments you have on our product. We read every comment on every registration card.

F. The *Nolo News*

As a registered user of a Nolo Press product, you will receive a free, two-year subscription to the *Nolo News*, our quarterly publication.

The *Nolo News* contains:

- articles on estate planning, consumer law, personal finance, small business law and other topics of interest

- the latest product news

- significant law changes (if any) that affect WillMaker users

- Nolo's famous lawyer jokes column, and

- a complete catalog of all our books and software.

If you buy other Nolo products or upgrade this product in the two-year period, you get two more years free. If your free period runs out, another two-year subscription costs $12.

G. Customer Service

Phone 510-549-1976

Hours 7 A.M. to 6 P.M. Pacific Time, Monday through Friday

E-mail NoloInfo@nolo.com

Nolo Customer Service representatives can answer questions on product availability, prices, software upgrades, product features, customer registration, policies, procedures and other non-technical topics.

Change of Address

If you move, please send a letter with both your old and new addresses and, if possible, the mailing code on your *Nolo News* mailing label to:

> Customer Service
> Nolo Press
> 950 Parker Street
> Berkeley, CA 94710-9867
> ATTN: CHANGE OF ADDRESS

Defective or Damaged Products

If you are a registered user and either of your disks is damaged or defective, we'll replace it free of charge. Send the defective disk and a brief explanation to:

> Customer Service
> Nolo Press
> 950 Parker Street
> Berkeley, CA 94710-9867
> ATTN: REPLACEMENT DISK

H. Technical Support

Nolo Press offers free technical support to registered WillMaker users.

Phone   510-549-4660

Hours   9 A.M. to 5 P.M. Pacific Time, Monday through Friday

E-mail   NoloTec@nolo.com

If you have technical questions or problems operating this program, read Part 7, Section B, before contacting the Nolo Technical Support Department.

PART 2

Installing and Starting WillMaker

A. Installing WillMaker

You will need approximately 6 MB of free space on your hard disk to install WillMaker 6 for Macintosh and its accompanying help files.

   To install WillMaker:

1. Start up your Macintosh.

2. Insert WillMaker Disk 1 into your floppy disk drive.

3. Double-click the **Installer** icon.

4. Follow the instructions that appear on screen.

5. When installation is finished, eject the WillMaker floppy disk by dragging it into the Trash.

6. Double-click the **WillMaker 6** folder icon to open it. You should see this:

7. Double-click the **Read Me First i**con to read important information that didn't make it into this Users' Guide. You can print the Read Me First file by choosing Print... from the File menu.

8. Double-click the **WillMaker 6** application icon to start the program.

READ THE READ ME FILE

The WillMaker 6 folder that's created upon installation contains a file called Read Me First. Double-click on the **Read Me First** icon to see important information that didn't make it into this manual.

You should read this file *before* you start up WillMaker.

B. Starting WillMaker

Once you've installed WillMaker on your hard disk, you're ready to start the program.

To start WillMaker:

1. Start up your Macintosh.

2. Open the folder that contains the WillMaker 6 application by double-clicking it.

3. Double-click the **WillMaker 6** application icon.

The program will start and you should see the opening screen shown below. If the opening screen doesn't appear, consult Part 7 of the Users' Guide.

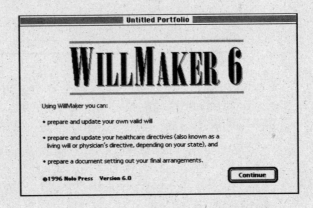

BEFORE YOU BEGIN USING WILLMAKER 6

Before you begin using the program and creating your documents, we strongly advise you to:
- read the Legal Guide section of this manual to learn about the documents you are about to create
- read Part 3 of the Users' Guide to learn how to work with WillMaker portfolio files, and
- read Part 5 of the Users' Guide when you're ready to start making documents.

C. Quitting WillMaker

You can quit WillMaker by:

- choosing Quit from the File menu (COMMAND-Q).

If you've made any changes since the last time your portfolio data file was saved, these changes will be automatically saved if the Automatically Save Changes feature is on. (See Part 3, Section A3.) If you try to quit when Automatically Save Changes is turned off, you'll be asked whether you want to save your changes before quitting.

PART 3

Working With WillMaker Portfolio Files

All of the data you enter to create WillMaker documents is stored on your hard disk in your "portfolio." This chapter explains how to create and work with WillMaker portfolio files.

A. Creating and Using Portfolios Files

Once you've started the program and gone through some introductory screens, you will be asked to create your first portfolio—the file that contains the set of three documents you'll produce.

You create your portfolio by entering your name when you get to the screen shown here:

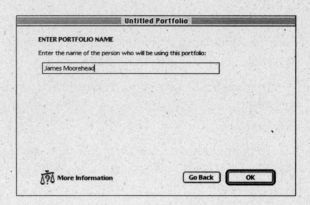

Type your full name, then click **OK** or press RETURN. If the Automatically Save Changes option is on (see Section 3, below), you'll then see a standard Macintosh save file dialog box. If the Automatically Save Changes option is off, you won't see the save file dialog box until you choose Save or Quit from the File menu.

Unless you specify otherwise, the portfolio file will be named "Portfolio of [the name you previously entered]" and stored in the WillMaker 6 application folder on your hard disk.

Click **Save** in the dialog box to create the portfolio file. The portfolio name now appears in the title bar of the WillMaker program window.

If you need to create more than one portfolio, see Section 1, below.

If you are upgrading to WillMaker version 6 and want to work on a portfolio file you created using version 5, see Section C, below.

1. Creating Additional Portfolios

You can create as many WillMaker portfolios as you want. However, WillMaker and its manual are copyrighted, and the licensing agreement prohibits you from preparing wills for people outside your immediate family or for commercial or nonprofit purposes. (If you are interested in licensing WillMaker for commercial or nonprofit purposes, see the WillMaker License in the front of this manual.)

To make a will for another person in your immediate family, including your spouse, domestic partner, children or parents, you must make a new portfolio.

To do this, choose New from the File menu (COMMAND-N). If a portfolio is already open, you'll be asked to close it before you can open a new one.

You will then go through the program's opening sequence of orientation screens before you are asked to enter the new portfolio's name, as described above.

2. Opening Previously Created Portfolios

VERSION 5 WILLS CAN'T BE CONVERTED TO VERSION 6

If you are upgrading from WillMaker version 5, read Section C for important information about opening WillMaker 5 portfolio files.

To open a portfolio that you created earlier with this program:

1. Choose Open... from the File menu (COMMAND-O). If a portfolio file is already open, you'll be prompted to close it before you can open a different file.

    You'll then see a standard Macintosh open file dialog box that lists the portfolios that are stored in the WillMaker 6 folder.

2. Select the portfolio you want to open by clicking it.

3. Click **Open**.

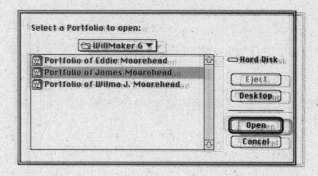

If you have not yet started WillMaker, you can open a portfolio by double-clicking its icon in the WillMaker 6 application folder. This will launch WillMaker and display the "Documents in Your Portfolio" screen listing the status of the documents in that portfolio. (See Section B2, below.)

3. Saving Your Data

There are two ways to save the data you enter into your portfolio file as you work on it:

- automatically, or
- manually.

To automatically save your file and any changes made to it, leave the Automatically Save Changes command in the File menu turned on. When you start up WillMaker for the first time, this feature is on—so if you open the File menu you'll see a check mark next to this command. You can turn Automatically Save Changes off by selecting it; when turned off, the check mark no longer appears. We strongly suggest you leave it turned on.

If Automatically Save Changes is turned off, choose Save from the File menu (COMMAND-S) to manually save your file and any changes made to it. The Save command is available only if Automatically Save Changes is turned off.

4. Protecting Your Portfolio With a Password

To make sure no one else can gain access to your portfolio file, you can lock it by assigning a password. To lock a portfolio file, choose Lock Portfolio from the File menu, and enter the password you want to use.

 Remember Your Password

Once locked, your portfolio file cannot be opened without first entering the correct password. It is your responsibility to remember the password. While you can later unlock your file (by choosing Unlock Portfolio from the File menu) or change its password (by choosing Change Portfolio Password from the File menu), you can only do so while the file is open.

B. The Documents in Your Portfolio

Once you have created your WillMaker portfolio, you will see a list of documents in your portfolio:

- your will
- your healthcare directives, and
- your final arrangements document.

These documents are described in more detail in Part 5, Section A.

To work on a document, click on its name, then click **OK** or press RETURN. You'll then begin the interview for that document.

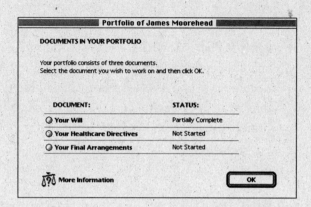

1. Switching Between Document Interviews in Your Portfolio

To return to the "Documents in Your Portfolio" screen at any time, choose Switch to Another Document from the Document menu. You can switch to a different document interview even if you haven't finished the interview for the document you're working on. When you re-enter a document interview that you've already started, you pick up right where you left off.

2. Your Document Status

The "Documents in Your Portfolio" screen shows the status of each document interview in the currently opened portfolio.

- **Not Started** You haven't started this document interview. If you select this document, you will see a few orientation screens that will familiarize you with what you are about to do. Then your interview will begin.

- **Partially Complete** You have started this document interview, but haven't completed it. When you re-enter this document interview, you will pick up where you left off previously.

- **Ready to Print**   You have completed the interview for this document and have entered enough information to print out a complete document. If you re-enter this document interview, you will go directly to a "Congratulations" screen, from which you can display, print or export your document, or review and modify the answers you gave in your interview. (See Part 6.)

C. Working With Portfolio Files Created With WillMaker 5

If you are upgrading from WillMaker for Macintosh version 5, read this section before using this new version of WillMaker to open a WillMaker 5 portfolio file.

YOUR WILL DATA IS NOT CONVERTED

As discussed in Part 1, Section A2, new options in the WillMaker 6 will make it impossible to convert the data from wills created with WillMaker 5.

- To take advantage of these new features, you must re-enter your data and make a new will using WillMaker 6.
- If you are not ready at this time to remake your will, or if you only want to make minor revisions to your existing will, keep a copy of the WillMaker 5 application on your hard disk so that you can edit your version 5 portfolio file.

We believe the benefits of the new options in WillMaker 6 far outweigh the inconvenience of re-entering your will data. Take the time to check out the new options available in the WillMaker 6 will—as you already know, it doesn't take very long to create a WillMaker document.

1. How to Open a Version 5 File

To open a WillMaker 5 file:

1. Choose Open… from the File menu.

   You'll then see a standard Macintosh open file dialog box asking you to select a file to open.

2. Locate and select the WillMaker 5 file you want to convert. (It is probably in the WillMaker 5 application folder.)

3. Click **Open**.

   You'll then see a prompt stating that your version 5 portfolio file has been converted.

4. Click **OK**.

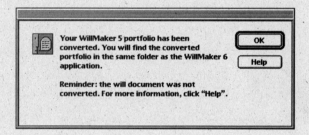

The newly converted data is automatically saved in a new WillMaker 6 file that is located in the same folder as the WillMaker 6 application.

2. Your Documents After Conversion

Your **healthcare** and **final arrangements** data is saved to the converted version 6 portfolio file. When you open the converted version 6 portfolio, the status of these documents is "Partially Complete" on the "Documents in Your Portfolio" screen. (See Section B2, above.) Review all the information entered in the document interview before using version 6 to print out and sign these documents.

As described in Section 1, above, your **will** data is not saved to the converted version 6 portfolio. That's why the status of your will is "Not Started" on the "Documents in Your Portfolio" screen. (See Section B2, above.)

D. Backing Up Your WillMaker Portfolio Files

As with all important computer files, you should keep an extra copy of your WillMaker portfolio files on a floppy disk, stored in a safe place, in case something should happen to the files on your hard disk. (You can reinstall the WillMaker program from the installation disks that came in this package.)

To back up a WillMaker portfolio file to a floppy disk:

1. Quit WillMaker by choosing Quit from the File menu (COMMAND–Q), and return to the Finder.

2. Locate the folder that contains the WillMaker 6 application.

3. Open the folder (if it's not already open) by double-clicking its icon.

4. Insert a floppy disk into your floppy disk drive.

5. Select the portfolio you want to copy by clicking once on it. If you want to copy several portfolios, hold down the SHIFT key and click on the additional portfolios you want to copy.

6. Drag the selected files onto the floppy disk icon.

When the files are copied, remove the floppy disk and store it in a safe place.

PART 4

Using Online Help

WillMaker 6's Help system offers three different kinds of assistance:

*   context-sensitive help for every WillMaker screen, explaining the legal and practical aspects of making and maintaining your documents (Section B)

*   an online version of the Legal Guide section of this manual (Sections B3 and D), and

*   an online version of the Users' Guide section of this manual (Sections C and D).

WILLMAKER'S HELP MENU

Appendix A at the end of this Users' Guide contains a complete listing of the commands and functions in WillMaker's Help menu, and all the other WillMaker menus as well.

A. Elements of the WillMaker Help System

In this section, you'll get a brief tour of some of the features included in the WillMaker for Macintosh help system. As discussed above, WillMaker's help system has three parts: context-sensitive help, the Legal Guide and the Users' Guide.

Menu bar
See Section 1

Button bar
See Section 2

Hypertext links
See Section 3

Title bar

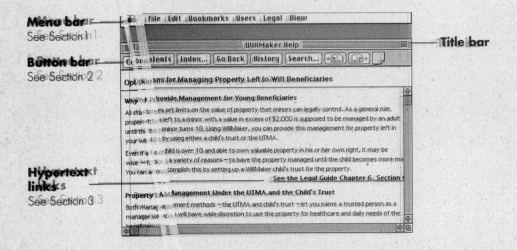

1. The Menu Bar

When a WillMaker help topic is on top, the menu bar changes.

The menus in the WillMaker Help system's menu bar contain many useful features:

File   Lets you print help topics, open and close the help file, and quit the WillMaker Help system.

Edit   Lets you copy help topic text into your clipboard and edit "sticky" notes you've attached to help topic.

Bookmarks   Lets you set a bookmark at the current help topic for fast and easy reference.

Users   Lets you access a specific chapter in the online Users' guide.

Legal   Lets you access a specific chapter in the online Legal guide.

View   Lets you hide or show the "sticky" notes you've added and change which help window is "on top."

Note Some menus in the WillMaker Help system's menu are only available from the main WillMaker Help window and cannot be accessed if the Table of Contents help window (see Sections B3 and C, below) is "on top."

2. The Button Bar

Use the WillMaker Help's main button bar to:

• view the main table of **contents** of the WillMaker Help system

- use an "electronic" **index** to find information in the online WillMaker manual (see Section D)

- **go back** to help topics you've viewed previously

- view the **history** of your help session—a sequential list of the help topics you've previously displayed

- **search** the online version of the WillMaker manual for a specific word or phrase (see Section D)

- browse the **previous** or **next** section of the online version of the WillMaker manual (see Section D)

- annotate help topics with "sticky" notes.

ANNOTATING HELP TOPICS WITH STICKY NOTES

To add a note to any help topic:

1. Click on the yellow **Notepad** in the button bar and drag it to the desired location in the current help topic.
2. Release the mouse button. Notice the cursor is flashing inside the Notepad.
3. Begin typing your notes—the **Notepad** gets bigger as you type. Since it does not automatically wrap the text, you'll need to press the RETURN key to continue typing on a new line. While the cursor is flashing inside the **Notepad**, you can access the standard text editing commands (Undo, Cut, Paste, Clear and Select All) found in the Edit menu.
4. When you're done typing, click outside the **Notepad** to save your notes.

You can hide or show your notes by choosing Show Notes from the View menu. A checkmark indicates that notes are shown; no checkmark means they are hidden.

To delete a note, use your mouse to grab and drag it back over the **Notepad** in the button bar. When the "hand" changes to a "trash can," release the mouse button.

3. Links to Other Related Topics

WillMaker help topics contain references to other related topics. For example, each context-sensitive help topic refers to more detailed discussions found in the online Legal Guide. (See Section B3.) These blue, underlined cross-references are hypertext links to jump from one help topic to another, making it easy to find all relevant information.

To view a related topic, just click on the underlined text that refers to it.

B. Getting More Information: Legal Help

Now that you're familiar with the Help system, let's see how to use it to assist you while answering interview questions.

1. Getting More Information for the Current Screen

WillMaker's Help system is context-sensitive. It "knows" what interview question you're working on and provides information to help you with the decisions you are about to make, such as whether you need to name an alternate beneficiary or which form of property management to set up.

To get more information about the screen you're currently working on:

* choose Help for This Screen from the Help menu (COMMAND-H), or
* click the **More Information** button at the lower left corner of the interview screen.

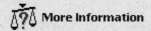 **More Information**

2. Using Screens That List Legal Topics

As you use WillMaker, you'll periodically encounter "More Information" screens. Such screens list the various legal help topics pertaining to the part of the interview you're about to work on. For example, during the will interview, before you are asked to make some choices about naming personal representatives, you'll see a screen entitled "More Information on Personal Representatives."

To view a help topic listed on a More Information screen, click on the listed topic.

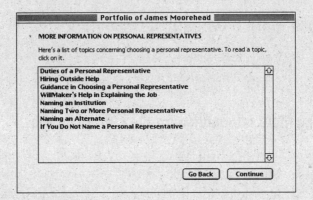

3. Viewing the Legal Guide Online

For even more detailed legal information, you can access an online version of the Legal Guide portion of the WillMaker manual.

To view the online Legal Guide:

1. Choose Legal Manual from the Help menu. You'll then see two windows: the Table of Contents window on the left and the main WillMaker Help window.

2. In the Table of Contents window, click on the chapter you want to read to view a list of topics (sections) in that chapter.

3. Click on an underlined topic to display it in the main WillMaker Help window on the right.

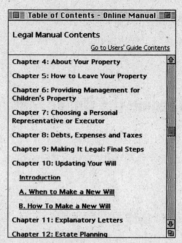

4. When finished, click the close box on the Help window, then click on the main WillMaker interview screen to bring it to the front.

    For additional tips on using the online legal guide, see Section D, below.

C. Getting Program Help on How to Use WillMaker

If you need help on the technical aspects of using WillMaker—such as what buttons to click, menus to select or keys to press—you can refer to the online version of this Users' Guide.

To view the online Users' Guide:

1. Choose How to Use WillMaker from the Help menu. You'll then see two windows: the Table of Contents window on the left and the main WillMaker Help window.

2. In the Table of Contents window, click on the part you want to read to view a list of topics (sections) in that part.

3. Click on an underlined topic to display it in the main WillMaker Help window on the right.

4. When finished, click the close box on the Help window, then click on the main WillMaker interview screen to bring it to the front.

D. Some Tips on Reading the Online Manual

Here's some additional tips on how to find information once you've already accessed the WillMaker Help system.

PREFIXES OF HELP TOPIC NAMES

As you use the WillMaker Help system, you may see lists of the names of topics (in the Index, Search Results or History lists). To help you tell what section of the Help system a topic is from, the topic names have these prefixes:

LG   a Legal Guide topic
UG   a Users' Guide topic
CAT a Nolo Press catalog topic

---

1. The Legal and Users' Menus

- To find information in the Legal Guide, pull down the Legal menu to select the chapter you want to read. When you select a chapter from this menu, you'll see (1) a list of the topics in the chapter you selected in the Table of Contents window, and (2) the first topic in the selected chapter in the main WillMaker Help window.

- To find information in the Users' Guide, pull down the Users menu to select the chapter you want to read. When you select a part from this menu, you'll see (1) a list of the topics in the part you selected in

the Table of Contents window and (2) the first topic in the selected
chapter in the main WillMaker Help window.

- When you're reading a Users' Guide or Legal Guide topic—and both
  a Table of Contents window and a WillMaker Help topic window are
  open—you many not be able to see the main WillMaker screen.
  That's because it's behind the Help windows.

  — When you're done reading a Users' Guide or Legal Guide topic,
    click the **close box** at the top of the Table of Contents window.
    Then click the main WillMaker interview screen to bring it back
    on top.

  — If you want to keep the WillMaker application and WillMaker
    Help windows open, use the Finder menu to switch back and
    forth between WillMaker and Help.

- While reading the manual on screen, use the **previous** and **next**
  buttons (with the open book icons) in the button bar to read the
  other sections of the current chapter or part. (See Section A2.)

2. Using the Manual's Electronic Index

To make it easy to look up information, we've included an "electronic"
version of the index found in the back of the WillMaker manual.

To use the online manual's index.

1. Click the **Index...** button to open the Index dialog box.

2. There are two ways to search for an indexed keyword or phrase:

   — scroll through the Index to look for your subject of interest, or

   — type in your subject of interest. As you type each letter, the
     indexed keyword or phrase that most closely matches what
     you've typed is highlighted in the Keyword column of the Index.

   To the right of each indexed keyword or phrase is the name of the
   topic it is discussed in (whether it's from the Legal Guide, Users'

Guide, the chapter and section). If the same topic is listed more than once, it means that this keyword is discussed in several places in the same topic.

3. When you find the indexed keyword you're after, double-click on it, or select it and then click the **Go To Topic** button.

Note The **Index...** button can only be used to find information in the online legal and users' manuals. The Index does not include context-sensitive help topics.

3. Searching for a Specific Word or Phrase

You can search the entire text of the online manual for a specific word or phrase. WillMaker Help will instantly find all topics containing your search keyword or phrase.

1. Click the **Search...** button on the WillMaker Help button bar to open the Search dialog box.

2. In the "Search For" field, type the word or words you want to search for, then click the **Search** button.

3. The Search Results dialog box appears listing all topics—in the Legal Guide, Users' Guide and Nolo catalog—that contain the search keyword or phrase. To jump to a listed topic, double-click it, or select it and then click the **View Topic** button in the Search Results dialog box.

The Search Results dialog box will stay on screen, so you can jump to every topic containing your search word or phrase. When you display a topic found in your search, all instances of the search word are highlighted.

Note The **Search** button can only be used to find information in the online legal and users' manuals. Context-sensitive help topics are not searched.

PART 5

Creating Documents:
The WillMaker Interviews

WE CAN'T EMPHASIZE THIS ENOUGH

The documents you are about to create are important legal documents. You won't be able to make informed decisions along the way unless you are familiar with the information discussed in the Legal Guide.

You may be used to consulting help only if you get stuck at some point in the program. But WillMaker's context-sensitive help system contains important information that every user must understand to use the program successfully.

- Click the **More Information** button on the lower left of the screen before you answer an interview question.
- Make use of screens that list related help topics (see Part 4, Section B) by reading all relevant topics before you going on to the next screen.
- If you need additional legal help, refer to the Legal Guide section of this manual. (You can read it on screen by choosing Legal Guide from the Help menu.)
- Read over each answer carefully before you confirm it by clicking **OK**. While you can always go back and change your answer, it's better to do it correctly the first time.

A. An Overview of the Three Document Interviews

WillMaker interviews you to get the information it needs to correctly generate your documents. There are three separate interviews, one for each document in your portfolio.

The **will** interview asks you about yourself, your family, your spouse (if any) and about what property you want to go to whom. If you give property to minors, you're asked who should take care of their property until they are old enough to manage it themselves. If you have children, it asks who you want to be their guardian while they are minors. You're also given a chance to forgive debts that people may owe to you, and to name a personal representative (executor) to make sure your property is distributed according to the wishes expressed in your will.

The **healthcare directives** interview asks you to set out specific instructions about the types of medical care you want should you be diagnosed as having a terminal condition or being in a permanent coma. Individual life-sustaining procedures are listed on the screen and described in the corresponding help topics for these screen. You can pick and choose which life-sustaining procedures you'd like, or simply indicate you'd like all or none of the life-sustaining procedures administered. You can also name a representative who can supervise your directions to your healthcare providers based on the document you produce with WillMaker.

The **final arrangements** interview asks you about your preferences and prior arrangements for your burial or cremation and accompanying ceremonies, and about any arrangements you may have made regarding organ donation.

You can start or stop an interview at any time, or switch between interviews by choosing Switch to Other Document from the Document menu. However, we suggest that you work on one interview at a time so as not to get confused.

B. Navigating Through Interview Screens: The Basics

In this section, you'll learn how to navigate through the interview by moving from screen to screen, and how to keep track of where you are in the interview process.

1. Moving to the Next Screen

Some screens don't request any input from you, but provide important information. Read the information, and then move on to the next screen by clicking **Continue** or pressing RETURN.

At other screens, you must make a choice, answer a question or enter some information before you can proceed. When you've given your answer, click **OK** to confirm your answer(s) and continue with the interview.

DEFAULT BUTTONS

OK   Continue

Whenever you see a button with a heavy black outline, most often the **OK** or **Continue** button, this is the default button. To activate the default button you can click it or press RETURN. For example, on the screen in which you choose your state, the **OK** button is surrounded by a thick black outline. So, if you press RETURN you move to the next screen and continue the interview.

LEAVING A QUESTION UNANSWERED

At times during the interview, the information requested is optional. You can leave your answer blank and continue on to the next screen.

Some screens require you to enter the requested information before you can continue on to the next one—you will not be able to leave these screens blank. If you are unable to or don't want to answer yet, you can:

- answer as best you can now, and return later to change it
- switch to another document by choosing Switch to Another Document from the Document menu, or
- quit the program (COMMAND-Q) and return to it later.

The next time you return to this document, the interview picks up where it last ended.

2. Moving Back to a Previous Screen

If you want to refer back to a previous part of the interview or change a previous answer, click the **Go Back** button at the lower right. That button takes you back one screen at a time. Keep clicking that button until you see the screen you want.

> **Go Back**

When you return to a screen where you made a choice or entered data, your answer is displayed.

If you change an answer and try to go back before confirming the new answer (by clicking **OK**), you'll see this warning:

> ⚠ Any changes or additions you have made on this screen will be ignored if you go back now.
>
> Are you sure you want to go back?
>
> Cancel　　OK　　Help

Note A few screens don't have a **Go Back** button. You cannot move backwards from these screens.

3. Keeping Track of Where You Are in the Document Interview

As you go through the WillMaker interview, you can see a "progress" report by choosing Where Am I? from the Document menu. You'll see a listing of the parts of the interview you're currently doing that tells you

*   what part you're at now
*   what parts you've completed
*   what parts remain before your documents can be assembled.

    Click on any part to view more detailed information about that part.

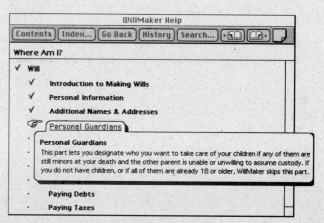

C. Answering Multiple Choice Questions

Many of the interview questions are multiple choice—two or more options are listed and you must select one or more answers. You can make your choice(s) by selecting one *radio button*, one item from a *list* or one or more *check boxes*.

To choose an answer with a *radio button*, click on it. A black dot in the option button next to your choice indicates that it's been selected. You must choose one of the options before you can continue with the interview.

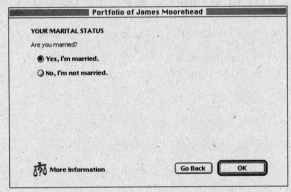

On the screen where you select your state, make your choice by

- double-clicking your state in the *list*, or
- clicking your state and then clicking **OK**.

Use the scroll bar or ARROW KEYS to see the entire list.

If you are not using a mouse, use the ARROW keys to select the item of your choice, then press the RETURN key.

You can select only one state. If you click on a different state, or highlight it by pressing an arrow key, your first choice is de-selected.

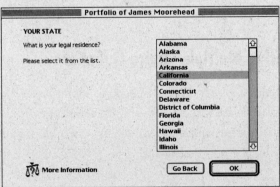

A few WillMaker screens have *check boxes* you can use to choose one or more of several options offered. Clicking on a check box marks the box with an X, or clears the X if it is already checked.

Remember that clicking another check box does not de-select a previous choice. You must select or de-select each choice one at a time. When you are sure your choices are correct, click on the **OK** button or press the RETURN key.

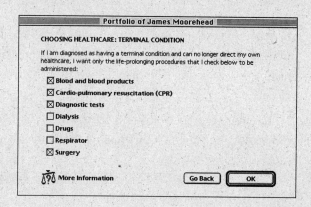

D. Entering Information

Some screens require you to type in information—a name, address, fraction, date or description of an item of property. At these screens, the box where you enter the requested information has a flashing cursor in it.

FOLLOW THE INSTRUCTIONS ON EACH SCREEN

This section contains general information on how to enter different kinds of information on a variety of screens. Each WillMaker screen, however, includes specific instructions for the type of information required—such as entering fractional shares or entering more than one name on separate lines. Be sure to read each screen's instructions on how to enter the requested information.

Note In addition to the screens discussed in this section, the will interview has a variety of screens where you enter information by creating and selecting from lists. These lists are discussed in Section E, below.

To enter your answer, just start typing. When you're done, confirm your answer by clicking **OK** pressing the RETURN key.

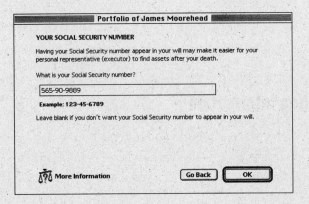

USING STANDARD EDITING COMMANDS

When the cursor is flashing in a text-entry box, you can use the standard text-editing commands included in WillMaker's Edit menu. (See the Appendix A at the end of this Users' Guide.)

1. Text-Editing Basics

Follow these general instructions on entering, deleting and editing your answers in text-entry boxes included on WillMaker interview screens.

To enter text in a text-entry box:

1. Click in the text box if the cursor is not already flashing in it.
2. Start typing. The text you type will be inserted at the location of the flashing cursor.

To delete your answer:

1. Select by clicking and dragging the mouse across the text you want to delete.
2. With the text still selected, press the DELETE key on the keyboard.

To edit your answer:

1. Place the cursor at the position you want to start editing by clicking the mouse there.
2. Start typing. The characters you type will be inserted at the location of the flashing cursor.

Note You can also use the DELETE key to make minor changes.

CHANGING AN ANSWER AFTER YOU HAVE LEFT THE SCREEN

If you have already answered an interview screen but want to change your answer, click the **Go Back** button until you are back at that screen. The cursor will be flashing at the beginning of the field containing your answer.

After you change your answer, click the **OK** button to confirm your new answer and move forward.

Note If "*BLANK*" appears in the text-entry box (because you chose not to answer the question), make sure that it's been deleted entirely before entering a new answer.

You can also review and change answers at the end of the interview, as described in Part 6, Section D.

2. Entering Names

Throughout WillMaker's interviews, you are asked to type in names—of family members, friends you want to inherit your property, etc. On some screens, you have the option of pasting in a name you entered previously, rather than retyping it. (See Section b, below).

a. Basic Rules for Entering Names

Follow these rules when entering names:

- Use full names, first name first.
- Use only one name for a person or organization.
  - If, for example, you use both a full name (or title) and a nickname (or abbreviation), the program assumes they are different and adds both to the Names List.
  - If you type in the same name, but with different capitalizations, you'll be asked which capitalization is correct, and the one you choose is saved.
- Carefully check the spelling before you leave screen. WillMaker does not "recognize" different spellings for the same name—it assumes they are different people and adds both to the Names List.
- Enter only one name per line. To begin a new line for an additional name, follow the on-screen instructions. (See Starting a New Line, below.)
- Whenever possible, use the Names List to paste in names that you've entered previously.

b. Pasting Names From the Names List

All names you enter during the course of your will interview are stored in a master Names List that is part of your portfolio file.

In the will interview, after entering information about your family and residence, enter any additional names you plan on using (see Section E2, below). In the remainder of the will interview, you can use the Names List to paste in the names that you entered previously.

To paste a name from the Names List:

1. Choose Paste From Names List from the Edit menu (COMMAND-L), or click the **Names List** button (when it's available). This opens a dialog box.

2. Select the name you want to paste by clicking it. To select more than one name, hold down the COMMAND key while clicking the names.

3. Click **Paste**. The names are inserted after any names that have already been entered.

For more about using WillMaker's Names List, see Section E2, below.

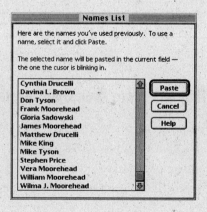

c. Starting a New Line (Multiple Names)

To answer some questions, you may need to start a new line. For example, if you want to name more than one personal representative (in the will interview), you need to enter each co-representative's name on a separate line.

To start a new line for an additional name, make sure your cursor is in the text-entry box and press RETURN.

Read the instructions on every interview screen to see whether you can enter multiple names, and how to do so.

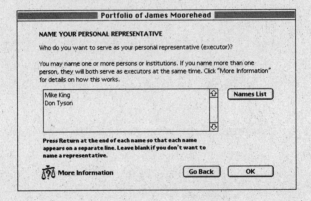

3. Answering Screens That Ask More Than One Question

While most WillMaker interview screens require you give one answer to a single question, there are screens that ask more than one related question. Such screens may have several text-entry boxes, or may be "mixed"—that is, you'll need to both enter text and select an option button.

To move to a text-entry box, just click in it or press TAB until that text-entry box is selected.

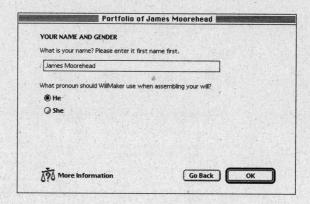

E. Using Lists in the Will Interview

Throughout the will interview, you will come across screens where your answers are compiled into a list. Such screens may include lists of names (of your children, grandchildren, or beneficiaries who may need the property you leave them managed by an older person) or of specific bequests of property.

Sometimes, you'll be adding to a blank list. Other times, you'll see a list that WillMaker compiled based on previous answers. (For example, the "List of Names" screen that appears at the end of the will interview includes every name you've entered.) You may be prompted to add to the list, or to select a listed item and enter additional information about that selection.

FOLLOW THE INSTRUCTIONS ON SCREEN

Each WillMaker list screen includes specific instructions for its use—such as how to add to a list of bequests or how to change property management arrangements for listed beneficiaries. Be sure to read the specific instructions on every WillMaker screen.

1. How to Use These Lists, Generally

When you first see a WillMaker list screen with an empty list, the default button is the **Add to List....** button.

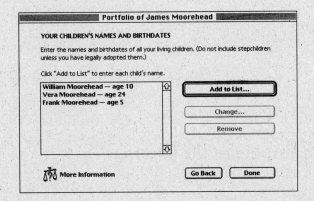

After clicking this button, you're asked to answer one or more questions in a pop-up dialog box. For example, after clicking **Add to List...** on the "Your Children's Names and Birthdates" screen, you're asked to enter the child's name, gender and date of birth.

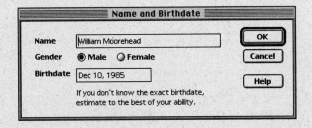

After you've entered the required information, you return to the list, which now includes the name you just entered. You can then use the other buttons on this screen to:

- **add** a new item to the list
- **change** an existing item
- **delete** an existing item from the list
- **go back** to the previous screen
- proceed to the next WillMaker interview screen when you're **done.**

To add a name, proceed or go back to another screen, click the appropriate button. If you choose to add a new item, you'll go to the same screen as when you added the first.

To change any part of your answer or delete a listed name entirely, first select it by clicking it, then click the appropriate button. If a button is dimmed and unavailable, it's because you haven't first made a selection from the list.

If the list is large, use the scroll bar or the Up and Down Arrows keys to see the entire list.

2. How WillMaker Stores Names—The Names List

All names you enter during the course of the will interview are stored in a master Names List that is part of your portfolio file.

In the will interview, after entering your name and those of your immediate family (if any), you'll see the "Other Names You Plan to Use in Your Will" screen. Although optional, we strongly urge you to use this screen to enter the names you plan on using. All names entered here, and throughout the interview, are added to the Names List.

The WillMaker's Names List:

- lets you paste a previously used name without retyping it each time you want to re-enter it (see Section D2, above)

- provides valuable information for your personal representative (executor), who will be responsible for carrying out the terms of your will (see Legal Guide, Chapter 7)

- ensures that correct pronouns are used throughout your document— that is, "she" and "her" for females, "he" and "his" for males, and "it" for organizations

- helps you make sure that:

  — you don't leave anyone out of your will by mistake, and

  — you've spelled a name the same way throughout.

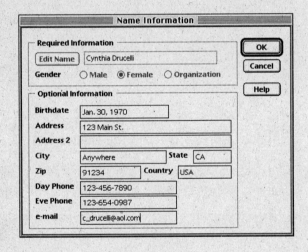

CLEANING UP THE NAMES LIST

At the end of the will interview, you'll see the "List of Names" screen. You can also display this screen by selecting **Names Entered in Your Will** at the "Review or Change Your Will" screen (see Part 6, Section D).

At this point you have the opportunity to:
- remove unused names
- make sure you've added personal information for every name, and
- update this information, if necessary.

To clean up the Names List, click the **Remove Unused Names** button. This purges the list of any names that were at one time entered but are no longer part of your will. If this button is dimmed and unavailable, it is because there are no unused names.

To make sure you've added personal information for every name you've used, or to update this information:

1. Click on the first name listed.
2. Click **Add Information...** to open the pop-up dialog box shown above.
3. Enter as much requested information as you can. When finished, click **OK**.
4. Repeat Steps 2 and 3 for every name listed.

If information about someone named in your will changes, you should update their personal information accordingly. This information will help your personal representative (executor) administer your will. (See Legal Guide, Chapter 7.)

3. Lists of Specific Bequests

In the will interview, you have the option of making specific bequests of property. There is no limit to how many separate bequests of specific personal or real property you can make in your WillMaker will. Bequests you make are compiled into a list.

For each specific bequest, enter:

- a description of the property you are leaving to the beneficiary
- the name(s) of a beneficiary(ies)
- directions for what should happen to the property if the primary beneficiary dies before you do.

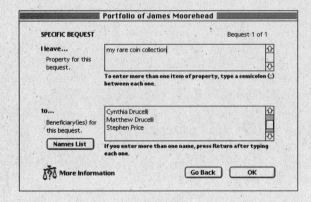

SOME TIPS ON MAKING SPECIFIC BEQUESTS

- If you want to include more than one item of property in the same bequest, type a semicolon in between each item. For example, "my Sony DAT recorder; my black leather sofa; $5000."
- If you want to name more than one person to share the same property item, enter each beneficiaries' name on a separate line. To start a new line, press RETURN before typing the next name. (You'll later be asked to designate each beneficiary's share.)
- Use the Names List to paste in a name you previously entered.

Each time you finish entering the required information, you come to the list of specific bequests you have made so far, which now includes the bequest you just made, numbered in the order you made them. To help you can keep track of what you've given to whom, you can view bequests by property or beneficiary by clicking the **Property** or **Beneficiary** button below the bequest list.

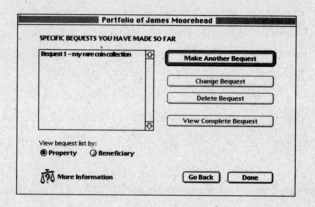

Use the other buttons on this screen to:

- **make another** bequest
- **change** the information contained in an existing bequest
- **delete** the bequest
- **view** how the bequest will be worded in your will
- **go back** to previous parts of the WillMaker interview
- proceed to the next subject of the interview when you're **done.**

To make another bequest, click the **Make Another Bequest** button, You'll repeat the series of screens you used to make your first bequest.

To change, view or delete a listed bequest, first select the bequest by clicking it, then click the appropriate button. If the **Change Bequest,**

Delete Bequest or **View Complete Bequest** button is dimmed and unavailable, it's because you haven't first made a selection from the list.

Example: Your first bequest is to leave your Barbie doll collection to your niece Gloria Sadowski. You proceed through a series of screens in which you describe the property ("my Barbie collection"), enter Gloria's name, and name who should get it if Gloria does not survive you.

When you have finished, "Bequest 1" is added to the bequest list. You can view the bequest by property (Bequest 1 - my Barbie collection), or by benefi-ciary (Bequest 1 - Gloria Sadowski). To view this bequest as it will appear in your will, select it, then click **View Complete Bequest***.*

To make another bequest, click the **Make Another Bequest** *button to cycle through the questions again. When you're finished making specific requests, click* **Done** *and continue on with the next part of the interview.*

4. Arranging Property Management for Minors and Young Adults

In the will interview, you have a chance to name who should manage the property you are leaving to beneficiaries who are too young to responsibly manage property for themselves. You will come to a list of all the beneficiaries you have named in your will.

For each young beneficiary you want to arrange property manage-ment for, you:

- select that beneficiary
- choose the kind of management you want (if your state allows more than one kind)
- enter the name of the trustee or custodian for the property the minor beneficiary will receive through your will
- name an alternate trustee or custodian, and
- specify the age at which the management terminates, if applicable.

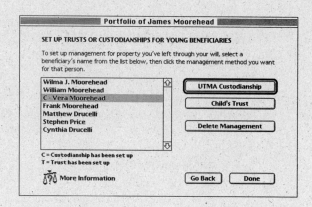

When you finish entering the required information, you'll come back to the list, which now indicates the kind of arrangement you've made for the listed beneficiary.

To delete an arrangement you've already made, select the name of the beneficiary you've made the arrangement for, then click **Delete Management**.

To proceed to the next subject of the WillMaker interview, click **Done**.

Example: Your niece Gloria's name appears on the beneficiaries list. Since the only property left to her is your Barbie collection, you decide not to arrange for management despite Gloria's age.

You do, however, want to set up a custodianship for your son Harold, who will inherit a large part of your estate. You proceed through a sequence of screens in which you

- *select Harold's name from the list*
- *click the **UTMA Custodianship** button, and*
- *name a custodian and an alternate custodian.*

*"C" now appears next to Harold's name on the list to signify that you've set up a custodianship for him. Since this is the only property arrangement you want to make, click **Done** and continue on with the next part of the interview.*

REVIEWING AND CHANGING A PROPERTY MANAGEMENT ARRANGEMENT

To review or change the details of an arrangement you've made, click the listed beneficiary's name. Then:

- if a "C" is next to the name, click **UTMA Custodianship** to review the specifics of the custodianship you've set up, or
- if a "T" is next to the name, click **Child's Trust** to review the specifics of the trust you've set up.

You can make any changes by typing in the appropriate text-entry box. Click **OK** to save your changes.

PART 6

Displaying and Printing
Your Completed Documents

Once you have entered all the information necessary to make your document, you come to a "Congratulations" screen. (The screen shown here is for the will document. The other two documents are similar.)

Portfolio of James Moorehead

CONGRATULATIONS!

Your will is complete.

> Display/Print...

> Export Document...

> Review/Change Answers

> Switch to Another Document

⚖ More Information

At this point, you can display your completed document on the screen and print it out.

A. Displaying Your Final Documents

Now you're ready to display your final document on the screen. To do this, click the **Display/Print...** button on the "Congratulations" screen.

1. What Documents Are Displayed

Each "document" that WillMaker produces is, in fact, a set of related documents.

Will	Instructions
	Will
	Self-Proving Affidavit (if applicable in your state)
	Letter to Your Personal Representative
Healthcare Directives	Instructions
	Living Will or Healthcare Directive
	Healthcare Proxy or
	Durable Power of Attorney for Healthcare
Final Arrangements	Instructions
	Final Arrangements Letter

After clicking **Display/Print...**, you'll see a listing of the documents in the document set you're working with. Make sure there's an X in the check box next to the documents you want to display, then click **OK**.

2. Viewing Your Documents

When a document is displayed in the Print Preview window, you can view each page of it, but cannot do any editing.

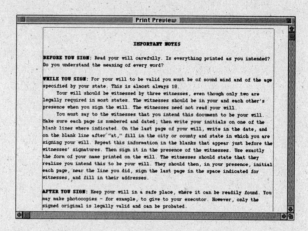

- Use the scroll bar to see the entire document.
- To close the Print Preview window and return to the "Congratulations" screen, click the **close box** at the upper-left corner of the Print Preview title bar.

WHY YOUR DOCUMENT MAY HAVE LINES OF "/////" AT THE END OF A PAGE

These "hash marks" are there as a precaution. WillMaker has built-in formatting that forces certain blocks of text to stay together on the same page.

For example, it is a requirement for making a legally valid will that a few lines setting out something of substance appear on the same page as your signature and the signatures of your witnesses. Often this results in a page break which leaves less than a full page of text on the previous page. When space is left at the bottom of the page, but there is more text of the document on the next page, it is customary to fill in the remaining "blank" lines with hash marks—the "/////" you see on the page.

This prevents someone from later tampering with your will and filling in the blank space with additional clauses after you have signed it.

While your document's displayed on screen, read it thoroughly, and make sure that the information is correct. If you'd rather proofread from paper, print a draft by choosing Print... from the File menu (see Section C, below).

- **If you want to change how the document looks,** choose Print Options... from the File menu (see Section B below).

- **If you want to change your answers,** click the **close box** at the upper-left corner. This will bring you back to the "Congratulations" screen. From there, click **Review/Change Answers** to change your answers (see Section D below).

- **If you're satisfied with the document as it is,** print it out by choosing Print... from the File menu (COMMAND-P) (see Section C, below).

B. Changing How Your Documents Look

You can change document's font, font size and page margins by choosing Print Options... from the File menu. You'll then see the print options dialog shown below.

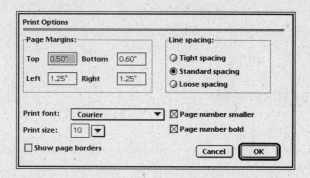

- **Page margins**   These margins are measured in inches. To fit more text on each page, decrease the margin sizes by typing in the margins you want.

- **Line spacing**   These options let you control how tightly spaced the printing of the document will be. To fit more text on a page, select **Tight spacing**.

- **Print font**   Pull down the font menu to select an available font.

- **Print size**   Pull down the size menu to select an available size for the selected font.

- **Page number smaller** and **page number bold**   Click these check boxes to change the appearance of the page number at the bottom of each page of your document.

- **Show page borders**   Click this check box to display each page of a completed document as a distinct page with margins shown as dotted lines. If the option is on and you're using a small Macintosh monitor, you may need to scroll the document to the right to see an entire line of text. This option only affects how the document is displayed on screen. You will need to close and then reopen the Print Preview window to see the effect of changing this setting.

Change the settings you want, then click **OK**. When you return to the displayed document, your changes will be reflected.

C. Printing Your Documents

You can only print a WillMaker document while it is displayed on screen. (See Section A, above, on displaying your documents.) While the Print Preview window is open, choose the Print... from the File menu (COMMAND-P).

You'll then see a standard Macintosh print dialog box. Click **OK** to print everything.

Note Entering page numbers in the **From** and **To** boxes in the printer dialog tells the program to print only the pages you specify. Keep in mind that the program counts from the first page actually printed, which will be the instruction page. Be sure to factor this in if you only want to print certain pages of a specific document.

After you print out the final documents, read the printed instructions and appropriate chapter of the Legal Guide for information on how to sign your documents and have them witnessed or notarized if necessary.

- For your will, see Chapter 9 of the Legal Guide.
- For your healthcare directions, see Chapter 13 of the Legal Guide.
- For your final arrangements, see Chapter 14 of the Legal Guide.

D. Reviewing or Changing Your Answers

If after displaying or printing your document, you find something that you want to change, click **Review/Change Answers** in the "Congratulations" screen. You will then see the "Review or Change" screen for the current document. (The screen shown here is for the will; the other two documents' screens are similar.)

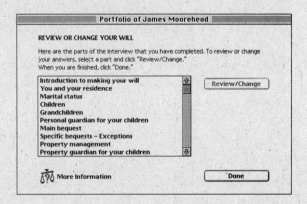

This screen lists the various parts of the WillMaker interview. To review a particular part, double-click on it, or first click on it and then click **Review/Change**.

For example, to go back to the part of the interview concerning where you live, double-click **You and your residence**. You'll return to the screen where you entered your name and gender, and your answers are shown.

If you want to change an answer, you can do so. At this point, you will cycle through the remaining screens for that section of the interview, eventually returning to the "Review or Change" screen. If, however, you have changed an answer that affects other choices you have made, such as your state of residence in your will, the program will make you review all of your answers for that document.

Use the "Review or Change" screens to update your will, healthcare directions or final arrangements whenever you deem it necessary. (See Chapter 10 of the Legal Guide for concerns about updating your will.)

IF YOU ENTERED A NEW NAME WHEN CHANGING YOUR WILL

If you added any new names when changing your will, you should use WillMaker's Names List feature to enter additional information about each new name. (See Part 5, Section D2 on using the Names List to add information about persons named in your will.) This can be done when, after making your change, you return to the "Congratulations" screen.

To add additional information for new names added while reviewing/changing your will:

1. At the "Congratulations" screen, click **Review/Change Answers**. You'll then see the "Review or Change Your Will" screen.
2. Select **Names Entered in Your Will** from the list of parts of the interview. You may need to scroll to the bottom of the list to find it.
3. Click the **Review/Change** button.
4. Click **Continue** until you reach the "List of Names" screen.
5. Select a name you just entered in the course of changing your document.
6. Click **Add Information...** to open the Name Information dialog box.
7. Enter the requested information, then click **OK** to close the dialog box and return to the "List of Names" screen.
8. Repeat Steps 5-7 for each new name entered.

E. Exporting Your Documents

You can export your completed document to a plain ASCII text (TXT) or rich text format (RTF) file on your hard disk.

There Is Really No Reason to Export Your Documents to a Text File

Most formatting, including font, font size and page margins, can be done from within WillMaker itself. (See Section B, above.) In addition, making any changes to the language of WillMaker documents can seriously affect the usefulness of your documents and create confusion, contradictions and legal problems. (See "If You Export a Document," below.)

To export your document:

1. Click the **Export Document...** button on the "Congratulations" screen. After you select which documents you want assembled, your document will be saved and you'll see the Export Document Text As dialog box.

2. Select the file format you want to export to by clicking either **Plain Text (ASCII)** or **Rich Text Format (RTF)** at the bottom of the dialog box.

3. Name the exported document text file.

4. Click **Save**.

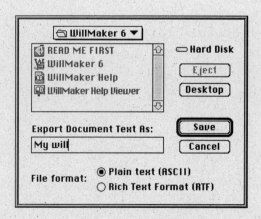

To print out the exported document, you will have to open the textfile with your word processor.

IF YOU EXPORT A DOCUMENT

- *Do not change the language of your documents under any circumstances.* If you have questions about the language in your documents, or if you would like to change the language in them, take the documents to an experienced estate planning attorney and get advice on how to accomplish your goals.
- Give each exported file a unique name (Step 3, above). If you don't, any file you have previously made with the same name will be erased.
- To use an exported file, you must use a word processing program to open it. Consult your word processor's manual if you are not sure how to do this. All word processors that can read plain text or rich text format files can load an exported file produced by WillMaker.
- Do not call Nolo Press Technical Support for instructions on how to operate your word processor. Consult the manual that came with your word processor on how to do the necessary operations.
- Carefully read any information in the exported file about how to place the proper headers and footers to correctly format your document. Be sure to delete these instructions from the exported file before printing out your final document.

PART 7

Problems Running WillMaker

A. Troubleshooting

This section of the manual briefly discusses some common technical difficulties you might encounter in running WillMaker.

On-screen help is also available by choosing How to Use WillMaker from the Help menu. If you haven't solved your problem, contact Nolo Tech Support. (See Section B, below.)

1. Problems Reading the Setup Disks

When you insert your WillMaker installation disk, you may get an alert message that says:

"The disk is unreadable: Do you want to initialize it?"

Eject the disk from the drive.

Check the disk drive by using another disk that you have used before. If the disk drive operates properly, then the installation disk you have received may be defective. To get a replacement free of charge, send the defective disk and a brief explanation to our customer service department. (See Part 1, Section G.)

2. Additional Error Messages

ERROR	WHAT IT MEANS	WHAT TO DO
The disk is write-protected.	The disk you are trying to save to is locked.	Unlock the disk by sliding back the write-protect tab so that the hole in the top corner is closed.
The disk is too full.	There is not enough space on your disk for WillMaker to save.	Delete some files on your hard disk and try again.
The disk seems to be damaged.	Something is wrong with your computer hardware.	Check out your hard disk with Apple's Disk First Aid.
A printer wasn't found. Please use the Chooser to select a printer, then try again.	In order for WillMaker to properly display a document, you must have chosen a printer.	Select a printer with the Chooser in the Apple menu.
Sorry. The clipboard contains too much text to paste into this field.	The clipboard contents won't fit in the active text edit field.	Try copying a smaller amount of text into the text field.
Sorry. The text on the clipboard contains return (new line) characters and not be pasted into this field.	The field you are trying to paste into allows only a single line of text; the text you copied contains returns.	Re-read the instructions for the current screen and type in your answer as a single line of text.
Sorry, an internal error occurred.	Something very serious is wrong with the program, either because of a disk error, memory error, or (gasp!) a bug.	Quit and restart the program and attempt to repeat what you did. The problem may clear up on its own. If not, try reinstalling the application. If that doesn't work, contact Nolo Technical Support.
Sorry, a required resource was not found.	Something very serious is wrong with the program, either because of a disk error, memory error, or (gasp!) a bug.	Quit and restart the program and attempt to repeat what you did. The problem may clear up on its own. If not, try reinstalling the application. If that doesn't work, contact Nolo Technical Support.

ERROR	WHAT IT MEANS	WHAT TO DO
Sorry. That file is damaged and cannot be opened.	Your portfolio file has been corrupted.	Use a backup file.
Sorry. The file was created by different version of Will-Maker and cannot be opened.	WillMaker 6 for Macintosh cannot read files created by WillMaker 4 or earlier.	You will have to redo your will entirely.
Sorry. That file was created with a later version of Will-Maker and cannot be read.	You are trying to open a file created by a later version of WillMaker.	Buy the upgrade.
Sorry, this file cannot be read by WillMaker.	You are trying to open or convert a file that is not recognized by WillMaker.	If you are sure the file you are attempting to use is a WillMaker data file, try a backup copy. If that doesn't work, contact Nolo Technical Support.
WillMaker can open only one document at a time; only the first document you selected will be opened.	You tried to open more than one portfolio from the Finder.	Open one portfolio at a time. Close the current file before opening another.
Sorry, you can't print a WillMaker document from the Finder.	You selected a WillMaker port-folio and chose "Print" from the Finder's File menu.	Open the portfolio from within WillMaker, and follow the interview to its end, where you are allowed to print.
There isn't enough memory to complete the operation.	The program ran out of memory.	Quit WillMaker and give it a larger memory space to work in (with the Finder's **Get Info** command).
Sorry. You are trying to open too many files at once.	Your computer has too many files open.	Try quitting other applications.
The file is locked, or is on a locked disk.	WillMaker was not allowed to open a file because it didn't have permission to open it, either because it is in use, or it is locked.	Check to make sure this disk is not locked, and the file has not been locked from the Finder.

B. Calling Nolo Press Technical Support

If you have problems that are not cleared up in the Troubleshooting section, call Nolo Press Technical Support: (510) 549-4660 between 9 A.M. and 5 P.M. Pacific Time, Monday through Friday.

When you call, try to be in front of the computer with which you are having the problem. And please have the following information ready:

- version of WillMaker *(should be 6.0 or higher)*
- the point in the program where the problem occurred .
- whether you can duplicate the problem
- version of the Macintosh you are running (which you can get by choosing About The Finder or About This Macintosh from the Apple menu when the Finder is the top application)
- the model Macintosh you are using
- the brand and model of printer—if you are having trouble printing
- amount of RAM, and
- any extensions or INITs you are running.

Appendix

A. WillMaker Menus

1. File Menu

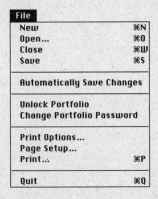

New (COMMAND-N)

Use this command to create a new WillMaker portfolio file. See Part 3, Section A1.

Open... (COMMAND-O)

Use this command to open a WillMaker portfolio file by selecting it from a file open dialog box. See Part 3, Section A2.

Close (COMMAND-W)

Use this command to close the currently opened portfolio file without exiting the program.

Save (COMMAND-S)

Use this command to manually save your currently opened portfolio file. This command is available only if there are changes to be saved. See Part 3, Section A3.

Automatically Save Changes

Selecting this item toggles the Automatically Save Changes option on or off. This option automatically saves your work each time you complete a section of the program (each "section" of the program is about three to

six screens of related information). If this option is on, a check mark
appears next to it. If it is off, no check mark appears and you must
manually save your work using the Save command in the File menu.
When you install WillMaker, this option is on. See Part 3, Section A3.

Lock/Unlock Portfolio

Use this command to lock your portfolio and give it a password. If your
portfolio is locked, no one can open it without first entering the password. If you want to unlock a file you've locked, you'll need to first
enter the password you assigned it. See Part 3, Section A4.

Change Portfolio Password

Use this command to change your password. This command is available
only if you have previously locked your portfolio. See Part 3, Section A4.

Print Options...

Use this command to change the formatting for your documents,
including page margins, line spacing, font type and font size.
We recommend keeping the default settings. See Part 6, Section B.

Page Setup...

Use this command to bring up the standard Macintosh page setup dialog
box.

Print... (Command-P)

Use this command to print out a completed WillMaker document. This
command is available only when a document is displayed in the Print
Preview window. See Part 6, SectionC.

Quit (COMMAND-Q)

Use this command to quit WillMaker. See Part 2, Section C.

2. Edit Menu

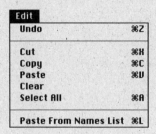

Undo (Command-Z)

Use this command to undo the last typing or editing you did, provided you haven't left the screen on which the changes were made.

Cut (Command-X)

Use this command to remove selected text and place it on the clipboard.

Copy (Command-C)

Use this command to copy selected text on the clipboard, without cutting it from the document.

Paste (Command-V)

Use this command to insert text that you have previously cut or copied at the blinking cursor, or to replace selected text with text that you have previously cut or copied.

Clear

Use this command to delete selected text without putting it on the clipboard (so the selected text will not be saved).

Select All (Command-A)

Use this command to select all the text in the currently active text field.

Paste From Names List (Command-L)

Use this command to see a list of all names you have previously entered in your documents. Pasting from the Names List ensures that names are spelled consistently throughout your documents, and helps you keep track of who you've already named. See Part 5, Sections D2 and E2.

3. Document Menu

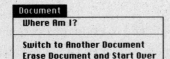

Where Am I?

Use this command to see your progress for the current document interview—where you are now, what you've done, and what remains to be done. See Part 5, Section B3.

Switch to Another Document

Use this command to change between your will, healthcare directives and final arrangements document interviews. This command takes you to the "Documents in Your Portfolio" screen, from which you select a document to switch to. See Part 3, Section B2.

Erase Document and Start Over

Use this command to erase the data in the current WillMaker document you are working on (will, healthcare directives or final arrangements) without erasing the other two documents in your portfolio.

4. Help Menu

Help
How To Use Help
Help for This Screen   ⌘H   Legal Manual
How to Use WillMaker   Keyboard Shortcuts
About Nolo Press   Nolo Press Catalog

How to Use Help

Use this command to open a help screen describing how to use the WillMaker's help system.

Help for This Screen (Command-H)

Use this command to display useful legal information so you can make informed decisions throughout the WillMaker interview. Context-sensitive legal help is available for every WillMaker 6 screen. See Part 4, Section B1.

Legal Manual

Use this command to access an online version of the Legal Guide portion of this manual. See Part 4, Section B3.

How to Use WillMaker

Use this command to access an online version of the Users' Guide portion of this manual. See Part 4, Section C.

Keyboard Shortcuts

Use this command to see how to operate the program using a keyboard rather than a mouse. See Appendix B.

About Nolo Press

Use this command to learn a little about the people who made this product, and why we do what we do.

Nolo Press Catalog

Use this command to browse through Nolo's catalog of over 100 self-help legal publications. You'll find information on prices and current editions of books, software, video and audio tapes on business, consumer and family law.

B. Keyboard Commands

1. WillMaker Menu

Press...	To...
COMMAND-O	Open an existing portfolio file.
COMMAND-N	Create a new portfolio file.
COMMAND-W	Close the current portfolio file.
COMMAND-S	Save the current portfolio file when the Automatically Save Changes function is turned off.
COMMAND-P	Print a document displayed in the Print Preview window.
COMMAND-Q	Quit WillMaker.
COMMAND-L	Open the Paste From Names List dialog box.
COMMAND-H	Open Legal Help for the current screen.
COMMAND-Z	Undo the most recent text editing you have done on the current screen if the change has not been saved yet. (Note: Undo will not revert a button selection).
COMMAND-X	Cut selected text.
COMMAND-C	Copy selected text.
COMMAND-V	Paste contents of clipboard.
COMMAND-A	Select all text in current text box.

2. Moving Around an Interview Screen

Press...	To...
RETURN	Trigger the default button (if one exists) or create another line in a text-editing box.
ENTER	Trigger the default button (if one exists).
DELETE	Delete selected text.
ESC	Trigger **Cancel**, **Close** or **No** button in pop-up dialogs.
TAB	Select text in a text-editing box or move to the next text box (if there is one).
DOWN ARROW	Scroll down a list.
UP ARROW	Scroll up a list.

3. WillMaker Help System Menus

Press...	To...
COMMAND-O	Open another help file.
COMMAND-W	Close the help file.
COMMAND-P	Print the currently displayed help topic.
COMMAND-Q	Quit the WillMaker Help system.
COMMAND-Z	Undo the most recent text editing you have done to a "sticky" note.
COMMAND-X	Cut selected text from a "sticky" note.
COMMAND-C	Copy selected text to a "sticky" note.
COMMAND-V	Paste contents of clipboard into a "sticky" note.
COMMAND-A	Select all text in "sticky" note.

WILLMAKER®

LEGAL GUIDE

CHAPTER 1

About Wills

CHAPTER 2

About WillMaker Wills

CHAPTER 3

About You and Yours

CHAPTER 4

About Your Property

CHAPTER 5

How to Leave Your Property

CHAPTER 6

Providing Management for Children's Property

CHAPTER 7

Choosing a Personal Representative or Executor

CHAPTER 8

Debts, Expenses and Taxes

CHAPTER 9

Making It Legal: Final Steps

CHAPTER 10

Updating Your Will

CHAPTER 11

Explanatory Letters

CHAPTER 12

Estate Planning

CHAPTER 13

Healthcare Directives

CHAPTER 14

Final Arrangements

CHAPTER 15

Experts and Legal Research

Appendix

CHAPTER 1

About Wills

Making a will is an excellent way to ensure that your plans for leaving property to family, friends and organizations of your choice are carried out after you die. You can efficiently and safely write your own legal will using the WillMaker program. But before you start, it is a good idea to read this chapter and Chapter 2, which explain generally what a will can accomplish and how you can use WillMaker to meet your needs.

A. Making It Legal

For a will to be legally valid, both you—the person making the will—
and the will itself, must meet some technical requirements.

1. Who Can Make a Will

There are a few legal requirements that control who can make a valid
will. Before you start your computer and get WillMaker going, make
sure you qualify to make a will in the eyes of the law.

a. Age

To make a will, you must either be:

- at least 18 years old—with the exception of Wyoming residents,
  who must be at least 19 years old, or
- living in a state that permits people under 18 to make a will if
  they are married, in the military or otherwise considered legally
  emancipated. Georgia law, for example, permits people as young
  as 14 to make their own wills if they are married.

b. Mental competence

You must also be of sound mind to prepare a valid will. While this
sounds like a subjective standard, the laws generally require that you
must:

- know what a will is and what it does and that you are making
  one
- understand the relationship between you and the people who
  would normally be provided for in your will, such as a spouse or
  children

- understand the kind and quantity of property you own, and
- be able to decide how to distribute your belongings.

This threshold of mental competence is not hard to meet. Very few wills are successfully challenged based on the charge that the person making the will was mentally incompetent. It is not enough to show that the person was forgetful or absent-minded.

To have a probate court declare a will invalid usually requires proving that the willmaker was totally overtaken by the fraud or undue influence of another person—and that person then benefited from the wrongdoing by becoming entitled to a large amount of money or property under the will. Interestingly, the grand majority of undue influence contests are filed against attorneys who draw up wills in which they are named to take clients' property. If the person making the will was very old, ill, senile or otherwise in poor mental condition when he or she made the will, it is obviously easier to convince a judge that undue influence occurred.

 If a Contest Seems Possible

If you have any serious doubts about your ability to meet the legal requirements for making a will, or you believe your will is likely to be contested by another person for any reason, consult a lawyer. (See Chapter 15.)

2. Will Requirements

The laws in each state control whether a will made by a resident of the state is valid—and a will that is valid in the state where it is made is valid in all other states. Contrary to what many people believe, a will need not be notarized to be legally valid. But adding a notarized document to the will verifying that the will was signed and witnessed can be helpful when it comes times to file the will in probate court. This option is available in all but a handful of states. (See Chapter 9, Section B2.)

There are surprisingly few legal restrictions and requirements in the willmaking process. In most states, a will must:

- include at least one substantive provision—either giving away some property or naming a guardian to care for minor children who are left without parents

- be signed and dated by the person making it

- be witnessed by at least two other people who are not named to take property under the will, and

- be clear enough so that others can understand what the willmaker intended. Nonsensical, legalistic-sounding language such as: "I hereby give, bequeath and devise" is both unwise and unnecessary.

HANDWRITTEN AND ORAL WILLS

In a minority of states, unwitnessed, handwritten wills—called holographic wills—are legally valid. And a few states accept the historical holdover of oral wills under very limited circumstances, such as when a mortally wounded soldier utters last wishes.

But handwritten and oral wills are fraught with possible legal problems. Most obviously, after your death, it may be difficult to prove that your unwitnessed, handwritten document was actually written by you and intended to be your will. And it may be almost impossible to prove the authenticity of an oral will.

A properly signed, witnessed will is much less vulnerable to challenge by anyone claiming it was forged or fabricated. If need be, witnesses can later testify in court that the person whose name is on the will is the same person who signed it, and that making the will was a voluntary and knowing act.

B. Dying Without a Will

If you die without leaving a valid will, money and other property you own at death will be divided and distributed to others according to your state's intestate succession laws. These laws divide all property between the relatives who are considered closest to you according to a set formula—and completely exclude friends and charities.

These legal formulas often do not mirror most peoples' wishes. For example, dividing property according to intestate succession laws is often unsatisfactory if you are married and have no children, because most state laws require your spouse to share your property with your parents. And the situation is even worse for unmarried couples. No state intestate succession law gives an unmarried partner any property.

Also, if you have minor children, another important reason to make a will is to name a personal guardian to care for them. This is an important concern of most parents who worry that their children will be left without a caretaker if both die or are unavailable. (See Chapter 3, Section F.) Intestate succession laws do not deal with the issue of who will take care of your children, leaving it up to the courts and social service agencies to find and appoint a personal guardian.

C. Basic Decisions in Making a Will

Making a will is not difficult, but it is undeniably a serious and sobering process. Before you begin, get organized and focus on these important considerations:

- What do you own? (See Chapter 4.)
- Who would you like to get your property? (See Chapter 5.)

- Who is the best person to care for your minor children and who is best suited to manage property you leave them? (See Chapters 3 and 6.)

- Who should you name to see that your property is distributed according to your wishes after your death? (See Chapter 7.)

This manual offers guidance on how to use WillMaker to give legal effect to your decisions in all of these areas. The ultimate choices, however, are up to you.

D. Other Ways to Leave Property

A will is not the only way—and in some cases, not the best way—to transfer ownership of your property to another person upon your death. Most property passed by will must go through a legal process known as probate, in which:

- the will is filed with a court

- property is located and gathered by a personal representative, commonly known as an estate executor or administrator

- debts and taxes still owed are paid, and

- the remaining property is distributed as the will directs.

Probate has drawbacks. It can be lengthy, commonly taking a year or more. And it is usually expensive, since the services of lawyers are almost always required, and the services of other specialists such as appraisers may be needed as well. In many states, the lawyer handling the probate is allowed to collect a percentage of the total value of the estate—that is, the property owned by the deceased person at death. This fee arrangement typically means that a portion of your property you intended for family and friends goes instead to pay lawyers. (See Chapter 12, Section B2.)

If you are making a will—especially if you are older and own a fair amount of property—consider whether it makes sense for you to plan now to pay the least amount in probate fees by transferring valuable property in a way that avoids probate, and consider how best to use a will as part of a larger estate plan. (See Chapter 12, Section B3.)

 Beware of Estate Tax Concerns

With a few exceptions, the federal government will tax property in your estate that is worth more than $600,000 when you die, unless you are married and you pass the property to your spouse. Your state may also impose taxes on the property in your estate. Making tax-exempt gifts during your life, along with several other strategies, can reduce the size of your estate and by doing so, reduce its estate tax liability. (See Chapter 12, Section D.)

E. Doing Your Own Will

As a way to decide who gets your property, the will has been around in substantially the same form for about 500 years. For the first 450 years, self-help was the rule and lawyer assistance the exception. When this country was founded, or even during the Civil War, it was highly unusual for a person to hire a lawyer to set out formally what should be done with his or her property. However, in the past 50 years, the legal profession has scored a public relations coup by convincing many people that writing a will without a lawyer is like doing your own brain surgery.

Balderdash.

The hardest part of making a will is figuring out what property you own and who you want to get it when you die—questions you can answer best. WillMaker provides you with step-by-step legal guidance along the way.

But you may have a question about your particular situation that WillMaker does not answer. Or perhaps you have a very large estate—worth over $1 million—and want to engage in some sophisticated tax planning. Or you may simply be comforted by having a lawyer give your WillMaker will a once-over. Whenever you have concerns such as these or simply feel that you are in over your head, it may be wise to consult with someone who has knowledge and experience in wills and estate planning. (See Chapter 15.)

USING A COMPUTER FOR THE JOB

The computer has quickly proven to be an ideal tool for assisting informed consumers in making simple wills. It will never betray your confidences or urge you to do anything you do not feel is right. And it will not charge you a cent to revise your will should your needs change.

The reason computers are such efficient willmaking tools is that writing wills involves little more than systematically collecting answers to well-defined questions, then translating the answers into language developed over hundreds of years. WillMaker, which has been in wide and successful use for over a decade, prompts you to answer the necessary questions—and produces a will that fits your circumstances and is legal in your state.

CHAPTER 2

About WillMaker Wills

Because they reflect peoples' intentions of how and to whom they want to leave their property, wills can be as complex and intricate as life. While state laws broadly regulate the procedures for valid willmaking, you are generally free to write a will to meet your needs. Of course, this freedom can be dizzying to those who are not used to wading in the muck of legal documents.

WillMaker offers considerable guidance, so that the task of willmaking will be understandable and legal rules will not be trampled. The program works by having you systematically answer questions. As you will soon see, you either already have enough information to answer them easily, or you can quickly get your hands on it.

A. What You Can Do With WillMaker

This chapter gives you a quick survey of what you can and cannot do with the WillMaker program. Each topic is discussed in greater detail, both in the program information screens and in other chapters in the manual.

1. Tailor Your Will to Your Needs

WillMaker provides special screens and options for users based on the state in which they live, their marital status, whether they have children and whether the children are minors. Recognizing that some people have very simple wishes for leaving their property while other people's plans are more complex, WillMaker lets the user choose from among several approaches designed to meet these different needs. For instance, a married person may choose to:

- leave all property to his or her spouse
- leave most property to a spouse, with several specific property items going to people he or she names, or
- divvy property among many different people and organizations.

(See Chapter 5.)

2. Name a Guardian to Care for Your Children

You may use WillMaker to name a personal guardian to care for your minor children until they reach 18 in case there is no natural or adoptive parent to handle these duties. You may name the same guardian for all your children, or different guardians for different children. You will also have the opportunity to explain your choices in your will.

If your children need a guardian after your death, a court will formally review your choice. Your choice will normally be approved unless the person you name refuses to assume the responsibility, or the court becomes convinced that the best interests of your children would be better served if they were left in the care of someone else. (See Chapter 3, Section F.)

Example: Millicent names her friend Vera to serve as personal guardian in the event that her husband, Frank, dies at the same time she does or is otherwise unavailable to care for their three children. Millicent and Frank die together in an earthquake. The court appoints Vera as personal guardian for all three children since her ability to care for them has not been questioned. If Frank had written a will naming another person to serve as guardian, however, the court would have to choose between those nominated. For this reason, parents should choose the same people as personal guardians if that is possible.

3. Name Beneficiaries to Get Specific Property

WillMaker lets you make an unlimited number of separate gifts, called specific bequests, of cash, personal property or real estate to your spouse, children, grandchildren or anyone else—including friends, business associates, charities or other organizations. (See Chapter 5.)

Example: Using WillMaker, Robin leaves her interest in the family home to her spouse Lee, her valuable coin collection to one of her children, her boat to another child, her computer to a charity and $5,000 to her two aunts, in equal shares.

Example: Raymond, a lifelong bachelor, follows WillMaker's directions and leaves his house to his favorite charity. He divides his personal possessions among 15 different relatives and friends.

Example: Darryl and Floyd have lived together for several years. Darryl wants to leave Floyd all of his property, which includes his car, time-share ownership in a condominium, a savings account and miscellaneous personal belongings. He can use WillMaker to accomplish this.

4. Name Someone to Take All Remaining Property

If you have chosen an approach that lets you divvy your property by making specific bequests, WillMaker also allows you to name people or organizations to take whatever property is left over after you have made the specific bequests. This left-over property is called your residuary estate.

Example: Annie wants to make a number of small bequests to friends and charities, but to leave the bulk of her property to her friend Maureen. She accomplishes this by using the specific bequest screens to make the small gifts, and then names Maureen as residuary beneficiary. There is no need for her to list the property that goes to Maureen. The very nature of the residuary estate is that the residuary beneficiary—in this case, Maureen—gets everything that is left over after the specific bequests are distributed.

5. Name Alternate Beneficiaries

Using WillMaker, all beneficiaries you name will only take the property you leave them under your will if they survive you by 45 days. The reason that WillMaker imposes this 45-day rule is that you do not want to leave your property to a beneficiary who dies very shortly after you do, because that property will then be passed along to that person's inheritors. These beneficiaries are not likely to be the ones you would choose to receive your property.

To account for the possibility that your first choices of beneficiaries will not meet the survivorship requirement, WillMaker allows you to name alternate beneficiaries for any specific bequests and for your residuary property. (See Chapter 5.)

6. Name a Manager for Property Left to Children

You may leave property to your own or other peoples' children. Or your young children may receive property from some other source. But at your death, property left to minors—especially cash or other liquid assets—will usually have to be managed by an adult until the minors turn 18. And in many cases, it may be most prudent to have property left to minors managed for them until they are even older.

Property management involves safeguarding and spending the property for the young person's education, healthcare and basic living needs, keeping good records of these expenditures and seeing that income taxes are paid. Management ends at the age you specify in the will. What is left of the property is then distributed to the child.

WillMaker allows you to name a trusted person—or, if no one is available, you can name an institution such as a bank or trust company—to manage property left to young beneficiaries. The management methods available are different from state to state. (See Chapter 6, Section D.)

WillMaker also allows you to name a property guardian who will handle property that other people leave your children or property that you leave them outside of your will. (See Chapter 6, Section E.)

 ### Providing for Beneficiaries With Special Needs

It is common to set up management for property that will pass to a beneficiary who has a mental or physical disability, or who manages money poorly. The management provided under WillMaker is not sufficiently detailed to provide adequately for people with disabilities, or those with special problems such as spendthrift tendencies or substance abuse. If you need this type of management, consult an attorney who specializes in dealing with the needs of disabled people. (See Chapter 15.)

7. Cancel Debts Others Owe You

You can use WillMaker to relieve any debtors who owe you money at your death of the responsibility of paying your survivors. All you need to do is specify the debts and the people who owe them. WillMaker will then include a statement in your will canceling the debts. If a debt is canceled in this way, WillMaker also automatically wipes out any interest that has accrued on it as of your death. (See Chapter 8, Section A.)

Example: Cynthia has lent $25,000 at 10% annual interest to her son George as a downpayment on a house. She uses WillMaker to cancel this debt. At her death, George need not pay her estate the remaining balance of the loan, or the interest accrued on it.

8. Designate How Debts, Expenses and Taxes Are Paid

WillMaker allows you to designate a particular source of money or other specific assets from which your personal representative, or executor, should pay your debts, final expenses such as funeral and probate costs and any estate and inheritance taxes. (See Chapter 8, Section D.)

Example: Brent owns a savings account, a portfolio of stocks and bonds, an R.V. and two cars. He uses WillMaker to make a will—leaving his R.V. and stocks and bonds to his nephew, his cars to his niece and his savings account to his favorite charity, River Friends. He also designates the savings account as the source of payment of his debts and expenses of probate. Under this arrangement, River Friends will receive whatever is left in the savings account after debts and expenses of probate have been paid.

Example: Calvin's estate is valued at over $600,000. It is likely that his estate will owe some federal estate taxes when he dies. He uses WillMaker to specify that any estate tax he owes should be paid proportionately from all the property subject to the tax. If there is estate tax liability, the personal representative he designates will require that each of Calvin's beneficiaries pay part of the tax in the same proportion their bequest bears to the value of Calvin's estate as a whole.

9. Name a Personal Representative or Executor

With WillMaker, you can name a personal representative for your estate—that is, the property you own and leave at your death. This person or institution, called an executor in some states, will be responsible for making sure the provisions in your will are carried out and your property distributed as your will directs. WillMaker also produces a letter to your executor that generally explains what is required by the job.

The personal representative can be any competent adult. Commonly, people name a spouse or other close relative or friend or—for large estates or where no trusted person is able to serve—a financial institution such as a bank or savings and loan. You are free to name two or more people or institutions to share the job. (See Chapter 7.)

It is also wise to use WillMaker to name an alternate personal representative in case your first choice becomes unable or unwilling to serve.

Example: Rick and Phyllis both use WillMaker to complete wills naming each other as personal representative in case the other dies first. They both name Rick's father as an alternate personal representative to distribute their property in the event they die at the same time.

Example: Pat and Babs do not wish to burden their relatives with having to take care of their fairly considerable estate. Each names the Third National Bank as personal representative after checking that their estate is large enough so that this bank will be willing to serve.

B. What You Cannot Do With WillMaker

WillMaker produces a valid and effective will designed to meet the needs of most people. But there are some commonsense restrictions built into the program. Some of the restrictions are designed to prevent you from writing in conditions that may not be legally valid. Others are intended to keep the program simple and easy to use.

1. Make Bequests With Conditions

You cannot make a bequest that will take effect only if a certain condition comes true—an if, and or but such as "$5,000 to Ted if he stops smoking." Such conditional bequests are confusing and usually require someone to oversee and supervise the erstwhile inheritors to be sure the conditions are satisfied. If you doubt this, consider that someone would have to constantly check up on Ted to make sure he never took a puff.

So, to use WillMaker, you must first decide that you want to leave property to people outright; you cannot make them jump through hoops or change their behavior to get it.

 Takers Must Survive by 45 Days

To ensure that property goes to people you want to have it, WillMaker automatically imposes the condition that each of your beneficiaries must survive you by 45 days. If they do not survive by that amount of time, the property you had slated for them will pass instead to the person or institution you have named as a residuary beneficiary, or it will go to the one you have named to take your residuary estate.

2. Write Joint Wills

In the past, it was common for a married couple who had an agreed scheme for how to distribute all their property to write one document together: a joint will. But time has shown that setup to be crawling with problems.

WillMaker requires that each spouse make his or her own will, even if both agree about how their property is to be distributed. This limitation is not imposed to annoy people or defeat their intentions; there is solid legal reasoning behind it. Joint wills are intended to prevent the surviving spouse from changing his or her mind about what to do with the property after the first spouse dies. The practical effect is to tie up the property for years in title and probate determinations—often until long after the second spouse dies. Also, many court battles are fought over whether the surviving spouse is legally entitled to revoke any part of the will.

There are still some lawyers who will agree to write joint wills for clients, but they do so in the face of the risk that such wills may become cumbersome or even found invalid in later court challenges. For these reasons, it is best for both spouses to write separate wills—a bit more time-consuming, perhaps, but a lot safer from a legal standpoint.

3. Explain the Reasons for Leaving Your Property

Most of the time, the act of leaving property to people—or choosing not to—speaks for itself. Occasionally, however, people making wills want to explain to survivors the reasons they left property as they did. This might be the case, for example, if you opt to leave one of your two children more property than the other to equal out the loan you made during your lifetime to help one of them buy a house. Although the yearning to make such explanations is understandable, WillMaker does not allow you to do it in your will, because of the risk that you might add legally confusing language to the document.

However, there is an easy and legally safe way to provide your heirs with explanations for your bequests. You can draft a letter that you can attach to your will, explaining your reasons for leaving property to some people—or not leaving it to others. (See Chapter 11.)

4. Name Co-Guardians for Children or Their Property

WillMaker allows you to name one personal guardian to care for each of your minor children and one guardian to care for their property. While you may wish to choose different guardians for different children, you may not name two people to share the job of being a personal or property guardian. (See Chapter 6.)

At first glance, it may seem to be a good idea to divide up the job—naming two people or a married couple to agree to take on the responsibility of caring for your children or supervising their property if you die while they are still young. But a closer look reveals that naming co-guardians often presents more problems than it solves. For example, as life unwinds, the loving couple you named to jointly care for your children may divorce—making it impossible for them to be in the same room together, much less agree on the best way to raise a child. In such cases, courts are often called in to decide who is the most fitting guardian—a process that may be long, costly and very often heart-rending.

 Get on the Same Page

People who jointly own property or have children together should review their wills together to be sure they do not provide conflicting information—such as each naming different guardians for the children.

5. Control Property After Death

Bequests given in a WillMaker will must take effect as soon as you die. You cannot make a bequest by will with the property to be used for a person's life and then be given to a second person when the first person dies. Such an arrangement would involve too many variables for both willmakers and beneficiaries to handle.

Example: Emory wants his grandchildren to inherit his house, but wants his wife to first have the right to live in the house until her death. He cannot use WillMaker to accomplish this. Emory would have to leave his house in trust to his spouse for her life and then to his grandchildren upon his spouse's death. He should consult a lawyer to have the necessary trust prepared.

6. Set Up Trusts That Avoid Taxes

If your estate is large—$600,000 or more—or if you are elderly or ill, it may be important to use trusts to preserve your property for your beneficiaries. WillMaker does not allow you to set up the types of trusts commonly used to lessen federal estate taxes, such as marital life estate trusts or generation-skipping trusts. To do this, you will need to consult a lawyer. (See Chapter 12.)

7. Require Bond for Executors or Property Managers

A bond is like an insurance policy that protects the beneficiaries in the unlikely event that the personal representative wrongfully spends or distributes estate property. Because the premium or fee that must be paid for a bond comes out of the estate, leaving less money for the beneficiaries, most wills for small or moderate estates do not require one. Following this general practice, the will produced by the WillMaker program does not require a bond. Instead, take care to appoint someone you know to be trustworthy.

C. A Look at a WillMaker Will

You may wish now to take a look at a WillMaker will and instructions that print out with it. Do not be alarmed if the will does not exactly match the one you produce. Your WillMaker will is tailored to your property, circumstances and state laws. Nearly every paragraph, or clause, of the will used as an example here is explained in the brackets following it.

IMPORTANT NOTES

Before you sign Read your will carefully. Is everything printed as you intended? Do you understand the meaning of every word?

While you sign For your will to be valid you must be of sound mind and of the age specified by your state. This is almost always 18.

Your will should be witnessed by three witnesses, even though only two are legally required in most states. The witnesses should be in your and each other's presence when you sign the will. The witnesses need not read your will.

You must say to the witnesses that you intend this document to be your will. Make sure each page is numbered and dated; then write your initials on one of the blank lines where indicated. On the last page of your will, write in the date, and on the blank line after "at," fill in the city or county and state in which you are signing your will. Repeat this information in the blanks that appear just before the witnesses' signatures. Then sign it in the presence of the witnesses. Use exactly the form of your name printed on the will. The witnesses should state that they realize you intend this to be your will. They should then, in your presence, initial each page, near the line you did, sign the last page in the space indicated for witnesses, and fill in their addresses.

After you sign Keep your will in a safe place, where it can be readily found. You may make photocopies—for example, to give to your executor. However, only the signed original is legally valid and can be probated.

If there are major changes in your life, you should make and sign a new will and have it witnessed. Destroy the original of your old will and all copies. Changes that make it wise for you to make a new will include: having or adopting a child, moving to another state, the death of anyone named in your will, a change of marital status, and a significant change in the property you own.

Keep up to date Fill out the WillMaker registration card in the manual and send it to Nolo Press at the address below. If you do not have a copy of the manual include $69.95 for a full WillMaker package.

WillMaker Copyright 1995 by Nolo Press.
950 Parker St., Berkeley, CA 94710
(510) 549-1976

WILL OF JAMES MOOREHEAD

PERSONAL INFORMATION

I, James Moorehead, a resident of the State of California, Humboldt County, declare that this is my will. My Social Security Number is 123-45-6789.

REVOCATION OF PREVIOUS WILLS

I revoke all wills and codicils that I have previously made.

[This provision makes clear that this is the will to be used—not any other wills or amendments to those wills, called codicils, that were made earlier. To prevent this possible confusion, all earlier wills and codicils should also be physically destroyed.]

MARITAL STATUS

I am married to Wilma Jazmin Moorehead.

[Here you identify your spouse if you are married. If you are not married, this provision will not appear in your will.]

CHILDREN

I have the following children now living: William Moorehead, Vera Moorehead and Frank Moorehead.

[This part of your will should list all of your natural born and adopted children; your stepchildren should not be included here. By naming all your children, you will prevent a child from claiming that he or she was accidentally overlooked in your will. It will also ward off later claims that any child is entitled to take a share of your property against your wishes.]

GRANDCHILDREN

I have the following grandchild now living: Gloria Sadowski.

[This clause should list all of your grandchildren. By naming them all, you will prevent any of them from claiming that they were accidentally overlooked in your will. It will

also ward off later claims that any grandchild is entitled to take a share of your property against your wishes.]

FAILURE TO LEAVE PROPERTY

If I do not leave property in this will to one or more of my children or my grandchild named above, my failure to do so is intentional.

[This clause makes clear that if you do not leave a child—or a child of one of your children who is deceased—any property in your will, that decision was intentional rather than accidental. This language helps protect you against claims by such a child or grandchild that he or she was accidentally overlooked in your will when it comes time to distribute your property.]

DISPOSITION OF PROPERTY

I leave $20,000 to William Moorehead. If William Moorehead does not survive me, I leave this property to Davina L. Brown.

[This language leaves a specific item of property—$20,000—to William Moorehead. If Moorehead does not survive the willmaker, then Davina L. Brown will get the money.]

I leave my rare coin collection to Cynthia Drucelli, Mathew Drucelli and Stephen Price in the following shares: Cynthia Drucelli shall receive a 1/4 share. Mathew Drucelli shall receive a 1/2 share. Stephen Price shall receive a 1/4 share.

[This language leaves a specific item of property—a coin collection—to three people in unequal shares.]

I leave my collection of Nash cars to The City Motor Museum and Wilhemina Clark in equal shares. If Wilhemina Clark does not survive me, I leave his or her share of this property to Henley Simpson.

[This will leaves specific property to an organization and a person equally. Since the willmaker here was concerned only about providing for the possibility that the person would not survive to take the property, he named an alternate for her.]

I leave my residuary estate to my wife Wilma Jazmin Moorehead. If my wife Wilma Jazmin Moorehead does not survive me, I leave my residuary estate to my

Page 1   Initials: _____   _____   _____   _____   Date: _____

children William Moorehead, Vera Moorehead and Frank Moorehead in equal shares.

[This clause gives the residuary estate to Wilma Moorehead. Your residuary estate may be defined differently depending on your plans for leaving your property. If the person named here to take the residuary estate does not survive the willmaker, the residuary estate will pass to the three people named—the willmaker's children.]

SPECIFIC BEQUESTS OF PROPERTY

Specific bequest refers to a bequest of specifically identified property that I leave in this will.

[This paragraph simply defines the phrase specific bequest, which is used later in the will, so that the document and all its provisions can be easily understood.]

RESIDUARY ESTATE

Residuary estate means all property subject to this will that does not pass under a specific bequest.

[This paragraph simply defines the phrase residuary estate, which is used later in the will, so that the document and all its provisions can be easily understood.]

ENCUMBRANCES AND LIENS

All personal and real property that I leave in this will shall pass subject to any encumbrances or liens on property as security for the repayment of a loan or debt.

[This language explains that whoever inherits any real estate also inherits the mortgage and other legal claims against the property, such as liens. And anyone who inherits property that is subject to a loan, such as a car loan, gets the debt as well as the property.]

SURVIVORSHIP PERIOD

All beneficiaries must survive me for 45 days to receive property under this will. As used in this will, the phrase survive me means to live at least 45 days after my death.

[This language means that to receive property under your will, a person must be alive for at least 45 days after your death. Otherwise, the property will go to whomever you named as an alternate. This language permits you to choose another way to leave your property if your first choice dies within a short time after you do.

This will clause also prevents the confusion associated with the simultaneous death of two spouses, when it is hard to tell who gets the property they have left each other. Property left to a spouse who dies within 45 days of the first spouse, including a spouse who dies simultaneously, will go to the person or organization named as alternate.]

SHARED BEQUESTS

Any property I leave to two or more beneficiaries shall be shared equally by them unless this will provides otherwise.

If I leave property to be shared by two or more beneficiaries, and any of them does not survive me, I leave his or her share to the others equally unless this will provides otherwise.

[This language provides that for all specific and residuary bequests that are made to two or more people, the property shall be split equally between the people, unless the bequest itself says otherwise. If you want to give property to be split among people in unequal shares, you need to indicate that when you are describing the bequest by including the percentage share in parentheses after each beneficiary's name. Otherwise, it will be presumed that you wanted the property split equally.]

CUSTODIANSHIP UNDER THE UNIFORM TRANSFERS TO MINORS ACT

All specific bequests and residuary bequests made in this will to Frank Moorehead shall be given to Lynette Leander, to be held until Frank Moorehead reaches age 25, as custodian for Frank Moorehead under the California Uniform Transfers to Minors Act. If Lynette Leander is unwilling or unable to serve as custodian of property left to Frank Moorehead under this will, Hank Leander shall serve instead.

[This clause provides that all property left to the chiuld named in the clause will be managed by the person named as the custodian until the child turns the age indicated.

An alternate custodian is also named in case the first choice custodian is unable or unwilling to serve when the time comes.]

INDIVIDUAL CHILD'S TRUST

All property left in this will to Vera Moorehead shall be held in a separate trust for Vera Moorehead until she reaches age 34. This trust shall be managed under the trust administration provisions set forth in this will. The trustee of the Vera Moorehead trust shall be Wilma Jazmin Moorehead. If Wilma Jazmin Moorehead is unwilling or unable to serve, the trustee shall be Roberta Durango.

[This clause provides that all property given to the child named in the clause shall be held in trust—that is, managed strictly for the benefit of the child—by the person named as the trustee until the child turns the age indicated. An alternate trustee is also named in case the first choice trustee is unable or unwilling to serve when the time comes.]

Duties of the Trustee. The trustee of an individual child's trust shall manage and distribute the assets in the trust in the following manner.

Until the trust beneficiary reaches the age specified for final distribution of the principal, the trustee may distribute some or all of the principal or net income of the trust as the trustee deems necessary for the child's health, support, maintenance and education. Education includes, but is not limited to, college, graduate, post-graduate and vocational studies and reasonable living expenses.

[This clause lets the trustee spend the trust principal and income for the childts general living, health and educational needs. The clause gives the trustee great latitude in how this is done and what amount is spent.]

In deciding whether or not to make a distribution to a beneficiary, the trustee may take into account the beneficiary's other income, resources and sources of support.

[This clause lets the trustee withhold the trust principal or income from the trust beneficiary if, in the trustee's opinion, the beneficiary has sufficient income from other sources.]

Any trust income that is not distributed by the trustee shall be accumulated and added to the principal.

[Every trust involves two types of property: the property in the trust—called the trust principal—and the income that is earned by investing the principal. This clause assures that the trustee must add to the trust principal any income that is earned on the principal, unless the income is distributed to the trust beneficiary.]

Termination. An individual child's trust shall terminate as soon as one of the following events occurs:

- the beneficiary reaches the age stated above, in which case the trustee shall distribute the remaining principal and accumulated net income of the trust to the beneficiary
- the beneficiary dies, in which case the principal and accumulated net income of the trust shall pass under the beneficiary's will, or if there is no will, to his or her heirs, or
- the trust principal is exhausted through distributions allowed under these provisions.

[This clause sets out three events that may cause the trust to end. The first is when the minor or young adult reaches the age specified for the trust to end. If the trust ends for this reason, the minor or young adult gets whatever trust principal and accumulated income is left. The trust will also end if the minor or young adult dies before the age set for the trust to end. If the trust ends for this reason, the principal and income accumulated in the trust goes to whomever the young adult named in his or her will to get it, or if there is no will, to the minor or young adult's legal heirs—such as parents, brothers and sisters. A third occurrence that will cause the trust to end is when there is no trust principal left—or so little left that it's no longer financially feasible to maintain it.]

TRUST ADMINISTRATION PROVISIONS

All trusts established in this will shall be managed subject to the following provisions.

Bond. No bond shall be required of any trustee.
[The trustee will not be required to post bond to ensure that she carries out her duties faithfully.]

Court Supervision. It is my intent that any trust established in this will be administered independently of court supervision to the maximum extent possible under the laws of the state having jurisdiction over the trust.

[As a general rule, the management of a trust is a private matter and not subject to very much court supervision. However, to the extent that any state's laws require such supervision, this clause makes clear that supervision is not desired.]

Transferability of Interests. The interests of any beneficiary of all trusts established by this will shall not be transferable by voluntary or involuntary assignment or by operation of law and shall be free from the claims of creditors and from attachment, execution, bankruptcy, or other legal process to the fullest extent permitted by law.

[This important clause removes the trust principal and accumulated income from the reach of the minor or young adult's creditors—while it is being held in the trust. Also, this clause prevents the minor or young adult from transferring ownership of the principal or accumulated interest to others—again, while it is in the trust. Once property is distributed to the minor or young adult, however, there are no restrictions on what he or she can do with it.]

Powers of the Trustee. In addition to other powers granted a trustee in this will, a trustee shall have the powers to:

1) Invest and reinvest trust funds in every kind of property and every kind of investment, provided that the trustee acts with the care, skill, prudence and diligence under the prevailing circumstances that a prudent person acting in a similar capacity and familiar with such matters would use.

2) Receive additional property from any source and acquire or hold properties jointly or in undivided interests or in partnership or joint venture with other people or entities.

3) Enter, continue or participate in the operation of any business, and incorporate, liquidate, reorganize or otherwise change the form or terminate the operation of the business and contribute capital or loan money to the business.

4) Exercise all the rights, powers and privileges of an owner of any securities held in the trust.

5) Borrow funds, guarantee or indemnify in the name of the trust and secure any obligation, mortgage, pledge or other security interest, and renew, extend or modify any such obligations.

6) Lease trust property for terms within or beyond the term of the trust.

7) Prosecute, defend, contest or otherwise litigate legal actions or other proceedings for the protection or benefit of the trust; pay, compromise, release, adjust or submit to arbitration any debt, claim or controversy; and insure the trust against any risk and the trustee against liability with respect to other people.

8) Pay himself or herself reasonable compensation out of trust assets for ordinary and extraordinary services, and for all services in connection with the complete or partial termination of this trust.

9) Employ and discharge professionals to aid or assist in managing the trust and compensate them from the trust assets.

10) Make distributions to the beneficiaries directly or to other people or organizations on behalf of the beneficiaries.

[This list of powers should cover the gamut of activities that trustees might be called upon to exercise in administering any trust set up in this will.]

Severability. The invalidity of any trust provision of this will shall not affect the validity of the remaining trust provisions.

[This language that ensures that in the unlikely event that a court finds any individual part of this trust to be invalid, the rest of the document will remain in effect.]

PERSONAL GUARDIAN

If at my death a guardian is needed to care for William Moorehead, I name Madelyn Cosette as personal guardian. If this person is unwilling or unable to serve as personal guardian, I name Pierre Cosette to serve instead.

No personal guardian shall be required to post bond.

[This clause names someone to provide parental-type care for a minor child if there is no natural parent able to provide it. The clause also provides for an alternate to step in if the first choice is not able or willing to act when the moment comes. When making your own will, be aware that if there is a natural parent on the scene, that parent will be awarded custody of the children, even if you named someone else as personal guardian, unless a court concludes that the children would be at risk of harm. The clause also provides that the personal guardian need not provide a bond to secure faithful performance of his or her duties.]

PROPERTY GUARDIAN

If at my death a guardian is needed to care for any property belonging to William Moorehead, I name Madelyn Cosette as property guardian. If this person is unwilling or unable to serve as property guardian, I name Pierre Cosette to serve instead.

No property guardian shall be required to post bond.

[This clause appoints someone to manage property that the willmaker or other people leave to minor children outside of the will, as in a life insurance property or living trust. This person will also manage property left to minor children under a will if you or anyone else who leaves them property does not arrange for someone to manage it. You may also appoint an alternate property guardian in case your first choice is not able or willing to serve when the time comes. The clause also provides that the personal guardian need not provide a bond—a kind of insurance of good performance—to secure that he or she will act faithfully.]

FORGIVENESS OF DEBTS

I wish to forgive all debts specified below, plus accrued interest as of the date of my death: Ben Moorehead, 4/4/90, $250,000.

[Forgiving a debt is equivalent to making a bequest of money. It is a common way to equalize what you leave to all your children when you have loaned one of them some money—that is, the amount that you would otherwise leave that child can be reduced by the amount of the debt being forgiven.]

PERSONAL REPRESENTATIVE

I name Wilma Jazmin Moorehead to serve as my personal representative. If Wilma Jazmin Moorehead is unwilling or unable to serve as personal representative, I name Wilma Jazmin Moorehead to serve instead.

No personal representative shall be required to post bond.

[This clause identifies the choices for personal representative—that is, an executor—and an alternate representative who will take over if the first choice is unable or unwilling to serve when the time comes. You have the option of naming more than one.]

PERSONAL REPRESENTATIVE'S POWERS

If the probate of this will is necessary, I direct that my personal representative petition the court for an order to administer my estate under the provisions of the Independent Administration of Estates Act.

[This clause sets out the specific authority that the personal representative will need to competently manage the estate until it has been distributed under the terms of the will.

In a few states, including California and Texas, this clause will include the words of a specific state statute that gives a personal representative the maximum authority possible—without court supervision. In all other states, the will language expresses your desire that your personal representative work as free from court supervision as possible. This will cut down on delays and expense.

When you print out your will, a second paragraph will list a number of specific powers that your personal representative will have, if necessary. It also makes clear that the listing of these specific powers does not deprive your personal representative of any other powers that he or she has under the law of your state. The general idea is to give your personal representative as much power as possible, so that he or she will not have to go to court and get permission to take a particular action.]

PAYMENT OF DEBTS

Except for liens and encumbrances on property as security for the repayment of a loan or debt, I instruct my personal representative to pay all debts and expenses using the following assets in the order listed: Account #223-233-03039 in the Independence Bank, Pacific Branch.

[This clause states how debts will be paid. Depending on the choice you make when operating WillMaker, your debts may be paid either from specific assets you designate, or from your residuary estate—all the property covered by your will that does not pass through a specific bequest.]

PAYMENT OF TAXES

I instruct my personal representative to pay all estate and inheritance taxes assessed against property in my estate or against my beneficiaries using the following assets, in the order listed: Account #24225-393-1 at bank Tormeline.

[This clause states how any estate or death taxes owed by the estate or beneficiaries should be paid. This will usually apply only to people whose estate has a net value of $600,000 or more. Depending on the choice you make when operating WillMaker, your taxes may be paid from all of your property, from specific assets you designate, or by your personal representative according to the law of your state.]

NO CONTEST PROVISION

If any beneficiary under this will contests this will or any of its provisions, any share or interest in my estate given to the contesting beneficiary under this will is revoked and shall be disposed of as if that contesting beneficiary had not survived me and left no living children.

[This harsh-sounding clause is intended to discourage anyone who receives anything under the will from challenging its legality for the purpose of receiving a larger share.

The clause is often not very effective if a spouse or children are the ones doing the suing, but may be enforced against less closely-related beneficiaries. A few states have passed laws specifically stating that a no contest clause will not be enforced, but if your will has such a provision, the rest of it will be enforced as written.]

/////
/////

/////
/////

/////
/////

/////
/////

/////
/////

/////
/////

/////
/////

/////
/////

/////
/////

[These hashmarks will automatically appear to fill up the rest of the page so that the witnesses' signatures appear with some text of the will—one way to help guard against an unethical survivor tampering with the document.]

SEVERABILITY

If any provision of this will is held invalid, that shall not affect other provisions that can be given effect without the invalid provision.

[This is standard language that ensures that in the unlikely event that a court finds any individual part of your will to be invalid, the rest of the document will remain in effect.]

SIGNATURE

I, James Moorehead , the testator, sign my name to this instrument, this _____ day of _____, 19___, at _____.
I declare that I sign and execute this instrument as my last will, that I sign it willingly, and that I execute it as my free and voluntary act. I declare that I am of the age of majority or otherwise legally empowered to make a will, and under no constraint or undue influence.

_____

(Signed)

WITNESSES

We, the witnesses, sign our names to this instrument, and declare that the testator willingly signed and executed this instrument as the testator's last will.

In the presence of the testator, and in the presence of each other, we sign this will as witnesses to the testator's signing.

To the best of our knowledge, the testator is of the age of majority or otherwise legally empowered to make a will, is mentally competent and under no constraint or undue influence.

We declare under penalty of perjury that the foregoing is true and correct, this _____ day of _____, 19___, at _____.

Witness #1: _____
Residing at: _____
Witness #2: _____
Residing at: _____
Witness #3: _____
Residing at: _____

Page 12   Initials: _____   _____   _____   _____   Date: _____

About You and Yours

A. Identifying Information

As you go through WillMaker, you will first be asked to answer a number of preliminary questions about yourself and where and how you live. This section discusses those questions in the order in which they appear in the program.

1. Your Name and Gender

Enter your name—first, middle if you choose, then last—in the same form that you use on other formal documents, such as your driver's license or bank accounts. This may or may not be the name that appears on your birth certificate. If you customarily use more than one name for business purposes, list all of them in your WillMaker answer, separated by aka, which stands for "also known as."

There is room for you to list several names. But use your common sense. Your name is needed here to identify you and all the property you own. Be sure to include all names in which you have held bank accounts, stocks, bonds, real estate or other property. But you need not list every embarrassing nickname from your childhood, or names you use for non-business purposes.

WillMaker also asks you to select a pronoun by which you identify your gender. This is not because of rampant nosiness, but so that the screens you see while proceeding through the program and the language in your final document will be grammatically elegant.

2. Your Social Security Number

WillMaker prompts you to enter your nine-digit Social Security number. This is not a legal requirement, and you may choose not to provide it.

However, it is a good idea to supply the information, because the number is often helpful to your personal representative and others who must track down your records and property after your death. And the information may be especially helpful if you have a common name that may be easily confused with others.

B. Your Residence

You are asked to specify the state of your legal residence, sometimes called a domicile. This is the state where you make your home now and for the indefinite future.

This information is important for a number of willmaking reasons, so it is important to check your answer for accuracy. Your state's laws affect: marital property ownership, property management options for young beneficiaries, how your will can be admitted into probate and whether your property will be subject to state inheritance tax. (See Chapter 8, Section E.)

If you divide up the year living in two or more states and have business relationships in both, you may not be sure which state is your legal residence. Choose the state where you are the most rooted—that is, the state in which you:

- are registered to vote
- register your motor vehicles
- own valuable property—especially property with a title document, such as a house or car
- have checking, savings and other investment accounts, and
- maintain a business.

To avoid confusion, it is best to keep all or at least most of your roots in one state, if possible. For people with larger estates, ideally this should be in a state that does not levy an inheritance tax.

 Wills Valid in Continental U.S. Only

WillMaker produces valid wills in all of the continental United States except for Louisiana—and the program guides you by showing you screens geared specifically to the state of residence you indicate when using it.

Because the property and probate laws in Puerto Rico and Guam, for example, may differ from a state you have selected to use in making your will, we do not guarantee that a WillMaker will is valid there. However, some users who reside outside the U.S. do use WillMaker to help draft their wills and then have them looked over by an experienced local professional. In this way, WillMaker helps users answer questions and organize basic information about their property and beneficiaries that is commonly used in making wills.

1. Living Overseas

If you live overseas temporarily because you are in the Armed Services, your residence will be the Home of Record you declared to the military authorities. Normally, your Home of Record is the state you lived in before you received your assignment, where your parents or spouse live, or where you now have a permanent home. If there is a close call between two states, consider the factors listed above for determining a legal residence, or get advice from the military legal authorities.

If Your Choice Is Not Clear

If you do not maintain continuous ties with a particular state, or if you have homes in both the U.S. and another country, consult a lawyer to find out which state to list as your legal domicile when using WillMaker.

If you live overseas for business or education, you probably still have ties with a particular state that would make it your legal residence. For example, if you were born in Wisconsin, lived there for many years, registered to vote there and receive mail there in care of your parents who still live in Milwaukee, then Wisconsin is your legal residence for purposes of making a will.

2. Your County

Including your county in your will is optional, but recommended for convenience and as one additional way to help others identify you and to track down your property after your death.

Also, a county name may provide those handling your estate with important direction, because wills are probated through the court system of the county where you last resided, no matter where you died. The one exception is real estate: that property is probated in the court of the county in which it is located.

C. Marital Status

If you are married, review the property ownership laws affecting married people. (See Chapter 4, Section C.)

For most people, listing their proper marital status does not require much thought. But if you are unsure whether you are married or single according to law, it is important to clarify your status. The information below should help.

1. Divorced Individuals

Do not rely on word of mouth as evidence that you are legally divorced. Make sure you see a copy of the final order signed by a judge. To track down a divorce order, contact the court clerk in the county where you believe the divorce occurred. You will need to give the first and last names of you and your former spouse and make a good guess at what year the divorce became final. If you cannot locate a final decree of divorce, it is safest to assume you are still married.

If the divorce was supposed to have taken place outside the United States, that important bit of information may be difficult to verify and evaluate. If you have any reason to think that someone you consider to be a former spouse might claim to be married to you at your death because an out-of-country divorce was not legal, consult a lawyer. (See Chapter 15.)

2. Separated Individuals

Many married couples, contemplating divorce or reconciliation, live apart from one another, sometimes for several years. While this often feels like a murky limbo while you are living it, for willmaking purposes, your status is straightforward: You are legally married until a court issues a formal decree of divorce, signed by a judge. This is true even if you and your spouse are legally separated as declared in a legal document. Note that many separation agreements, however, set out rights and restrictions that may affect your ownership of property.

3. Common Law Marriages

It is uncommon to have a common law marriage. In most states, common law marriage does not exist.

But in the states listed below, couples can become legally married if they live together and either hold themselves out to the public as being married or actually intend to be married to one another. Once these conditions are met, the couple is legally married. And the marriage will still be valid even if they later move to a state that does not allow couples to form common law marriages there.

No matter what state you live in, if either you or the person you live with is still legally married to some other person, you cannot have a common law marriage.

The following states recognize some form of common law marriage:

Alabama
Colorado
District of Columbia
Georgia
Idaho (if created before1/1/96)
Iowa

Kansas

Montana

New Hampshire (for inheritance purposes only)

Ohio (if created before 10/10/91)

Oklahoma

Pennsylvania

Rhode Island

South Carolina

Texas

Utah

There is no such thing as a common law divorce; no matter how your marriage begins, you must go through formal divorce proceedings to end it.

4. Same Sex Marriages

No state currently legally recognizes marriages between people of the same sex—even where a religious ceremony has been performed. However, there is legislation pending in Hawaii which could make it the first state to legalize same-sex marriages.

 The Importance of Your Marital Status

You should make a new will whenever your marital status changes. (See Chapter 10, Section A.)

There are a number of reasons for this. WillMaker takes the user's marital status into account when asking questions and collecting information. If your marital status changes but your will does not, your new spouse or ex-spouse may get more or less of your property than you intend. For example, if you marry after making a will and do not provide for the new spouse, either in the will or through transfers outside the will, your spouse, in many states, may be entitled to claim up to half your property at your death.

Also, if you name a spouse in a will, then divorce or have the marriage annulled and die before making a new will, state laws will produce different, often unexpected results. In some states, the former spouse will automatically get nothing. In other states, the former spouse is entitled to take the property as set out in the will. And in a few states, courts will consider the entire will invalid.

5. Your Spouse's Name

WillMaker should prompt you for your spouse's name by asking for the name of your husband or wife. If the husband or wife label does not fit your situation, back up to the screen titled Your Name and Gender and correct your answer.

Enter your spouse's full name. As with your own name, list all names used for business purposes, following the tips suggested for entering your own name in Section A1.

D. Children

Becoming a parent is what may have motivated you to buckle down to the task of writing your will in the first place.

If you are the parent of young children, your will is the perfect place to address some driving concerns you are likely to have if you die before they are grown:

- who will care for them, and

- who will manage their property.

WillMaker lets you make these decisions separately. This gives you the option of placing the responsibilities in the hands of the same person, or if need be, naming different people. First, you are asked to address who you want to care for your children. Later in the program, you can grapple with the issue of providing property management for your own or other people's young children. (See Chapter 6, Section E.)

1. Identifying Your Children

It is important to name all your children when making your WillMaker will. This warning is backed by strong legal reasoning: If a minor or adult child is neither named in a will nor specifically disinherited, the law of most states assumes that you accidentally forgot to include that child. The effect is that the overlooked child has a right to the same share of your estate he or she would be entitled to had you left no will. This amount varies from state to state, often depending on your family composition, but would likely be a significant percentage of your property.

These laws are intended to protect both the interests of the accidentally forgotten child—termed a "pretermitted heir"—and the person making the will. This rule applies no matter how old your children are when you die—and no matter whether you specifically plan to leave them any property in your will.

Example: Bruno leaves nothing to his daughter Portia in his will because they have been estranged for years. He neither names her nor specifically disinherits her. When Bruno dies, Portia is 66 years old. Portia may be entitled to sue for a share of Bruno's estate as a pretermitted heir.

WillMaker protects you against the pretermitted heir rule by asking you to name all your children and then including the statement in your will that if you do not leave any property to one or more of these children, that decision is intentional. However, to go the last inch to make sure that no child can challenge your will under the pretermitted heir rule, it also makes excellent sense to leave each child some amount of property, no matter how small. Also, it is important to update your will to name any child you have at a later time.

WillMaker asks whether or not you have any children and, if so, it asks that you name all of them, including:

- children born to or adopted by you while you were married to your current spouse

- children born to or adopted by you when you were married to a previous spouse, and

- children born to or adopted by you when you were not married.

If you are the parent of a child who has been legally adopted by another person—or you have otherwise given up your legal parental rights—then you need not name that child in your will.

It is not necessary to name stepchildren that you have not adopted, since they are not entitled by law to a share of your property when you die. The pretermitted heir rule does not apply to them. Also, WillMaker offers a number of options that include your children as a group, and if you include stepchildren in the list and use one of these options, your will might contain provisions you did not intend.

However, you are free to leave your stepchildren as much property in your will as you wish. If you want to treat your children and stepchildren equally and not differentiate between them, when WillMaker asks how you wish to leave your property, choose the option labeled "Some other way." (See Chapter 5, Sections A and C.)

To list your children, enter their full names in the sequence and format you want the names to appear in your will.

 Don't Use "All My Children"

Some people are tempted to skimp on naming their children individually and want to fill in "all my children," "my surviving children," "my lawful heirs," or "my issue." Don't do it. That shorthand language can be confusing and may lead to pretermitted heir problems down the line.

2. Your Children's Birth Dates

WillMaker also asks you to enter your children's dates of birth—month, day, year—separated by a slashmark. The program will automatically compute their ages in years—an important consideration when you are asked to name a personal guardian and provide management for property you or others leave them.

E. Grandchildren

WillMaker asks you to name your grandchildren. Name all such grandchildren—including children your child legally adopted and those born while he or she was not married.

This question is asked because the rule that allows pretermitted children to sue to get a share of your estate also applies to grandchildren you may have overlooked in your will if their parent—that is, your child—dies before you do. (See Section D1.)

As it does for your own children, WillMaker automatically provides the statement that if you have not left any property to a grandchild, that is intentional—and therefore eliminates the problem. Again, you are free to leave the grandchild property if you choose. Also, if you have additional grandchildren after making your will, it is wise to make a new will that includes them.

KEEP YOUR WILL CURRENT

You should make a new will in the following two situations:

- If a child is born to or legally adopted by you after you make your will. You should draft a new will to list the new child. If you do not, that child may challenge your will as a pretermitted heir and sue to receive a share of what you leave.
- If one of your children dies before you do and leaves children of his or her own. The laws of many states require that you name and provide for the children of deceased children. If you do not, they are considered pretermitted heirs. To protect against this, make a new will, naming these grandchildren so that you can signal that you are aware that these grandchildren exist. You are still free to leave them as little or as much property as you wish in your will.

(See Chapter 10 for information on updating your will.)

F. Personal Guardians for Your Minor Children

Among the most pressing concerns of parents with minor children is who will care for the children if one or both of them die before the children reach 18.

Although contemplating the possibility of your early death can be wrenching, it is important to face up to it and adopt the best contingency plan for the care of your young children. If the other parent is available, then he or she can usually handle the task. But life is full of possibilities—some of them rather bleak. You and the other parent might die close together in time. Or you may currently be a single parent, and need to come to terms with what will happen if you do not survive until your children reach age 18.

This section discusses using WillMaker to choose a personal guardian to care for the children's basic health, education and other daily needs. Choosing a person to manage your children's property is discussed in Chapter 6.

1. Reasons for Naming a Personal Guardian

The general legal rule is that if there are two parents willing and able to care for the children, and one dies, the other will take over physical custody and responsibility for caring for the child. In many states, the surviving parent may also be given authority by a court to manage any property the deceased parent left to the children—unless the deceased parent has specified a different property management arrangement in a will.

But there is no ready fallback plan if both parents of a minor child die, or in the case of a single parent, there is not another parent able or willing to do the job. Using WillMaker, you can cover these concerns by naming a personal guardian and an alternate. The person you name will normally be appointed by the court to act as a surrogate parent for your minor children if:

- there is no surviving natural or adoptive parent able to properly care for the children, and
- the court agrees that your choice is in the best interests of the children.

If both parents are making wills, they should name the same person as guardian for each child—to avoid the possibility of a dispute and perhaps even a court battle should they die simultaneously. But remember, if one spouse dies, the other will usually assume custody and will then be free to make a new will naming a different personal guardian if he or she wishes. In short, in a family where both parents are active caretakers, the personal guardian named in a will cares for the children only if both parents die at the same time or close together. However, if you feel strongly that the other person is not the best person to care for the children, be sure to explain your reasoning when the WillMaker program prompts you to do so. (See Section F4.)

 One Guardian and Alternate Per Child

WillMaker allows only one person to be named as personal guardian and one person as alternate personal guardian for each of a parent's minor children. While it is legally permissible to name co-guardians, it is normally a poor idea because of the possibility that the co-guardians will later disagree or go separate ways.

NAMING DIFFERENT GUARDIANS FOR DIFFERENT CHILDREN

One obvious concern in choosing a personal guardian for your children is to keep them together if they relate well to each other as siblings. This suggests that it is best to name the same personal guardian for all the children. But sometimes, the children in a family are not particularly close to one another, but have strong attachments with one or more adults outside the immediate family. For instance, one child may spend a lot of time with a grandparent while another child may be close to an aunt and uncle. Also, in a second or third marriage, a child from an earlier marriage may be close to a different adult than a child from the current marriage. In these situations and others, logic dictates other advice: choose the personal guardian you believe would best be able to care for the child. This may mean that you will choose different personal guardians for different children.

2. Choosing a Personal Guardian

To qualify as a personal guardian, your choice must be an adult—18 in most states—and competent to do the job. For obvious reasons, you should first consider an adult with whom the child already has a close relationship—a stepparent, grandparent, aunt or uncle, older sibling, close friend of the family or even a neighbor. Whoever you choose, be sure that person is mature, good-hearted and willing and able to assume the responsibility.

3. Choosing an Alternate Personal Guardian

WillMaker lets you name a back-up or alternate personal guardian to serve in case your first choice for each child either changes his or her mind or is unable to do the job at your death. The considerations involved in naming an alternate personal guardian are the same as those you pondered when making your first choice: maturity, a good heart, familiarity with the children and willingness to serve.

4. Explaining Your Choice

Leaving a written explanation of why you made a particular choice for a personal guardian may be especially important if you are separated or divorced. You may have strong ideas about why the child's other parent, or perhaps a grandparent, should not have custody of your minor children. In an age when many parents live separately, the following predicaments are sadly common:

"I have custody of my three children. I don't want my ex-husband, who I believe is emotionally destructive, to get custody of our children if I die. Can I choose a guardian to serve instead of him?"

"I have legal custody of my daughter and I've remarried. My present wife is a much better mother to my daughter than my ex-wife, who never cared for her properly. What can I do to make sure my present wife gets custody if I die?"

"I live with a man who's been a good parent to my children for six years. My father doesn't like the fact that we aren't married and may well try to get custody of the kids if I die. What can I do to see that my partner gets custody?"

There is no definitive answer to these questions. If you die while the child is still a minor and the other parent disputes your choice in court, the judge will likely grant custody to the other natural parent, unless that parent:

- has legally abandoned the child by not providing for or visiting the child for an extended period, or
- is clearly unfit as a parent.

Example: Susan and Fred, an unmarried couple, have two minor children. Although Susan loves Fred, she does not think he is capable of raising the children on his own. She uses WillMaker to name her mother, Elinor, as guardian. If Susan dies, Fred, as the children's natural parent, will be given first priority as personal guardian over Elinor, despite Susan's will, assuming the court finds he is willing and able to care for the children. However, if the court finds that Fred should not be personal guardian, Elinor would get the nod, assuming she was fit.

TIPS ON WHAT TO INCLUDE

When deciding who should become a child's personal guardian, the courts of all states are required to act in the child's best interests. In making this determination, the courts commonly consider a number of facts, which you might want to include when explaining your choice for personal guardian.

- Who the parents nominated to become the personal guardian
- Whether the proposed personal guardian will provide the greatest stability and continuity of care for the child
- Which person will best be able to meet the child's needs, whatever these happen to be
- The quality of the relationship between the child and the adults being considered for guardian
- The child's preferences to the extent these can be gleaned
- The moral fitness and conduct of the proposed guardians.

It is usually difficult to prove that a parent is unfit, absent serious and obvious problems such as chronic drug or alcohol abuse, mental illness or a history of child abuse. The fact that you do not like or respect the other parent is never enough, by itself, for a court to deny custody to him or her. But if you honestly believe the other natural parent is incapable of caring for your children properly—or simply will not assume the responsibility—you should reinforce that belief by explaining why you elected to name other people as guardians and alternates.

Example: Justine and Paul live together with Justine's minor children from an earlier marriage. The natural father is out of the picture, but Justine fears that her mother, Tamira, who does not approve of unmarried couples living together, will try to get custody of the kids if something happens to her. Justine wants Paul to have custody because he knows the children well and loves them. She can use WillMaker to name Paul as personal guardian and add a statement making the reasons for this choice clear.

If Justine dies and Tamira goes to court to get custody, the fact that Justine named Paul will give him an advantage. If he is a good parent, he is likely to get custody in most states.

CUSTODY DIFFICULTIES FOR LESBIANS AND GAY MEN

Many lesbians and gay men are parents. If only one of the couple is a lesbian or gay, and there is later an acrimonious divorce, there may also be a difficult legal battle over who gets custody of the children. In a court fight over custody, judges are supposed to consider all factors and arrive at a decision in the "best interests of the child."

This means that virtually any information about a parent's lifestyle, sexual orientation and behavior can be brought out in court. In many states, especially in the south and midwest, evidence of a parent's lesbian or gay sexual identity is still a legally accepted reason for denying custody. If you anticipate a contested custody case, you will find guidance in *A Legal Guide for Lesbian and Gay Couples*, by Curry, Clifford and Leonard (Nolo Press).

CHAPTER 4

About Your Property

This chapter discusses the grist of willmaking: what you own, how you own it and what legal rules affect how you can leave it. Once you have considered the information about property in this chapter, you will be ready to use WillMaker to leave it to others—a task discussed in detail in Chapter 5. If you have children, see Chapter 6 for a discussion of their rights to inherit property and your right to disinherit them.

Many of you will not need the information in this chapter. If you plan to leave your property in a lump—that is, without leaving specific property items to specific people—it makes little difference what you own and how you own it. That will be sorted out when you die, and the people you have named to take "all" your property will get whatever you own—and they will not get what you do not own.

This chapter is important for you to read if:

- you are married—and this includes everyone who has not received a final decree of divorce—and plan to name someone other than your spouse to receive all or most of your property, or

- you plan to leave specific property items to specific people or organizations.

A. Property Not Affected by Your Will

Your will does not affect property that you have already arranged to leave by another method. For example, property in a living trust or a pay-on-death account, in joint tenancy, or in a retirement account or insurance policy where you have named the beneficiary, is not affected by your will.

Example: Laverne owns her house in joint tenancy with her daughter Linda. Later, she makes a will, leaving all of her property to her son Philip. At Laverne's death, Linda gets the house.

1. Property Held in Joint Tenancy

Two or more people can own property—real estate or personal property such as securities or a bank account—in joint tenancy with right of survivorship. When one of them dies, his or her share automatically goes to the surviving owner, called a joint tenant. A joint tenant cannot use a will to leave his or her share of the property to someone else.

If, however, you want to end a joint tenancy while you are alive, it is easy. You need only sign a new deed changing the way the property is held from joint tenancy to tenancy in common. (See Section B5.) Each person still owns the same share, but because a tenancy in common does not include any automatic right of survivorship, each owner is then free to leave his or her share of the property by will.

Normally, joint tenancies with right of survivorship are created by language in the document—a deed, title document or bank account certificate—that controls how the property is owned. To find out whether you own property in joint tenancy, examine the title document for the words "joint tenants," "joint tenancy," or "joint tenancy with right of survivorship." In Oregon, the words "tenancy in common with the right of survivorship" are required. And if you find just the notation "JT WROS," that too, means joint tenancy with right of survivorship.

STATES THAT HAVE RESTRICTED OR ABOLISHED JOINT TENANCY

The following states have limited or abolished joint tenancy. If you live in one of these states and believe you may have a joint tenancy ownership, make sure you understand what it means. Pay special attention to the state rules about whether the joint tenancy property passes automatically at death.

Alabama	No right of survivorship unless it is expressly indicated.
Alaska	No joint tenancy in real estate, except for husband and wife.
Florida	No right of survivorship unless it is expressly indicated.
Kentucky	No right of survivorship unless it is expressly indicated.
North Carolina	No right of survivorship unless it is expressly indicated.
Oregon	No joint tenancy for any property, but the right of survivorship may be created by express agreement between the joint owners. Transfers to husband and wife are considered tenancies by the entirety.
Pennsylvania	No right of survivorship unless it is expressly indicated.
South Carolina	No right of survivorship unless it is expressly indicated.
Tennessee	No joint tenancy for any property, but right of survivorship may be created by express agreement between joint owners. Transfers to husband and wife are considered tenancies by the entirety.
Texas	No joint tenancy for any property, but right of survivorship may be created by written agreement between joint owners.
Virginia	No right of survivorship unless it is expressly indicated.
Washington	No right of survivorship unless it is expressly indicated.
West Virginia	No right of survivorship unless it is expressly indicated.

If You Die the Sole Owner

If the other joint owners die before you do, and you end up the sole owner, you can of course change your will, or make a new one, to add the property and name someone to receive it. If you do not, the property will pass to the person or organization named in your will to receive any property not left to specific people or organizations.

2. Property Held in Tenancy by the Entirety

This form of ownership is basically the same as joint tenancy with right of survivorship discussed above, but is limited to married couples. The certificate of title for the property must specify that it is held as a tenancy by the entirety for this type of ownership to exist. When one spouse dies, the entire interest in the property goes automatically to the other.

Before tenancy by the entirety property can be changed to some other form of property ownership, both spouses must agree to the change.

Nearly half the states recognize tenancy by the entirety, but several of them—Alaska, Indiana, Kentucky, Michigan, New Jersey, New York, North Carolina, Oregon, Virginia and Wyoming—allow it only for real estate. In Kentucky, the deed must expressly state that there is a right of survivorship. If not, the spouses take the property as tenants in common (Ky. Rev. Stat. 381.050).

STATES WITH TENANCY BY THE ENTIRETY OWNERSHIP

Alaska	Massachusetts	Oklahoma
Arkansas	Michigan	Oregon
Delaware	Mississippi	Pennsylvania
District of Columbia	Missouri	Rhode Island
Florida	New Jersey	Tennessee
Hawaii	New York	Vermont
Indiana	North Carolina	Virginia
Kentucky	Ohio	Wyoming
Maryland		

3. Pay-on-Death Bank Accounts and U.S. Government Securities

These accounts are held in your name, but with a direction to pay the balance to another person at your death. You can change this pay-on-death form of ownership while you are alive, but if you die with property owned in this way, the person you designated on the bank's or government's registration form, when you set up the account will inherit it.

Example: Marc opens a bank account and deposits $5,000 in it. He states, on the bank's form, that whatever funds are in the account at his death should be turned over to his son, Jordan. Later, when he makes his will, he leaves the account to his nephew, but he does not change the way the account is registered at the bank. His son, not the nephew, will receive the money in the account.

4. Property You Place in a Trust

Property you place in a trust passes automatically to the beneficiary named in the trust document—not under the terms of your will. This includes property placed in a revocable living trust.

5. Property Left in Retirement Accounts

IRAs, Keoghs, 401(k) and similar retirement plans allow you to name a beneficiary and alternate beneficiary to take what remains in your account at your death. Once you name a beneficiary on the forms provided by the account administrator, your will have no affect on it. If you want to change the beneficiary, you must notify the retirement account administrator.

6. Life Insurance and Annuities

Proceeds of life insurance and annuity policies automatically go to the person or institution you named as beneficiary of the policy. If your first choice dies before you, the proceeds go to any alternate beneficiary you named. Your will does not affect insurance money unless you named your own estate as the beneficiary.

B. Property You Own With Others

If you are not married, and you own property with someone else, you probably own it in tenancy in common. This is the most common way for unmarried people to own property together. Each co-owner is free to sell or give away his or her interest during life or leave it to another at death in a will. To tell whether or not you own property as tenancy in common, check the deed or other title document; it should specifically note that the property is held as a tenancy in common.

If you are married, a whole host of legal rules may affect what property you own jointly and separately. (See Section D.)

C. Property on Which You Owe Money

Using WillMaker, if you leave property on which you owe money, the beneficiary who inherits it will also inherit the debt. This means the beneficiary of the property is responsible for paying off the debt.

D. Property Ownership Rules for Married People

Most married people leave all or the greatest share of their property to their surviving spouses at death. For them, the nuances of marital property law are not important, since the survivor gets the property, anyway.

But if you plan to leave your property to several people instead of or in addition to your spouse, the picture becomes more complicated. Under your state's laws, your spouse may own some property you believe is yours. And if you do not own it, you cannot give it away— either now or at your death. Questions of which spouse owns what property are important if your spouse does not agree to your plan for property disposition.

There are two issues to consider:

- What do you own?
- Will your spouse have the right to claim a share of your property—up to half, in some states—after your death? (See Section E.)

This section will help you determine what you own and so can leave to others in your will. To figure it out, you need to know a little about the laws of your state. When it comes to property ownership, states are broadly divided into two types: community property states and common law property states.

COMMUNITY PROPERTY STATES

Arizona	New Mexico
California	Texas
Idaho	Washington
Nevada	Wisconsin*

COMMON LAW STATES

All other states

*While Wisconsin is not technically a community property state, its marital property law resembles those found in community property states.

1. Community Property States

If you live in a community property state, there are a few key rules to keep in mind while making your will.

- You can leave your separate property to anyone you wish.

- You can leave half of the community property, which you and your spouse own together, to anyone you wish.

- After your death, your spouse keeps the other half of the community property.

a. Your separate property

In community property states, your separate property is:

- all property you owned before marriage

- any property you acquire after permanent separation, and

- property you receive during marriage by gift or inheritance, as long as it is kept separate from community property.

b. Community property

Generally, community property includes all earnings either spouse brings in during a marriage, plus the property bought with those earnings during the marriage. Each spouse owns half of the couple's community property.

Specifically, community property includes:

- all employment income received by either spouse during marriage. The one major exception to this rule is that all community property states except Washington allow spouses to treat income earned during marriage as separate property. But the spouses must sign a written agreement to do so and then actually keep that income separate—for example, in separate bank accounts.

- all property bought with employment income received by either spouse during their marriage—but not after permanent separation, and

- all property that, despite originally being separate property, is transformed into community property under state laws. Separate property turns into community property when one spouse gives it to the couple—for example, by putting a separately owned home in community property ownership. Or, a spouse who owns separate property may let it get so mixed together (commingled) with community property that it is no longer possible to tell the difference between the two.

Example: John has $10,000 in the bank when he marries Elsie. This is his separate property. Over the next several years, John deposits a number of community property paychecks in this account and regularly withdraws money to pay bills—some of them for the couple's living expenses, some to pay for John's optimistic habit of betting on the New England Patriots. The account balance fluctuates from $2,000 to $20,000. The separate property money in this account has been so commingled with community property that now the entire account is considered community property. That means John owns only half of the money.

CLASSIFYING PROPERTY IN COMMUNITY PROPERTY STATES: SOME EXAMPLES

Property	Community or Separate	Why
A computer you inherited while married	Separate; you can leave it in your will	Inherited property belongs only to the person who inherited it.
A car you bought before you got married	Separate; you can leave it in your will	Property owned before marriage is not community property.
A boat you bought with your income while married and registered in your name	Community; you can leave only your half-interest in your will	It was purchased with community property income (income earned during the marriage).
The family home you and your spouse own together	Community; you can leave your half-interest in your will	It was purchased with community property income (income earned during the marriage).
A loan that your brother owes you	Community; you can leave your half-interest in your will	The loan was made from community property funds and belongs half to you and half to your spouse.
A fishing cabin you inherited from your father	Separate; you can leave it in your will	Inherited property belongs belongs only to the person who inherited it.
Stock you and your spouse bought with savings from your spouse's earnings during marriage	Community; you can leave your half-interest in your will	It was purchased with one spouse's earnings, which are community property.

State Differences in Categorizing Property

States have slightly different rules on what is classified as community property. One of the biggest differences is how income earned by separate property is treated. In Idaho and Texas, it is considered community property. In Arizona, California, Nevada, New Mexico and Washington, any income earned by separate property is separate property.

c. Property that is difficult to categorize

Normally, classifying property as community or separate property is easy. But in some situations, it can be a close call. There are several potential problem areas.

Businesses. Family businesses can create complications, especially if they were owned before marriage by one spouse and expanded during the marriage. The key is to figure out whether the increased value of the business is community or separate property. If you and your spouse do not have the same view of how to pass on the business, it may be worthwhile to get help from a lawyer or accountant.

Money from a personal injury lawsuit. Usually, but not always, awards won in a personal injury lawsuit are the separate property of the spouse receiving them. There is no easy way to characterize this type of property. If a significant amount of your property came from a personal injury settlement, research the specifics of your state's law or ask an estate planning expert.

Pensions. Generally, the part of a pension gained from earnings made during the marriage is considered to be community property. This is also true of military pensions. However, some federal pensions—such as Railroad Retirement benefits and Social Security retirement benefits—are not considered community property because federal law deems them to be the separate property of the employee earning them.

2. Common Law Property States

Common law property states are all states other than Arizona, California, Idaho, Nevada, New Mexico, Texas, Washington and Wisconsin.

In these states, you own:

- all property you purchased using your property or income, and
- property you own solely in your name if it has a title slip, deed or other legal ownership document.

In common law states, the key to ownership for many types of valuable property is whose name is on the title. If you and your spouse take title to a house together—that is, both of your names are on the deed—you both own it. That is true even if you earned or inherited the money you used to buy it. If your spouse earns the money, but you take title in your name alone, you own it.

If the property is valuable but has no title document, such as a computer, then the person whose income or property is used to pay for it owns it. If joint income is used, then you own it together. You can each leave your half in your will, unless you signed an agreement providing for a joint tenancy or a tenancy by the entirety. (See Section A.)

Example: Will and Jane are married and live in Kentucky, a common law property state. They have five children. Shortly after their marriage, Jane wrote an extremely popular computer program that helps doctors diagnose illness. She has received royalties averaging about $200,000 a year over a ten-year period. Jane has used the royalties to buy a car, boat and mountain cabin—all registered in her name alone. The couple also owns a house as joint tenants. In addition, Jane owns a number of family heirlooms which she inherited from her parents. Throughout their marriage, Jane and Will have maintained separate savings accounts. Will works as a computer engineer and has deposited all of his income into his account. Jane put her unspent royalties in her account, which now contains $75,000.

Jame owns...	Will owns...
the savings account listed in her name alone	the savings account listed in his name alone
one-half interest in the house (which, because it is held in joint tenancy, will go to Will at Jane's death)	one-half interest in the house (which, because it is held in joint tenancy, will go to Jane at Will's death)
the car, boat and cabin, since there are title documents listing them in her name. If there were no such documents, she would still own them because they were bought with her income.	
her family heirlooms	

Example: Martha and Scott, who are married, have both worked for 30 years as schoolteachers in Michigan, a common law state. Generally, Scott and Martha pooled their income and jointly purchased a house, worth $200,000 (in both their names as joint tenants), cars (one in Martha's name and one in Scott's), a share in a vacation condominium (in both names as joint tenants), and household furniture. Each maintains a separate savings account, and they also have a joint tenancy checking account containing $2,000. In addition, Scott and his sister own a piece of land as tenants in common.

Martha owns...	Scott owns...
her savings account	his savings account
half-interest in the house and condo (which, because they are held in joint tenancy, will go to Scott at Martha's death)	half-interest in the house and condo (which, because they are held in joint tenancy, will go to Martha at Scott's death)
her car	his car
half the furniture	half the furniture
	a half-interest in the land he owns with his sister

3. Moving From State to State

Complications may set in when a husband and wife acquire property in a common law property state and then move to a community property state. Californi, Idaho and Washington treat the earlier-acquired property as if it had been acquired in the community property state. The legal jargon for this type of property is quasi-community property.

The other community property states do not recognize the quasi-community property concept for willmaking purposes. Instead, they go by the rules of the state where the property was acquired. If you and your spouse move from a non-community property state into California or Idaho, all of your property is treated according to community property rules. However, if you move to any of the other community property states from a common law state, you must assess your property according to the rules of the state where the property was acquired.

Couples who move from a community property state to a common law state face the opposite problem. Generally, each spouse retains one-half interest in the community property the couple accumulated while living in the community property state. However, if there is a conflict after your death, it can get messy; courts dealing with the issue have not been consistent.

 If You Move

If you move from a community property state to a common law one, and you and your spouse have any disagreement as to who owns what, it may be wise to check with a lawyer. (See Chapter 15.)

E. Your Spouse's Right to Inherit From You

If you intend to leave your spouse very little or no property, you may run into some legal roadblocks. All common law property states (see list in Section D2) protect a surviving spouse from being completely disinherited—and most assure that a spouse has the right to receive a substantial share of a deceased spouse's property.

Community property states do not give surviving spouses this kind of protection. Instead, they try to protect spouses while both are still alive, by granting each spouse half ownership of property and earnings either spouse acquires during the marriage. (See Section D1.)

 Leaving Little to a Spouse

If you do not plan to leave at least half of your property to your spouse in your will and have not provided for him or her generously outside your will, consult a lawyer unless your spouse willingly consents in writing to a plan leaving a large part of your estate to others—perhaps children, charities or grandchildren.

In a common law state, a shortchanged surviving spouse usually has the option of either taking what the will provides, called taking under the will, or rejecting the gift and instead taking the minimum share allowed by state law, called taking against the will. In some states, your spouse may have the right to inherit the family residence, or at least use it for his or her life. The Florida constitution, for example, gives a surviving spouse the deceased spouse's residence.

Of course, these are just options; a spouse who is not unhappy with the share he or she receives by will is free to let it stand. And in some states, one spouse can give up all rights to inherit any property by completing and signing a special document. If you want to make that type of arrangement, consult a lawyer. (See Chapter 15.)

FAMILY ALLOWANCES

Some states provide additional, relatively minor protection such as family allowances and probate homesteads. These vary from state to state in too much detail to discuss here. Generally, however, these devices attempt to assure that your spouse and children are not totally left out in the cold after your death, by allowing them temporary protection—such as the right to remain in the family home for a short period, or funds—typically, living expenses while an estate is being probated.

Laws protecting spouses vary among the states. In most common law property states, a spouse is entitled to one-third of the property left in the will. In a few, it is one-half. The exact amount of the spouse's minimum share often depends on whether there are also minor children and whether the spouse has been provided for outside the will by trusts or other means.

Example: Leonard's will leaves $50,000 to his second wife, June, and the rest of his property, totaling $400,000, to May and April, his daughters from his first marriage. June can choose instead to receive her statutory share of Leonard's estate, which will be far more than $50,000. To the probable dismay of May and April, their shares will be substantially reduced; they will share what is left of Leonard's property after June gets her statutory share.

In many common law states, how much the surviving spouse is entitled to receive depends on what that spouse receives both under the will and outside of the will—for example, through joint tenancy or a living trust. The total of both of these is called the augmented estate.

While the augmented estate concept is rather complicated, its purpose is easy to grasp. Basically, all property of a deceased spouse, not just the property left by will, is taken into account in determining whether a spouse has been left the minimum statutory share. This makes sense because many people devise ways to pass their property to others outside of wills to avoid probate fees. (See Chapter 12, Section B.)

Example: Alice leaves $10,000 to her husband, Mike, and $7,000 to each of her three daughters in her will. However, Alice also leaves Mike real estate worth $500,000 through a living trust. The total Mike receives from the augmented estate—$510,000—is more than half of the value of Alice's total property, so he would have nothing to gain by exercising his option of ignoring the will and taking his statutory share instead.

FAMILY PROTECTION IN COMMON LAW STATES

Alabama	Spouse has right to $1/3$ of augmented estate
Alaska	Spouse has right to $1/3$ of augmented estate
Arkansas	Spouse entitled to percentage, which varies if there are children; usually $1/2$ if no children, $1/3$ if children
Colorado	Spouse has right to up to $1/2$ of augmented estate, depending on the length of the marriage
Connecticut	Surviving spouse has right to use $1/3$ of deceased spouse's real property for life
Delaware	Spouse has right to $1/3$ of estate
District of Columbia	Spouse has right to up to $1/2$ of estate, depending on what the surviving spouse's intestate share would have been
Florida	Spouse has right to 30% of estate
Georgia	Spouse entitled to percentage, which varies if there are children; usually $1/2$ if no children, $1/3$ if children
Hawaii	Spouse has right to $1/3$ of estate
Illinois	Spouse entitled to percentage, which varies if there are children; usually one-half if no children, one-third if children
Indiana	Spouse entitled to percentage, which varies if there are children; usually $1/2$ if no children, $1/3$ if children
Iowa	Spouse has right to $1/3$ of estate
Kansas	Spouse has right to up to $1/2$ of augmented estate, depending on the length of the marriage
Kentucky	Spouse has right to use $1/3$ of deceased spouse's real property for life

Maine	Spouse has right to $^1/_3$ of augmented estate
Maryland	Spouse entitled to percentage, which varies if there are children; usually $^1/_2$ if no children, $^1/_3$ if children
Massachusetts	Spouse entitled to percentage, which varies if there are children; usually $^1/_2$ if no children, one-third if children
Michigan	Spouse has right to up to $^1/_2$ of estate
Minnesota	Spouse has right to $^1/_2$ of estate (through December 31, 1995); up to $^1/_2$ of augmented estate, depending on length of marriage (after December 31, 1995)
Mississippi	Spouse has right to up to $^1/_2$ of estate, depending on what surviving spouse's intestate share would have been
Missouri	Spouse entitled to percentage, which varies if there are children, usually $^1/_2$ if no children, $^1/_3$ if children
Montana	Spouse has right to up to $^1/_2$ of augmented estate, depending on the length of the marriage
Nebraska	Spouse has right to $^1/_2$ of augmented estate
New Hampshire	Spouse entitled to percentage, which varies if there are children; usually $^1/_2$ if no children, $^1/_3$ if children
New Jersey	Spouse has right to $^1/_3$ of augmented estate
New York	Spouse has right to $50,000 or $^1/_3$ of the net estate, whichever is greater
North Carolina	Spouse has right to up to $^1/_3$ of the net estate, depending on what surviving spouse's share would have been
North Dakota	Spouse has right to $^1/_3$ of augmented estate
Ohio	Spouse entitled to percentage, which varies if there are children; usually $^1/_2$ if no children, $^1/_3$ if children

Oklahoma	Spouse has right to $1/2$ interest in all property acquired by the joint work of spouses during marriage
Oregon	Spouse has right to $1/4$ of estate
Pennsylvania	Spouse has right to $1/3$ of estate
Rhode Island	Spouse has right to 100% of deceased spouse's real property, subject to any encumbrances existing at his or her death
South Carolina	Spouse has right to $1/3$ of estate
South Dakota	Spouse has right to $100,000 or $1/3$ of augmented estate, whichever is greater
Tennessee	Spouse has right to $1/3$ of estate
Utah	Spouse has right to $1/3$ of augmented estate
Vermont	Spouse has right to use $1/3$ of deceased spouse's real property for life
Virginia	Spouse entitled to percentage, which varies if there are children; usually $1/2$ if no children, $1/3$ if children
West Virginia	Spouse has right to up to $1/2$ of augmented estate, depending on the length of the marriage
Wyoming	Spouse entitled to percentage, which varies if there are children; usually $1/2$ if no children, $1/3$ if children

How to Leave Your Property

The heart of willmaking is deciding who gets your property when you die. For many, this is an easy task: You want it all to go to your spouse, your kids, your partner or your favorite charity. For others, it's a little more complicated—for example, you want most of it to go to your spouse, partner, child or charity, but you also want certain items to go to other people. You may even have a fairly complicated scheme in mind that involves divvying your property among a number of people and organizations.

Chapter 4 introduced some basic concepts about your property and your ability to leave it in your will. This chapter explains how to put your plan into effect using the WillMaker program. WillMaker is designed to accommodate your wishes. If you want to leave all or most of your property to a spouse, loved one or favorite charity, the program offers you some shortcuts. And WillMaker also accommodates more complex wishes.

After you name who you want to get your property, WillMaker lets you name alternates—that is, who should get property if your first choices do not survive you.

You do not need to read all of this chapter to figure out how to write the will you want. Start with the discussion that is tailored to your situation:

- If you are married with children: Section A

- If you are married without children: Section B
- If you are unmarried with children: Section C
- If you are unmarried without children: Section D

A. If You Are Married With Children

Many married people have simple willmaking needs. They want to leave all or most of their property to their spouses. As alternates for their spouses, they may want to choose their children, or name another person or organization. WillMaker lets you choose any of those paths easily. And if you do not want to make your spouse the main beneficiary of your will, that option is available, too.

1. Choosing Your Beneficiaries

WillMaker will prompt you to choose one of three approaches to leaving your property:

- leave everything to your spouse
- leave most of your property, with some specific exceptions, to your spouse, or
- make a plan that may or may not include your spouse.

The third option offers flexibility. You should choose it if you want to divide up your property more evenly among a number of beneficiaries, or if you want to give all or most of your property to someone other than your spouse. If you choose it, be sure that you understand the rules governing what you own and the rights of your spouse. (See Chapter 4, Section D.)

Example: Anne and Robert are a married couple with one young child. Anne wants a simple will, in which she leaves all of her property to Robert. She chooses the first option—everything to your spouse—to get a will that reflects her wishes.

Example: Arnie wants his wife to receive most of his property when he dies, but he has a valuable violin that he wants to go to his best friend, Eddie, and a coin collection that he wants his nephew to receive. Arnie chooses the second option—most to your spouse. Then, later in the program, he can name Eddie to receive his violin and his nephew to receive his coin collection.

Example: Sylvia is married to Fred. She wants to leave him her share of their investment portfolio and family business, but also wants to leave a number of specific property items to her many different friends, relatives and charities. She chooses the third option when using WillMaker. The program then prompts her to list specific property items and the person or organization she wants to receive each one. Before she does, Sylvia reviews Chapter 4 to make sure she understands what property is appropriate to leave in her will.

 When You Can Skip Ahead

If you do not want to name your spouse to receive all or most of your property, skip the rest of this section and go to Section E for a discussion of what comes next.

2. Choosing Alternates for Your Spouse

If you choose your spouse to receive all or most of your property, your next task will be to choose an alternate for your spouse.

The will you create with WillMaker provides that all beneficiaries—including your spouse—must survive you by 45 days to receive the property you leave them. This is a standard will provision, called a survivorship requirement. It is based on the assumption that if a beneficiary survives you by only a few days or weeks, you would prefer the property to go to another beneficiary that you choose and name in your will.

The alternates you choose will receive the property only if your spouse dies less than 45 days after you do.

Depending on your previous choices, WillMaker offers two or three options for alternates. You can name:

- your child or children, or
- alternate beneficiaries you name.

These two approaches to naming alternates are shortcuts. If your spouse does not survive you by 45 days or more, then alternates will receive all the property that would have gone to your spouse. You need not specify which items go to which beneficiaries.

If you named your spouse to receive all your property, you also have a third option: You can make a completely new plan for leaving your property—or Plan B—which will take effect only if your spouse does not survive you by at least 45 days. If you choose to make Plan B, you can divvy up your property among a number of alternate beneficiaries.

Each of these approaches to naming alternates is discussed below.

a. Designating your children as alternates

It is common for married people with children to simply leave all or most of their property to the surviving spouse and name the children as alternates for the spouse. This means if your spouse does not survive you by 45 days, the property your spouse would have received will pass to your child or children.

If you have more than one child, you will also need to decide how the children should share the property.

If any of your children are 18 or older, you can specify the share each will receive. Later in the program, you will have the option of designating someone to manage a child's share if he or she is still a young adult when you die. (See Chapter 6.)

Example: Meg and Charlie have three grown children. When Charlie makes his will, he leaves everything to Meg and names the children as alternates for her. He directs that all three children should receive equal shares of his property.

If any of your children are minors—that is, under 18 years old—you may:

- specify the share each child will receive; later, you may designate how each child's share will be managed and doled out if a child is under 35 when you die, or

- direct that the property be held in one undivided fund, called a pot trust; under this option, the person you select to serve as trustee will use the assets in the trust for all your children as needed, until your youngest child turns an age you choose.

(See Chapter 6 for a discussion of these methods for managing property left to children.)

Example: Julia and Emanuel have three school-aged children. When Julia makes her will, she names Emanuel to inherit most of her property and leaves a few small items to her sister. As alternates for her husband, she picks her children. But because they are too young to manage money or property, later in the program she names her sister to manage any property the children may inherit while they are still young.

Example: Barry and his wife Marta have two young daughters close in age. In his will, Barry leaves Marta all his property and chooses the children as alternate beneficiaries. He also picks the pot trust option and names his mother as trustee. If Marta does not survive him by a least 45 days, all of Barry's property will go into a trust for the two girls, administered by Barry's mother.

WillMaker also lets you name a second level of alternates—that is, alternates who will take the property a child would have received, if that child does not survive you. You can name an alternate for each child, or simply designate that the survivors receive any property that would have gone to a deceased child.

b. Naming alternates

If you decide to specify alternates to receive the property left to your spouse, you may name whomever you want. You are not constrained, as with the first option, to naming only your children as alternates. For instance, you may name a charity, or some of your children. If your spouse does not survive you by 45 days, the alternates you name will receive the property your spouse would have received. If you name more than one person or organization, you may specify what share each is to receive.

Example: Celeste is married with two grown children. The children have both been provided for nicely with money from trusts, and are financially secure.

In her will, Celeste leaves her husband most of her property, with a few exceptions of some heirlooms for her children. As an alternate for her husband, she names the university where she taught for many years.

You can also name a second level of alternates—that is, alternates to take the property should both your spouse and a first level of alternate you name all die before you do. You can name a back-up alternate for each first-choice alternate. If you named more than one first-level alternate, you may designate that the survivors receive any property that would have gone to a deceased alternate.

c. Making an alternate plan

This option—Plan B—is available only if you choose to leave all your property to your spouse.

It lets you create a whole new plan to take effect if, and only if, your spouse doesn't survive you by 45 days. This option is for people who think like this: I want to leave all my property to my spouse, period. But in case my spouse does not survive me, I want to make a whole new plan from the ground up—my Plan B—that does not include my spouse. Then, if my spouse survives me, he gets all my property. But if not, I'll have been able to divide my property just as if I weren't married.

Your Plan B can include as many specific bequests as you wish. (See Section E.) After you have made all your specific bequests, you can also name someone to take the rest of your property. This is called your residuary beneficiary. (See Section F.) Again, all of these Plan B bequests will take effect only if your spouse does not survive you by 45 days.

Example: Sean wants to leave all his property to Eva, his wife, if she's alive when he dies. But thinking about what he would want to happen if Eva were not around to take everything, he decides that he would want to divide his property among several friends, relatives and charities.

When he sits down with WillMaker to make his will, Sean names Eva to get all his property. Then, when it's time to name alternates, he chooses the Plan B option and leaves $10,000 to a local food bank, his piano to his niece and the rest of his property to his brother.

B. If You Are Married Without Children

Many married people have simple willmaking needs. They want to leave all or most of their property to their spouses. Then, as alternates for their spouses, they may name one or more other people or organizations. WillMaker lets you choose this path easily. And if you do not want to make your spouse the main beneficiary of your will, that option is available, too.

1. Choosing Your Beneficiaries

WillMaker will prompt you to choose one of three approaches to leaving your property:

- leave everything to your spouse
- leave most of your property, with some specific exceptions, to your spouse
- make a plan that may or may not include your spouse.

The third option offers flexibility. You should choose it if you want to divide up your property more evenly among a number of beneficiaries, or if you want to give all or most of your property to someone other than your spouse. If you choose it, be sure that you understand the rules governing what you own and the rights of your spouse. (See Chapter 4, Section D.)

Example: Mark and Abby are a young married couple with no children. Mark wants simply to leave everything to Abby in his will. He chooses the first option—everything to your spouse—so that his will reflects his intentions.

Example: Paul wants his wife to receive most of his property when he dies, but he wants his golf clubs to go to his best friend, Eric, and wants his niece to take his photography equipment. Paul chooses the second option—most to your spouse. Then, later in the program, he can name Eric to receive his golf clubs and his niece to receive the photography equipment.

Example: Eleanor is married to William. She wants to leave William her share of their investment portfolio and family business, but also wants to leave a number of specific items to different friends, relatives and charities. She chooses the third option when using WillMaker. The program then prompts her to list specific property items and the person or organization she wants to receive each of them Before she does, Eleanor reviews Chapter 4 to make sure she understands what property is appropriate to leave in her will.

 When You Can Skip Ahead

If you do not want to name your spouse to receive all or most of your property, skip the rest of this section and go to Section E for a discussion of what comes next.

2. Choosing Alternates for Your Spouse

If you choose your spouse to receive all or most of your property, your next task will be to choose an alternate for your spouse.

The will you create with WillMaker provides that all beneficiaries—including your spouse—must survive you by 45 days to receive the property you leave them. This is a standard will provision, called a survivorship requirement. It is based on the assumption that if a beneficiary survives you by only a few days or weeks, you would prefer the property to go to another beneficiary that you choose and name in your will.

The alternates you choose will receive the property only if your spouse does not live at least 45 days longer than you do.

The simplest ways to provide for an alternate are:

- to name one person or organization to receive everything your spouse would have received, or

- to name more than one person or organization to share it all. If you go that route, the alternates will receive all the property that would have gone to your spouse. You need not specify which items go to which beneficiaries.

If, however, you named your spouse to receive all your property, you have a second option: You can make a completely new plan for leaving your property—Plan B—which will take effect only if your spouse does not survive you by 45 days. If you choose to make a new plan, you can divvy up your property among several alternate beneficiaries.

These approaches to naming alternates are discussed below.

a. Naming alternates

You may name whomever you want as the alternate for your spouse. For instance, you may name a charity, friend or relative. If your spouse does not survive you by 45 days, the alternates you name will receive the property your spouse would have received. If you name more than one person or organization, you may specify what share each is to receive.

Example: In her will, Sharon leaves her husband, Alex, most of her property, with a few exceptions of some small items for friends. As an alternate for Alex, she names the charity at which she volunteered for many years.

You can also name a second level of alternates—that is, alternates to take the property should both your spouse and a first level of alternate you name fail to survive you. You can name a back-up alternate for each first-choice alternate. If you named more than one first-level alternate, you may designate that the survivors receive any property that would have gone to a deceased alternate.

b. Making an alternate plan

This option is available only if you choose to leave all your property to your spouse.

It lets you create a whole new plan to take effect if, and only if, your spouse doesn't survive you by 45 days. This option is for people who think like this: I want to leave all my property to my spouse, period. But in case my spouse does not survive me, I want to make a whole new plan from the ground up—my Plan B—that does not include my spouse. Then, if my spouse survives me, he gets all my property. But if not, I'll have been able to divide my property just as if I weren't married.

Your alternate plan—Plan B—can include as many specific bequests as you wish. (See Section E.) After you have made all your specific bequests, you can also name someone to take the rest of your property. This is called your residuary beneficiary. (See Section F.) Again, all of these Plan B bequests will take effect only if your spouse does not survive you by 45 days.

Example: Sean wants to leave all his property to Eva, his wife, if she's alive when he dies. But thinking about what he would want to happen if Eva were not around to take everything, he decides that he would want to divide his property among several friends, relatives and charities.

When he sits down with WillMaker to make his will, Sean names Eva to take everything. Then, when it's time to name alternates, he chooses the Plan B option and leaves $10,000 to a local food bank, his piano to his niece, and everything else to his brother.

C. If You Are Unmarried With Children

If you are a single parent, your children probably figure prominently in your plans for distributing your property after your death. With that in mind, WillMaker offers some shortcuts when making your will.

1. Choosing Your Beneficiaries

WillMaker will prompt you to choose one of three approaches to leaving your property:

- leave everything to your child or children
- leave most of your property, with some specific exceptions, to your child or children, or
- make a plan that may or may not include your children.

The third option offers flexibility. You should choose it if you want to divide up your property more evenly among a number of beneficiaries, or if you want to give all or most of your property to someone other than your children. If you choose it, be sure that you understand the rules governing what you own. (See Chapter 4, Section D.)

Example: Raquel is a divorced mother of two young children. She wants to leave all her property to the children, in equal shares. She chooses the first option.

Example: Carlo, a widower, has one son, who is now 40 years old. Carlo wants to leave most of his property to his son, but also make a few small bequests to charities. He chooses the second option. Then, later in the program, he can name the charities and the amounts he wants to leave to each.

Example: Brenda has three children, all of whom are grown and well-off financially. She wants to leave a number of specific property items to her children but also to many different friends, relatives and charities. She chooses the third option when using WillMaker. The program then asks her to list specific property items and the person or organization she wants to receive each one. Before doing this, Brenda reviews Chapter 4 to make sure she understands what property may appropriately be left in her will.

 When You Can Skip Ahead

If you do not want to name your child or children to receive all or most of your property, skip the rest of this section and go to Section E for a discussion of what comes next.

2. Designating Children's Shares

If you have more than one child, you must decide how you want them to share the property they receive through your will.

If any of your children are adults—that is, 18 or older—you can specify the share each will receive. Later in the program, you will have the option of designating someone to manage a child's share if he or she is still a young adult when you die. (See Chapter 6.)

Example: Charlie has three grown children. When Charlie makes his will, he names the children to receive everything. He directs that all three children should receive equal shares of his property.

If any of your children are minors—that is, under 18 years old—you may:

- specify the share each child will receive; later, you may designate how each child's share will be managed and doled out if a child is under 35 when you die, or

- direct that the property be held in one undivided fund, called a pot trust; under this option, the person you select to serve as trustee will use the assets in the trust for all your children as needed, until your youngest child turns an age you choose.

(All of these methods for managing property left to children are discussed in Chapter 6.)

Example: Tess has three children, two teenagers and one 26-year-old. When she makes her will, she leaves the children most of her property and leaves a few small items to her sister. Because her oldest child is self-supporting, she leaves him just a 1/5 share, and leaves the two younger children 2/5 each. Later in the program, Tess names her sister to manage any property the two younger children come to own while they are still young.

Example: Frank has two young sons close in age. In his will, he leaves them all his property. He then picks the pot trust option and names his sister as trustee. That means that if the boys inherit Frank's property while they are still young, all of it will go into a trust for them, administered by Frank's sister.

3. Choosing Alternates for Your Children

If you choose your child or children to receive all or most of your property, your next task will be to choose an alternate for your child.

 When You Can Skip Ahead

If you do not want to name your child or children to receive all or most of your property, skip the rest of this section and go to Section E for a discussion of what comes next.

The will you create with WillMaker provides that a beneficiary must survive you by 45 days to receive property through the will. This is a standard will provision, called a survivorship requirement. It is based on the assumption that if a beneficiary survives you by only a few weeks, you would prefer the property to go to another beneficiary that you name in your will.

The alternates you choose for a child will receive the property only if the child does not survive you by at least 45 days.

 When You Need Not Choose

If you chose a pot trust, you don't need to name alternates. If one child does not survive you, the other surviving children will still share the property.

If you have one child, you can either:

• name one or more alternates for that child, or

- make a plan that may or may not include your child and other people or organizations.

If you have more than one child and have assigned each child a share, you can either:

- name one or more alternates for each child, or
- designate that if one child doesn't survive you, the survivors should take the deceased child's share.

If you chose a pot trust, you need not name alternates. If any child does not survive you, the others will share the property.

a. Naming alternates

You may name whomever you want—for instance, a charity, friend or relative— as the alternate for a child. If the child does not survive you by 45 days, the alternates will receive the property he or she would have received. If you name more than one alternate, you may specify what share each is to receive.

Example: In her will, Sharon leaves her daughter most of her property and gives the rest to friends. As an alternate for her daughter, she names her daughter's two young children.

b. Survivors

Rather than name alternates for each of your children, you may want to provide that whatever property you leave them will go to all the children who survive you.

Example: In his will, Patrick leaves his daughter and two sons all of his property. He specifies that each should receive an equal share. When WillMaker asks him to name alternates for the children, he chooses that specifies the survivors should take the share.

D. If You Are Unmarried Without Children

As a single person, you are free to leave your property to any person or organization you choose. You may have one beneficiary in mind—perhaps a partner or an organization you value highly. WillMaker gives you the choice of simply leaving everything to that one beneficiary, and then choosing an alternate beneficiary as well. If you don't want to name one main beneficiary of your will, that option is available, too.

1. Choosing Your Beneficiaries

WillMaker will prompt you to choose one of two approaches to leaving your property:

- leave everything to one person, or
- leave your property to a group of beneficiaries or divide it among several.

The first option gives you a shortcut in the process of making your will. The second option can be more involved. If you choose it, be sure that you understand what kinds of property should be left in a will, and what might be passed to your survivors in other ways. (See Chapter 4, Section A.)

Example: Fernando and Robert have been together for many years. When Fernando makes his will, he wants all his property to go to Robert. He chooses the first option—leave everything to one person—to make a will that reflects his wishes.

Example: Theresa, whose husband died several years ago, wants to divide her money and possessions among her many different friends, relatives and charities. She chooses the second option. WillMaker then asks her to list specific property items and the person or organization she wants to receive

each one. Before she does, Sylvia reviews Chapter 4 to make sure she under-
stands what property is appropriate to leave in her will.

 When You Can Skip Ahead

If you do not want to name one beneficiary to receive all or most of your property, skip the rest of this section and go to Section E for a discussion of what comes next.

2. Choosing Alternates

If you choose one person or organization to receive all or most of your property, your next task will be to choose an alternate for that beneficiary.

The will you create with WillMaker provides that all beneficiaries must survive you by 45 days to receive the property you leave them. This is a standard will provision, called a survivorship requirement. It is based on the assumption that if a beneficiary survives you by only a few days or weeks, you would prefer the property to go to another beneficiary that you choose and name in your will.

The alternates you choose will receive the property only if your main beneficiary does not survive for at least 45 days after you die.

WillMaker offers two options for alternates. You can:

- name alternate beneficiaries, or
- make an alternate plan, Plan B, which will take effect only if your main beneficiary does not survive you by 45 days. This way, you can divvy up your property among several alternate beneficiaries.

a. Naming alternates

If you decide to specify alternates to receive the property left to your main beneficiary, you may name whomever you want. For instance, you may name a charity or a group of friends. If you name more than one person or organization, you may specify what share each is to receive.

If your main beneficiary does not survive you by 45 days, the alternates you name will receive the property he or she would have received.

Example: Christine is not married and has no children. She is very close to her sister Karen, and wants to leave all her property to her.

In her will, Christine names Karen as her main beneficiary. As alternates for her, she names Karen's two children.

If you name one alternate beneficiary, you can also name a second level of alternates—that is, alternates to take the property should both your main beneficiary and the alternate not survive you by 45 days or more. If you named more than one first-level alternate, however, the survivors will receive any property that would have gone to a deceased alternate.

Example: In his will, Michael leaves everything to his friend Denise. As alternates for Denise, he names two other friends, Jeff and Jack. If both Denise and Jeff do not survive Michael, Jack will receive all of Michael's property.

b. Making an alternate plan

This option lets you create a whole new plan to take effect only if your main beneficiary does not survive you by 45 days. Your alternate plan—Plan B—can include as many specific bequests as you wish. (See Section E.)

After you have made all your specific bequests, you can also name someone to take the rest of your property. This is called your residuary beneficiary. (See Section F.)

Example: Sven wants to leave all his property to Jeannette, his companion, if she's alive when he dies. But thinking about what he would want to happen if Jeannette were not around to inherit everything, he decides that he would want to divide his property among several friends, relatives and charities.

When he sits down with WillMaker to make his will, Sven names Jeannette to take all of his property. Then, when it's time to name alternates, he chooses the Plan B option and leaves $10,000 to a local food bank, his piano to his niece and everything else to his brother.

E. Making Specific Bequests

This section discusses how to make specific bequests—that is, leave specific property items to specific people or groups. You should read this section if you:

- left most of your property to a main beneficiary, but want to leave some items to others

- want to divide your property among several beneficiaries, without leaving most or all of it to one main beneficiary, or

- left everything to one beneficiary, but instead of naming one alternate for that beneficiary, you want to make a Plan B to take effect if your main beneficiary doesn't survive you.

WillMaker lets you make an unlimited number of separate specific bequests. For each one, you must provide this information:

- a description of the item—for example, a house, cash, an heirloom or a car, and

- the names of the people or organizations you want to inherit the items, and

- if you wish, the name of an alternate beneficiary, who will receive specific property if your first-choice beneficiary does not survive you by 45 days. You can name multiple alternate beneficiaries; if you do, they will share the property.

1. Describing the Property

The first part of making a specific bequest is to describe the property you want to pass to a certain beneficiary or beneficiaries you have in mind. For example, if you want to leave your guitar to your best friend, you would begin by entering a brief description of the guitar, such as "my 1959 Martin guitar."

When describing an item, be as concise as you can, but use enough detail so that people will be able to identify and find the property. Most often, this will not be difficult: "my Baby Grand piano," "my collection of blue apothecary jars," or "my llama throw rug" are all the description you will need for tangible items that are easy to locate. If an item is very valuable or could be easily confused with other property, make sure you include identifying characteristics such as location, serial number, color or unique feature.

TIPS ON DESCRIBING PROPERTY IN YOUR WILL

Here is some help in how to identify different types of property with enough detail to prevent confusion.

- *Household furnishings.* You normally need not get very specific here, unless some object is particularly valuable. It is enough to list the location of the property: "all household furnishings and possessions in the apartment at 55 Drury Lane."

- *Real estate.* You can simply provide the street address, or for unimproved property, the name by which it is commonly known: "my condominium at 123 45th Avenue," "my summer home at 84 Memory Lane in Oakville," "the vacant lot next to the McHenry Place on Old Farm Road." You need not provide the legal description from the deed.

- *Bank, stock and money market accounts.* List financial accounts by their account numbers. Also, include the name and location of the organization holding the property: "$20,000 from savings account #22222 at Independence Bank, Big Mountain, Idaho," "my money market account #23456 at Beryl Pynch & Company, Chicago, Illinois," "100 shares of General Foods common stock."

- *Personal items.* As with household goods, it is usually adequate to briefly describe personal items and group them, unless they have significant monetary or sentimental value. For example, items of extremely valuable jewelry should normally be listed and identified separately, while a drawer full of costume jewelry and baubles could be grouped.

Do Not Include Property That Will Pass By Other Means

Before describing the property you wish to leave in a specific bequest, take a moment to reflect on what property you are legally able to pass in your will. If you have already arranged to leave property outside your will by using legal devices such as life insurance, pay-on-death bank accounts or living trusts, do not include that property in a specific bequest. (See Chapter 4, Section A.)

2. Naming Beneficiaries

The second step in making a specific bequest is to name one or more beneficiaries. If you have already entered the name of a beneficiary in the names list, select the name from the list and paste it in the beneficiary field. (See the Users' Manual for help.)

People. Beneficiaries' names need not be the names that appear on their birth certificates; as long as the names you use clearly identify the beneficiaries, all is well.

Organizations. You may want to leave property to a charity or a public or private organization—for example, the American Red Cross, the Greenview Battered Women's Shelter or the University of Illinois at Champaign-Urbana.

The organization you name need not be set up as a nonprofit, unless you wish your estate to qualify for a charitable estate tax deduction. (See Chapter 12, Section C.) It can be any organization you consider worthy of your bequest. The only limitation is that the organization must not be set up for some illicit or illegal purpose.

When naming an organization, be sure to enter its complete name, which may be different from the truncated version by which it is commonly known. Several different organizations may use similar names—and you want to be sure your bequest goes to the one you have in mind. Someone at the organization will be more than happy to help you get it straight.

Minors or Young Adults. If any of the beneficiaries you name is a minor (under 18) or young adult (under 35), you will have a chance, in a later part of WillMaker, to choose someone to manage the property for them until they are older. (See Chapter 6.)

Multiple Beneficiaries. If you name two or more beneficiaries to share a specific bequest, you will later be asked to specify each person's share. To avoid possible tiffs among your beneficiaries, the property you plan to leave them either should be property that is easily divided—a sum of money or an investment portfolio—or property that you intend to be sold so that the proceeds can be split, such as undeveloped real estate or a valuable collection. For property that requires discretion to divide—family antiques, for example—it may be wiser to leave items separately.

3. Specifying Shares

If you name a group of beneficiaries to receive specific property, WillMaker will ask you whether you want them to receive equal or unequal shares of the property. If you want it shared unequally, the shares must add up to one. WillMaker will warn you if your computations are off.

Example: Fred Wagner wants to leave an undeveloped real estate parcel to his three children, Mary, Sue and Peter. Because he has already paid for Mary's graduate school education, he wants to give Sue and Peter greater percentages of the property in case they want to go back to school, too. He lists his children and the share of his property to which they are entitled this way: Mary Wagner ($^1/_5$), Susan Wagner ($^2/_5$) and Peter Wagner ($^2/_5$).

DO NOT PLACE CONDITIONS ON BEQUESTS

Don't place conditions on any of your bequests; it risks making a confusing and even unenforceable will.

Here are some examples of what not to do:

- "I leave my gold Rolex to Andres, but only if he divorces his current wife, Samantha." Such a bequest would not be considered legally valid, since it actually encourages the break-up of a family.
- "I leave my dental office equipment to Claude, as long as he sets up a dental practice in San Francisco." The reason this bequest is unwieldy becomes obvious once you think ahead to the need for constant supervision. Who would be responsible for tracking Claude's dentistry career and making sure he ends up in San Francisco? What if Claude initially practices in San Francisco, using the equipment he was willed, then moves to grow grapes in the Napa Valley? Must he give up the equipment? To whom?
- "I leave my vintage Barbie doll collection to Collette, if the dolls are still in good condition." Who is to judge whether the dolls are in good condition? What happens if they aren't?

If you are determined to place conditions on beneficiaries or property, consult a lawyer who is experienced in drafting bequests that will adequately address these complex "what if" arrangements.

4. Naming Alternates

WillMaker automatically puts one condition in your will: to receive property, a beneficiary must survive you by 45 days. WillMaker assumes that if a beneficiary only survives you by a few days or weeks, you would prefer the property to pass to an alternate or residuary beneficiary named in your will, rather than have the property pass along with the beneficiary's other property.

With WillMaker, you can name one or more alternate beneficiaries to take the bequest if your first choices do not survive you by 45 days.

Example: Joan leaves her horse to her brother Pierre. In case Pierre does not survive her by 45 days to be eligible to receive this bequest, Joan names her sister Carmen as Pierre's alternate beneficiary.

If you name multiple beneficiaries to receive property, you can name an alternate for each beneficiary.

Example: Gideon leaves his house to his three nephews, Aaron, Thomas and Zeke, in equal shares. In case Aaron does not survive him by 45 days, Gideon specifies that the house should then go to the survivors, Thomas and Zeke. In case Thomas does not survive him by 45 days, Gideon names his brother Horace to take Thomas's share. In case Zeke does not survive him by 45 days, Gideon specifies that Aaron and Horace should take Zeke's share.

PROVIDING FOR PETS

You cannot legally name a pet as a beneficiary in your will; the law considers pets to be property. But if you own a pet, you may well be concerned that it receives a good home and good care after your death. Because of WillMaker's proscription against leaving bequests with conditions on them, you cannot leave, for example, "$100 to Suzy Anderson, to be spent for my cat, Felix."

However, because a pet is legally considered to be property, you can leave it to another person in your will. It is also permissible—and common practice—to leave some money to the caretaker, explaining in a letter attached to your will that you want the money to be used for the pet's care. (See Chapter 11, Section B5, for a sample letter.) Of course, you should get the caretaker's agreement first—or he or she could end up as the unwilling recipient of an animal that needs care and a good home.

5. Reviewing Specific Bequests

When you complete a specific bequest—that is, you have identified the property, named the beneficiary and named an alternate beneficiary—WillMaker will display the first-choice beneficiary's name on the screen. You can also view this list by property. You can then add a new bequest, or review, change or delete any of the bequests you have already made.

F. Naming Residuary Beneficiaries

WillMaker will ask you to name a beneficiary for your residuary estate only if:

- you chose not to name one main beneficiary to receive most or all of your property, or

- after leaving all your property to one beneficiary, you chose to create an alternate plan, or Plan B, in case your first choice does not survive you. In this case, you name a residuary beneficiary as part of your alternate plan.

If you left all or most of your property to one or more beneficiaries, they will receive property that does not pass in a specific bequest or by means other than your will. In effect, they will automatically become your residuary beneficiary.

Example: When Mikki makes her will, she leaves all her property to her husband, Tyler. By the time she dies, 15 years later, she has acquired a new car, stocks and other items. Everything goes to her husband.

1. What a Residuary Beneficiary Receives

Your residuary beneficiary receives anything that does not go, for one reason or another, to the beneficiaries you named to receive specific bequests.

Specifically, the residuary beneficiary receives:

• property you overlook when making your will

• property that you acquire after you make your will, and

• property that does not go to the person you named to get it in a specific bequest—for example, because that person died before you did and you did not name an alternate beneficiary, or the alternate also failed to survive you.

Example: In her will, Sara, a widow, leaves many different items to many different beneficiaries—books to her daughter, jewelry to a friend, a car to her nephew and so on. She doesn't name alternate beneficiaries for these specific bequests, but she names her daughter as residuary beneficiary.

When Sara dies, some years after making the will, the friend to whom she left the jewelry has already died. The jewelry goes to Sara's daughter, as does the other property that Sara acquired since making her will.

There is no need to describe, in your will, the property the residuary beneficiary will receive. By definition, your residuary estate is the rest of your property that does not pass outside of your will or in a specific bequest, so it is impossible to know exactly what it will include. When your executor inventories your entire estate after your death, he or she will identify the contents of your residuary estate.

2. How to Name Residuary Beneficiaries

You can name one or more individuals, organizations or a combination of both as residuary beneficiaries. Use the Names List to select and paste the name if it is already on the list. (See the User's Guide for help.)

If you name more than one residuary beneficiary, WillMaker will ask you what shares you want the beneficiaries to receive.

Example: After making a large number of specific bequests in his WillMaker will, Maurice leaves his residuary estate to his four children, Clara, Heinrich, Lise and Wiebke. He wants Lise and Wiebke each to receive 30% (3/10) of the property and the other two children to receive 20% (2/10) each. So he indicates that he wants to leave the residuary estate in unequal shares, and enters the desired shares on the screen provided for this purpose.

If any of the beneficiaries you name is a minor (under 18) or young adult (under 35), you will have a chance, in a later part of WillMaker, to choose someone to manage the property for them until they are older. (See Chapter 6.)

3. Naming Alternates

WillMaker also asks you to choose an alternate residuary beneficiary, in case your first choice does not survive you by 45 days.

 When You Need Not Bother

You do not have to name an alternate residuary beneficiary, and not everyone is concerned about this issue. Younger people in reasonably good health are usually confident that they can address a beneficiary's premature death by updating their wills. However, many married people are concerned about what will happen if they die close together in time. And older people in poor health may fear that they won't have an opportunity to update their wills if their first choice beneficiaries die before they do.

Example: After making many specific bequests, Alfredo leaves his residuary estate to his daughter, Vanessa. He then specifies that if Vanessa does not survive him, her share should go to her two children—Alfredo's grandchildren. If Vanessa does not survive Alfredo, and Alfredo does not write a new will, Vanessa's children would each inherit one-half of Alfredo's residuary estate.

Example: Jack makes a large number of specific bequests to friends and relatives, and then leaves his residuary estate to his friend, Joe. He names another friend, Josette, as alternate residuary beneficiary. Josette will inherit property under Jack's will only if Joe does not survive Jack by 45 days and there is property left over after the property left in specific bequests is distributed.

CHAPTER 6

Providing Management for Children's Property

Except for items of little value, minors are not permitted by law to receive property directly. Instead, that property will have to be distributed to and managed by a responsible adult. It is of vital importance to both your own children and other young beneficiaries you want to take your property at your death that you arrange for this management yourself, in your will, rather than leave it up to a court to appoint and supervise a property manager.

A. Property Management for Your Own Children

WillMaker enables you to establish management for property that your minor children receive from you:

- under your will, or
- outside of your will—for example, through a living trust or a life insurance policy.

For property received under your will, this management may last until the minor turns an age you choose, up to 35 years old. For property that your minor children receive outside of your will, the management provided by WillMaker lasts until the children become adults—18 years old in most states.

If you are a parent, you may choose to leave your property directly to your spouse or partner and trust him or her to use good judgment in providing for your children's needs. Even if you do this, however, you are not necessarily freed from the need to provide property management. To plan for the possibility that your spouse or partner dies close in time to you, you may want to name your children as alternate beneficiaries. You can then appoint a trusted adult as manager for the property they could inherit.

Finally, once you choose a person to manage the property, you must decide what you want to happen when your children reach the age of 18. You can choose to have what property is left by that time handed over in one lump sum, or for property left in your will, you may provide that the property management continue until the children are somewhat older.

EXPLAINING YOUR BEQUESTS TO YOUR CHILDREN

Using WillMaker, you are free to divide up your property among your children as you see fit. If your children are already responsible adults, your prime concern will likely be about fairness—given the circumstances and the children's needs. Often, this will mean dividing your property equally among your children. Sometimes, however, the special health or educational needs of one child, the relative affluence and stability of another or the fact that you are estranged from a child will be the impetus for you to make an uneven distribution.

Doing this can sometimes raise serious angst—a child who receives less property may conclude that you cared for him or her less. To deal with this, you may wish to explain your reasons for dividing your property unequally. Because of the risk of adding illegal or confusing language, WillMaker does not allow you to make this explanation in your will. Fortunately, there is a sound and sensible way to express your reasons and feelings. Simply prepare a separate letter to accompany your will. (See Chapter 11.)

B. Property Management for Other Children

It often also makes good sense to establish management for property you plan to leave to other minor children in your will—for example, your grandchildren, nieces and nephews. That way, you free their parents, or other adults responsible for them, from the expensive and time-consuming burden of having to go to court to get legal authority to manage that property. Here, too, you can use WillMaker to provide property management that lasts until the young beneficiary is 35 years old.

And there also may be a good reason to provide property management for beneficiaries who are 18 or over. For example, those considering young adults as beneficiaries may want to defer distribution of inherited property until a later age. You can use WillMaker to postpone distributing property left to any young adult—yours or someone else's—until the beneficiary reaches an age you choose, through 35 years old.

C. An Overview of Property Management

This section presents an overview of basic property management considerations. Section D discusses how to use WillMaker to put your management choices into your will.

Property management consists of naming a trusted adult to be in charge of caring for and accurately accounting for the property that a young beneficiary takes under your will until the beneficiary turns a specific age. The property being managed for the young beneficiary must be held, invested or spent in the best interest of the beneficiary. In other words, someone other than the young beneficiaries will decide if their inheritances will be spent on college tuition or a new sports car.

1. Property Management for Minors

Except for property of little value—that worth less than $2,000 or so—minors may not directly control property they inherit under a will. This legal rule is most important if the property is:

- cash or other liquid assets—for example, a savings account that can easily be spent, or

- property that comes with a title document—for example, real estate.

Property of this type must be managed by an adult for the minor's benefit until he or she turns 18. If you do not provide for this management in your will, the court will do it for you—an expensive and time-consuming alternative requiring court supervision of how the property should be managed or spent.

And from a practical standpoint, it may be important for you to provide management for property you leave to minors where that property is unique or valuable—for example, a collection of rare coins that you do not want squandered or damaged.

In addition, you may want to provide that management for property left to a minor continues beyond age 18—the age at which a court-established guardianship ends. WillMaker allows this management to last up to and including age 35.

WHAT HAPPENS IF THE MINOR DOES NOT INHERIT PROPERTY

If you arrange for property management for a minor, but the minor never actually becomes entitled to the property, no harm is done. The management provisions for that minor are ignored. For instance, suppose you identify a favorite niece to take property as an alternate beneficiary, and provide management for that property until the niece turns 25. If the niece never gets to take the property because your first choice beneficiary survives you, no property management will be established for her, since none will be needed.

2. Property Management for Young Adults

If you are leaving valuable property to someone who is in his or her late teens or early twenties, you may justifiably wish to delay the time the young beneficiary actually gets to use it. WillMaker lets you extend the time property left to young adults is managed until they reach an age up to and including 35.

D. Property Management Under WillMaker

WillMaker offers four basic legal approaches to property management for minors and young adults:

- the Uniform Transfers to Minors Act—for property left in your will—in those states that have this law (see Section D1)

- the WillMaker children's trust—for property left in your will—as an alternative to the UTMA and as an option for willmakers who live in states that have not adopted the UTMA (see Section D2)

- the WillMaker pot trust—for property left to your children in your will—if at least one of your children is under 18 (see Section D3), and

- a property guardianship—for property that passes to your minor children outside of your will (see Section E).

1. The Uniform Transfers to Minors Act

The Uniform Transfers to Minors Act (UTMA) allows you to name a custodian to manage property you leave to a minor. The management ends when the minor reaches age 18 to 25, depending on state law.

States are free to adopt or reject the UTMA, which is a model law proposed by a group of legal scholars who make up the Uniform Law Commission. So far, the grand majority of states have adopted the UTMA—many making minor changes to it. While it is likely that the UTMA will be universally adopted, that will take a few more years.

STATES THAT HAVE NOT ADOPTED THE UTMA

At present, the UTMA has not been adopted in these states: Delaware, Michigan, New York, South Carolina and Vermont.

If you are a resident of one of these states, you can set up property management for any minor or young adult beneficiary using the WillMaker children's trust, discussed in Section 2, below. If at least one of your children is under 18 years old, you may also use the WillMaker pot trust, discussed in Section D3.

If the UTMA has been adopted in your state, you may use it to specify a custodian to manage property you leave a minor in your will until the age at which the laws of your state require that it be turned over to the minor. Depending on your state, this varies from 18 to 21; Alaska, California and Nevada allow you to extend management until 25. The WillMaker program keeps track of the state you indicate as your residence and tells you whether the UTMA is available, and if so, the age at which property management under it must end.

AGE LIMITS FOR PROPERTY MANAGEMENT IN UTMA STATES

State	Age at Which Minor Gets Property
Alabama	21
Alaska	25
Arizona	21
Arkansas	18 to 21
California	25
Colorado	21
Connecticut	21
District of Columbia	18
Florida	21
Georgia	21
Hawaii	21
Idaho	21
Illinois	21
Indiana	21
Iowa	21
Kansas	21
Kentucky	18
Maine	18 to 21
Maryland	21
Massachusetts	21
Minnesota	21
Mississippi	21
Missouri	21
Montana	21
Nebraska	21
Nevada	25
New Hampshire	21
New Jersey	18 to 21
New Mexico	21
North Carolina	18 to 21
North Dakota	21
Ohio	21
Oklahoma	18
Oregon	21
Pennsylvania	21
Rhode Island	18
South Dakota	18
Tennessee	21
Texas	21
Utah	21
Virginia	18 to 21
Washington	21
West Virginia	21
Wisconsin	21
Wyoming	21

Among the powers the UTMA gives the custodian are the rights to collect, hold, manage, invest and reinvest the property, and to spend "as much of the custodial property as the custodian considers advisable for the use and benefit of the minor." All of these actions can be taken without getting prior approval from a court. The custodian must also keep records so that tax returns can be filed on behalf of the minor and must otherwise act prudently in controlling the property.

SPECIAL RULE FOR LIFE INSURANCE

Often the major source of property left to children comes from a life insurance policy naming the children as beneficiaries. If you want the insurance proceeds for a particular child to be managed, and you live in a state that has adopted the UTMA, instruct your insurance agent to provide you with the form necessary to name a custodian to manage the property for the beneficiary under the terms of this Act.

2. The WillMaker Children's Trust

The WillMaker children's trust, which can be used in all states, is a legal structure you establish in your will. If you create a trust, any property inherited by a minor beneficiary will be managed by a person or institution you choose to serve as trustee until the beneficiary turns an age you choose—through age 35. The trustee's powers are listed in your will. The trustee may use trust assets for the education, medical needs and living expenses of the minor or young adult beneficiary. All property you leave to a beneficiary for whom a trust is established will be managed under the terms of the trust.

Because management under the WillMaker children's trust can be extended through age 35, it is also suitable to use for property left to young adults. (The pros and cons of management options are discussed in Section D4.)

3. The WillMaker Pot Trust

The WillMaker pot trust is a legal structure you can establish in your will. However, instead of creating a separate trust for the property you leave to each child, as with the other trust options, you create one trust for all the property you leave to your children. You name a single trustee to manage the property for the benefit of the children as a group, without regard to how much is spent on an individual child. For example, if there are three children and one of the children needs funds for an expensive medical procedure, all of the property could be spent on that child, even though the other children would receive nothing. While this potential result may seem unfair, it in fact mirrors the reality faced by many families: some children need more money than others.

The pot trust will last until the youngest child turns 18. If there is a significant age gap between your children, the oldest children may have to wait many years past the time they become adults before they receive their share of the property. For instance, if one of your children is 5 and another child is 17, the 17-year-old will have to wait at least until he or she turns 30 to receive his or her share of the property left in the trust—since the 5-year-old will have to turn 18 before the property can be distributed to the older child.

 All or None Must Go in Pot

The WillMaker pot trust option is available only for property you leave to all of your children as a group. However, in some cases, a person with both minor and adult children may wish to use the pot trust for the minor children and one of the other property management options for the adult children. While this may be a sensible approach, the WillMaker program does not allow it, primarily to avoid making the program overly complex. If you do want to use the pot trust for some but not all of your children, you will need to see a lawyer.

4. Choosing Among Management Options

For each minor or young adult to whom you leave property in your will, you must decide which management approach to use—the UTMA, children's trust or the pot trust. Because all of these are safe, efficient and easy to put in place, any of them can be used for many situations. This section helps you decide which is best for you and yours.

a. Using the UTMA

As a general rule, the less valuable the property involved and the more mature the child, the more appropriate the UTMA is because it is simpler to use than the children's trust and pot trust. There are a couple of reasons for this.

Because the UTMA is built into state law, banks, insurance companies, brokerage firms and other financial institutions know about it and should make it easy for the custodian to carry out property management duties. To set up a children's trust or pot trust, the financial institution would have to be given a copy of the trust document and may tie up the proceeding in red tape to be sure the trustee is acting under its terms.

Also, a custodian acting under the UTMA need not file a separate income tax return for the property being managed; it can be included in the young beneficiary's return. However, with a children's trust or a pot trust, both the beneficiary and the trust must file returns.

Because the UTMA requires that management end at a relatively young age, if the property you are leaving is worth $50,000 or less—or the child is likely to be able to handle more than that by age 21 (25 in Alaska, California and Nevada), use the UTMA. After all, $50,000 is likely to be used up long before management under the UTMA ends—at least in most states.

b. Using the WillMaker children's trust

Generally, the more property is worth, and the less mature the young beneficiary, the better it is to use the children's trust, even though doing so creates a bit more work for the property manager than does the UTMA. For example, in a children's trust, the property manager must file a separate tax return for the trust. However, if a minor or young adult stands to inherit a fairly large amount of property—such as $200,000 or more—you might not want it all distributed by your state's UTMA cut-off age, which is usually 18 or 21. In such circumstances, you will be better off using the WillMaker children's trust. Remember, under the children's trust, management can last until an age you choose—through age 35.

c. Using the WillMaker pot trust

As a general rule, the pot trust only makes sense when the children are young and grouped fairly close in age. For instance, if one of your children was 30 and another child of a later marriage was 2, the 30-year-old would have to wait until age 46 to receive the property—the time the 2-year-old would turn 18. However, the pot trust option is available to you as long as you have one minor child, even if one or more of your children are adults.

 Property Management Needs Not Covered by WillMaker

The property management features offered by WillMaker—the UTMA, children's trust and pot trust—are similar and provide the property manager with broad management authority adequate for most minors and young adults. However, they are not designed to:

- provide skilled long-term management of a business
- provide for management of funds beyond age 35 for a person with spendthrift tendencies or other personal habits that may impede sound financial management beyond young adulthood, or
- meet a disadvantaged beneficiary's special needs. A physical, mental or developmental disability will likely require management customized to the beneficiary's circumstances, both to perpetuate the beneficiary's way of life and to preserve the

property, while assuring that the beneficiary continues to qualify for government benefits.

For all these situations, specific trust provisions custom-tailored to the needs of the beneficiary and your wishes should be drafted by an attorney experienced in this type of work.

E. Property Guardians

The UTMA, WillMaker children's trust and pot trust are good management for property that minor or young adult beneficiaries receive under your will. However, if you have minor children and they receive property of significant value outside of your will, a court will usually have to step in and appoint a guardian to manage the property under court supervision until the children turn 18.

The two most common ways that children receive property outside of a will are from life insurance or through a living trust. (See Chapter 12, Section B.) While it is possible to provide for management of this type of property through your life insurance agent under the UTMA or within the living trust itself, often no such management is established and a property guardianship is required.

In addition, property received by your children from other sources—the lottery, a gift from an aunt or uncle, earnings from playing in a rock band—may also need to be managed by a property guardian.

It is always better to specify who will be managing any such property that your minor children come to own. Otherwise, the court will appoint someone who may or may not have your children's best interests in mind. If you are using the WillMaker children's trust, pot trust, or the UTMA to provide management for property you are leaving to your children in your will, the person you have named as trustee or custodian would also be a good choice for property guardian. Another possible choice is the person you chose to be personal guardian, if you think he or she will handle the property wisely for the benefit of the minor. You also may wish to choose someone else entirely. (See Section F.)

F. Naming Property Managers

You may name one person and one successor, who will take over if your first choice is unable to serve, to manage the property. If you use the UTMA, these people will be called the custodian and successor custodian. If you use the WillMaker children's trust or the WillMaker pot trust, they will be called the trustee and successor trustee.

Choosing someone to manage your children's finances is almost as important a decision as choosing someone to take custody of them after your death—and oftentimes, you will choose the same person to handle both tasks. Name someone you trust, who is familiar with managing the kind of assets you leave to your children, and who shares your attitudes and values about how the money should be spent. (See Section F2.)

 Parents Do Not Get the Job Automatically

You may be surprised to learn that the child's other parent, even if you remain married to him or her, probably will not be able to automatically step in and handle property you leave your children in your will. Rather, unless you provide for management in your will, that other parent usually will have to petition the court to be appointed as the property manager and then handle the property under court supervision until the children turn 18. So, if you want your children's other parent to manage the property you are leaving your children, name him or her as the trustee or custodian. Of course, you may wish someone else to manage the property, and with rare exceptions, your choice will be honored.

Whoever you choose as custodian or trustee, it is essential to get his or her consent first. This will also give you a chance to discuss, in general terms, how you would like the property to be managed to be sure the manager you select agrees with your vision and fully understands the beneficiary's needs.

1. Selecting an Institution as Property Manager

If you are using the UTMA, you must name a person as custodian; you cannot name an institution. The WillMaker children's trust and pot trust, however, allow an institution to serve as trustee. Still, it is rarely a good idea to pick a bank or other institution as trustee. Most banks will not accept a trust with less than $200,000 worth of liquid assets.

When banks do agree to take a trust, they charge large management and administrative fees. All trustees are entitled to reasonable compensation for their services—paid from trust assets. But family members or close friends often waive payments or accept far less than banks when chosen to act as trustee. If you cannot find an individual you think is suitable for handling your assets and do not have enough property to be managed by a financial institution, you may be better off not creating a trust.

Also, note that it is common for banks to manage the assets of all trusts worth less than $1,000,000 as part of one large fund, while charging fees as if they were individually managed. Any trustee who invests trust money in a conservatively-run mutual fund can normally do at least as well at a fraction of the cost.

2. Guidance in Choosing a Property Manager

There are a few general principles to follow when choosing a property manager.

As a general rule, your choice for custodian or trustee should live in or near to the state where the property will be managed. Some states require property managers to live in the state where the trust is created. If you are using the trust option and wish to select a trustee who lives in a different state than you do, try to select an in-state person as the successor trustee. Then, if your first choice is prevented by the law of your state from serving, the alternate trustee will be able to step in and do the job.

You need not worry about finding a financial wizard to be your property manager. Under all options allowed by WillMaker, the property manager—custodian or trustee—has the power to hire professionals to prepare accountings and tax returns and to give investment advice. Anyone hired for such help may be paid out of the property being managed. The custodian or trustee's main jobs are to manage the property honestly, make basic decisions about how to take care of the assets wisely and sensibly mete out the money to the trust beneficiary.

It is usually preferable to combine the personal care and property management functions for a particular minor child in the hands of one person. Think first who is likely to be caring for the children if you die, and then consider whether that person is also a good choice for property manager. If you must name two different people, try to choose people who get along well; they will have to work together.

If you believe that the person who will be caring for the minor is not the best person to handle the minor's finances, consider an adult who is capable and is willing to serve.

For property being left to young adults, select an honest person with business savvy to manage the property.

Example: Orenthal and Ariadne agree that Ariadne's sister, Penny, should be guardian of their kids should they both die, but that the $100,000 worth of stock the three kids will inherit might better be handled by someone with more business experience and who will be better able to resist the children's urgings to spend the money frivolously. In each of their wills, they name Penny as personal guardian of the children, but also create trusts for the property they are leaving to their children. They name each other as trustees, and Orenthal's mother, Phyllis, who has investment and business knowledge and lots of experience in handling headstrong adolescents, as the alternate trustee, after obtaining her consent. Orenthal and Ariadne also decide that one of their children, who is somewhat immature, should receive his share of the estate—at least the portion not already disbursed for his benefit by the trustee—upon turning 25, and the other two children should get their shares when they turn 21.

G. Choosing an Age to End Management

If you choose a property guardian to manage property received by your minor children outside of your will, that management will terminate when each child turns 18.

For management under the UTMA, the age at which management terminates is seldom an issue. In all but a few states; the management terminates automatically at age 18 or 21, depending on the state; in Alaska, California and Nevada, it can be from 21 to 25. (See Section D1, above.)

Under the WillMaker children's trust, however, you may select any age up to 35 for the management to terminate. There is no general rule that will direct you in choosing an age for a particular beneficiary to get whatever trust property has not been spent on the beneficiary's health, welfare and educational needs. That will depend on:

- the amount of money or other property involved

- how much control you would like to impose over it

- the beneficiary's likely level of maturity as a young adult. For small children, this may be difficult to predict, but by the time most youngsters reach their teens, you should have a pretty good indication, and

- whether the property you leave, such as rental property or a small business, needs sophisticated management that a young beneficiary is unlikely to master.

H. Examples of Property Management Options

Here are some examples of how the WillMaker property management options might be selected. The following scenarios are only intended as suggestions. Remember, if you live in a state that has not adopted the

UTMA, your only property management options may be the WillMaker children's trust or the pot trust.

Example 1

Married
Adult children age 25 and older

You want to leave all your property, worth $150,000, to your spouse and name surviving children as alternate beneficiaries. As long as you think the children are all sufficiently mature to handle their share of the property if your spouse does not survive you, answer no when WillMaker asks if you wish to set up property management.

Example 2

Married
Children aged 19, 21 and 23

You want to leave all your property, which is worth $300,000, to your spouse and name your surviving children as alternate beneficiaries. You sensibly opt for property management in case the children get the property—if you and your spouse both die—and establish a children's trust for each child, to end at age 30. You name your financially experienced brother as trustee. You can leave each of the children the same amount of property, or you can leave varying amounts. You would not want to use the UTMA even if available in your state because it requires that property management end at age 21, or 25 in a few states.

Example 3

Married

Children aged 2, 5 and 9

You want to leave all your property, which is worth $150,000, to your spouse and name your children as alternate beneficiaries. You use the property management feature and select the pot trust option to manage the property if it passes to your children. You name your wife's mother—the same person you have named as personal guardian—as trustee, and name your brother as alternate personal guardian and alternate trustee. The property will be managed by the custodian until the age you choose, 18 to 21.

You also name your wife's mother as property guardian if management is needed for property your minor children receive outside of your will.

Later, when your children are older and you have accumulated more property, you may wish to make a new will and switch from the pot trust approach to the children's trust—and create a separate trust for each child to last until a later age you choose, up to age 35, for one or more of the children. You may wish to name different trustees for each child.

Example 4

Single or married

Two minor children from a previous marriage and one minor child with your present partner

You want to leave all your property, which is worth $150,000, directly to your children. You can use either the UTMA or the trust for each child, and name separate custodians or trustees, if you wish. You also have the option of using the pot trust. You should also name a property guardian to manage any property your minor child might get outside of your will.

Beware of Spouse's Property Rights

If you are married, your spouse may have a right to claim a portion of your property, so it is usually unwise to leave it all to your children unless your spouse agrees with that plan. (See Chapter 4, Section C.)

Example 5

Single or married

Two adult children from a previous marriage—ages 23 and 27—and one minor child with your present partner

You decide to divide $300,000 equally among the children. To accomplish this, you establish a trust for each child from the previous marriage and put the termination age at 30. You name your current spouse, who gets along well with the children, as trustee and a local trust company as alternate trustee. Because your third child is an unusually mature teenager, you choose the UTMA for this child and select 21 as the age at which this child takes any remaining property outright. You appoint your wife as custodian and your sister as successor custodian.

Example 6

Married or single

One daughter of your own, age 32, and three minor grandchildren

You want to leave $50,000 directly to each of the grandchildren. You establish a custodianship under the UTMA for each grandchild, and name your daughter as custodian and her husband as successor custodian.

CHAPTER 7

Choosing a Personal Representative or Executor

Using WillMaker, you can name a personal representative—also called an executor. That person will have legal responsibility, after your death, for safeguarding and handling your property, seeing that debts and taxes are paid and distributing what is left to your beneficiaries as your will directs.

> ### MAKE YOUR WILL AND RECORDS ACCESSIBLE
>
> As the willmaker, you can help with the personal representative's first task: locating your will. Keep the original in a fairly obvious place— a desk, file cabinet, safe deposit box. And make sure your personal representative has access to it.
>
> Should you need help in getting organized, *Nolo's Personal RecordKeeper* by Pladsen and Warner (Nolo Press) is a software program that helps you keep a complete inventory of all your legal, financial and personal records.

A. Duties of a Personal Representative

Serving as a personal representative is a job that can be fairly easy, or it can require a good deal of time and patience—depending on the amount of property involved and the complexity of the plans for it.

Your personal representative will have a number of duties, most of which do not require special expertise and can usually be accomplished without outside help. A personal representative typically must:

- obtain certified copies of the death certificate
- locate will beneficiaries
- examine and inventory the deceased person's safety deposit boxes
- collect the deceased person's mail
- cancel credit cards and subscriptions
- notify Social Security and other benefit plan administrators of the death
- learn about the deceased person's property—which may involve examining bankbooks, deeds, insurance policies, tax returns and many other records

- get bank accounts released or, in the case of pay-on-death accounts, get them transferred to their new owner, and

- collect any death benefits from life insurance policies, Social Security, veterans' benefits and other benefits due from the deceased's union, fraternal society or employer.

In addition to these mundane tasks, however, the personal representative will typically have to:

- file papers in court—usually called a probate court—to start the probate process and obtain the necessary authority to act as personal representative

- handle the court-supervised probate process—which involves transferring property and making sure the deceased's final debts and taxes are paid, and

- prepare final income tax forms for the deceased, and if necessary, file estate tax returns for the estate.

For these tasks, it may be necessary to hire an outside professional who will be paid out of the estate's assets—a lawyer to initiate and handle the probate process and an accountant to prepare the necessary tax forms. But in some states, because of simplified court procedures and adequate self-help law materials, even these tasks can be accomplished without outside assistance.

B. Naming a Personal Representative

Glancing through the list of the personal representative's duties mentioned above should tip you off about who you know that might be the best person for the job. The prime characteristics are honesty, good organization skills and a finesse with keeping track of details. For many tasks, such as collecting mail and finding important records and papers, it may be most helpful to name someone who lives nearby or who is familiar with your business matters.

1. Guidance in Choosing a Personal Representative

The most important guideline in naming a personal representative is to choose someone you trust enough to give access to your personal records and finances after your death. Many people choose someone who is also named to inherit a substantial amount of property under their wills. This is sensible because a person with an interest in how your property is distributed—a spouse, partner, child, or close family member—is also likely to do a conscientious job as personal representative. And he or she will probably also come equipped with knowledge of where your records are kept and an understanding of why you want your property split up as you have directed.

Whoever you select, make sure the person is willing to do the job. Discuss what the position requires with your choice as personal representative before naming him or her in your will.

WillMaker offers you help with the task of educating your personal representative. You have the option of printing out a document titled The Personal Representative's Role, which you can give to the person you name to serve. That document offers guidance on the personal representative's duties, which may include:

- deciding whether or not probate court proceedings are needed, and if so, filing the will in the local probate court
- deciding whether certain items may legally be transferred immediately to the people named to inherit them
- sending notice of the probate proceeding to the beneficiaries named in the will and if necessary, to certain close relatives

- finding and securing the deceased person's assets and managing them during the probate process

- handling day-to-day details, such as terminating leases and other contracts, and notifying banks and government agencies of the death

- setting up an estate bank account to hold money that is owed to the deceased person

- paying continuing expenses, debts and taxes, and

- supervising the distribution of property to the people or organizations named in the will.

While it is almost always best to choose a trusted person for the job, you may not know anyone who is up to the task—especially if your estate is large and complicated and your beneficiaries are very old, very young, or just inexperienced in financial matters. If so, you can select a trust management firm to act as your personal representative.

If that is your leaning, first be sure the institution you choose is willing to act. Most will not accept the job unless your estate is fairly large—worth at least $250,000 and often more. Also, understand that institutions charge a hefty fee for acting as personal representative—usually both a percentage of the value of property to be managed and a number of smaller fees for routine services such as buying and selling property.

You may also name one person or institution as alternate in case your first choice is unable or refuses to act when the time comes. (See Section C.)

Naming Two or More Executors

Some people want to name two or more personal representatives to serve jointly, and so WillMaker allows this option.

However, naming two or more executors to share the task is often not wise. Joint personal representatives may each act without the other's consent—and if they later disagree, your estate may be the loser because of lengthy probate delays and litigation expenses.

HOW YOUR PERSONAL REPRESENTATIVE— AND OUTSIDE EXPERTS—GET PAID

The laws of every state provide that a personal representative may be paid out of the estate. Depending on your state law, this payment may be:

- based on what the court considers reasonable
- a small percentage of the gross or net value of the estate, or
- set according to factors specified in your state's statutes.

When the personal representative either stands to inherit a large portion of the estate or is a close family relative, it is common for him or her to do the work without being paid. Some willmakers opt to leave their personal representatives a specific bequest of money in appreciation for serving.

However, any outside experts who are used will almost always be paid out of the estate. The amount outside experts—including lawyers—are paid is totally under the control of the personal representative. However, most states set out maximum fees that may be charged by lawyers and other professionals—usually a percentage of the value of the estate.

Beware of Lawyers' Fees

Lawyers commonly misrepresent to prospective clients that the maximum fee allowed by statute is the statutory fee that they are required to charge for their services. In fact, lawyers are perfectly free to charge by the hour or to set a flat fee that is unrelated to the size of the estate. One of the most important tasks that your personal representative can perform is to negotiate a reasonable fee with any lawyer he or she may pick to help probate your estate. Be sure you explain this to your choice for personal representative.

2. If You Do Not Name a Personal Representative

If you do not name a personal representative in your will, the document will still be valid as a will. But your decision will not have been a wise one. It will most often mean that a court will have to scurry and scrounge to come up with a willing relative to serve. If that fails, the court will probably appoint someone to do the job who is likely to be unfamiliar with you, your property and your beneficiaries. People appointed by the court to serve are called administrators.

The laws in many states provide that anyone who is entitled under the will to take over half a person's property has first priority to serve as personal representative. If no such person is apparent, courts will generally look for someone to serve among the following groups of people, in the following order:

Surviving spouse
Children
Grandchildren
Greatgrandchildren
Parents

Brothers and sisters
Grandparents
Uncles, aunts, first cousins
Children of deceased spouse
Other next of kin
Relatives of a deceased spouse
Conservator or guardian
Public administrator
Creditors
Any other person

C. Naming an Alternate

In case you name someone to serve as executor who dies before you do or for any other reason cannot take on the responsibilities, you should name an alternate to serve instead.

In choosing an alternate personal representative, consider the same factors you did in naming your first choice. (See Section B1.)

■

CHAPTER 8

Debts, Expenses and Taxes

Money matters have a way of living on—even after your death. But you can easily guide your survivors through the vexing process of dealing with your debts and expenses by including clear instructions in your will.

In your will, you can:

- forgive debts that others owed you during your lifetime
- designate what property should be used to pay debts you owe at death, and
- designate what property should be used to pay state and federal death taxes owed by your estate or due on the property in it.

A. Forgiving Debts Others Owe You

You can choose to release anyone who owes you a debt from the responsibility of paying it back to your estate after you die. You can cancel any such debt—oral or written. If you do, your forgiveness functions much the same as giving a gift; those who were indebted to you will no longer be legally required to pay the money they owed.

Of course, keep in mind that releasing a person or institution from the debt they owe you may diminish the property that your beneficiaries receive under your will.

1. Caution for Married People

If you are married and forgiving a debt, first make sure you have the full power to do so. For example, if the debt was incurred while you were married, you may only have the right to forgive half the debt. There is a special need to be cautious about this possibility in community property states. If your debt is a community property debt, you cannot cancel the whole amount due unless your spouse agrees to allow you to cancel his or her share of the debt—and puts that agreement in writing.

2. Describing the Debt

WillMaker prompts you to describe any debt you wish to cancel—including the name of the person who owes it, the approximate date the debt was incurred and the amount you wish to forgive.

This information is important so that the debt can be properly identified.

EXPLAINING YOUR INTENTIONS

Forgiving a debt is likely to come as a pleasant surprise to those living with the expectations that they must repay it. And you will probably give the gesture considerable thought before including such a direction in your will. While the final document will contain a brief clause stating your intention, you may wish to explain your reasoning beyond this bald statement. If you wish to do so, it is best to write your explanation in a brief letter that you attach to your will. (See Chapter 11.)

B. Liabilities at Your Death

If you live owing money, chances are you will die owing money. If you do, your personal representative will be responsible for rounding up your property and making sure all your outstanding debts are satisfied before any of the property is put in the hands of those you have named to get it. The property you own at your death—or your estate—may be liable for: several types of debts, expenses and taxes.

1. Debts You Owe

When you leave this credit-happy world, you will likely go out with debts you have not fully paid—personal loans, credit card bills, mortgage loans, income taxes. Whether such debts pass to the beneficiary along with the property, or must be paid out of the estate depends upon how the debt is characterized. (See Section C.)

2. Expenses Incurred After Your Death

There are several expenses incurred after you die—including costs of funeral, burial and probate—which may take your survivors by surprise if you do not plan ahead for paying them.

Funeral and burial expenses, for example, typically cost several thousand dollars. And for those who do not plan ahead, the costs may soar even higher. (See Chapter 14 Section B.) In addition, probate and estate administration fees typically run about 5% to 7% of the value of the property you leave to others in your will. Unless you specify otherwise, the fees will be paid according to the maximum suggested in the law of your state.

3. Estate and Inheritance Taxes

If your net estate is more than $600,000 at death, it will likely owe federal estate taxes. It may also owe state death taxes; some states tax estates and some do not. (See Chapter 12, Section E.) Unless you specify otherwise in your will, in most states, the taxes will normally be paid proportionately out of the estate's liquid assets. This means that a Gbeneficiary's property will be reduced by the percentage that the property bears to the total liquid assets. Liquid assets include bank accounts, money market accounts and marketable securities. Real estate and tangible personal property such as cars, furniture and antiques are not included. This could cause a problem if, for example, you left your bank account with $50,000 in it to a favorite nephew and your death tax liability—most of which resulted from valuable real property left to another beneficiary—gobbled up all or most of it. (See Section E.)

C. Types of Debts

There are two basic kinds of debts with which you need be concerned when making a will—secured and unsecured.

1. Secured Debts

Secured debts are any debts owed on specific property that must be paid before title to that property fully belongs to its owner.

One common type of secured debt occurs when a major asset such as a car, appliances or a business is paid for over a period of time. Usually, the lender of credit will retain some measure of legal ownership in the asset—termed a security interest—until it is paid off.

Another common type of secured debt occurs when a lender, as a condition of the loan, takes a security interest in property already owned by the person applying for the money. For instance, most finance companies require their borrowers to agree to pledge "all their personal property" as security for the loan. The legal jargon for this type of security interest is a non-purchase money secured debt—that is, the debt is incurred for a purpose other than purchasing the property that secures repayment.

Other common types of secured debts are mortgages and deeds of trust owed on real estate in exchange for a purchase or equity loan, tax liens and assessments that are owed on real estate, and in some instances, liens or legal claims on personal and real property created as a result of litigation or home repair.

If you are leaving property in your will that is subject to a secured debt, you may be concerned about whether the debt will pass to the beneficiary along with the property, or whether it must be paid by your estate.

a. Debts on real estate

WillMaker passes all secured debts owed on real estate along with the real estate.

Example: Paul owes $50,000 under a deed of trust on his home, signed as a condition of obtaining an equity loan. He leaves the home to his children. The deed of trust is a secured debt on real property and passes to the children along with the property.

Example: Sonny and Cati, a married couple, borrow $100,000 from the bank to purchase their home, and take out a deed of trust in the bank's favor as security for the loan. They still owe $78,000 and are two years behind in property tax payments. In separate wills, Sonny and Cati leave their ownership share to each other and name their children as alternates to take the home in equal shares. The deed of trust is a purchase money secured debt and, if the children get the property, they will also get the mortgage—and responsibility for paying the past due amount in taxes.

b. Debts on personal property

All debts owed on personal property pass to the beneficiaries of the personal property.

Example: Phil drives a 1985 Ferrari. Although the car is registered in Phil's name, the bank holds legal title pending Phil's payment of the outstanding $75,000 car note. Phil uses WillMaker to leave the car to his long-time companion Paula. The car note is a secured debt and will pass to Paula with the car.

Example: Carla borrowed $10,000 from a finance company to pay her income taxes. To get the money, she signed an agreement pledging "all her property" as collateral for repayment. Carla has a daughter, Juliet, and a son, Mark. Carla uses WillMaker to leave Juliet a precious doll house collection that has been passed down through the family for five generations, and leaves Mark the rest of her property. When Carla dies, she still owes $9,000 on the loan. The $9,000 debt is payable out of Carla's estate. Carla can either provide how this—and any other debts—should be paid, or she can leave this decision up to her personal representative.

WHEN THE DEBT EXCEEDS THE PROPERTY VALUE

Because the property is usually worth more than any debt secured by it, an inheritor who does not want to owe money can sell the property, pay off the debt and pocket the difference. However, at times, relying on this approach is not satisfactory—especially when it comes to houses. For example, if you leave your daughter your house with the hope that it will be her home, you will probably not want her to have to sell the house because she cannot meet the mortgage payments. If you think a particular beneficiary will need assistance with paying a debt owed on property, try to leave the necessary money or valuable assets to him or her as well.

2. Unsecured Debts

Unsecured debts are all debts not tied to specific property. Common examples are medical bills, most credit card bills, student loans, utility bills and probate fees. These debts and expenses must be paid by your personal representative or executor.

D. Paying Debts and Expenses

WillMaker offers two options for paying debts, including the expenses of probate. You can:

- designate a particular asset or assets to be used or sold to pay debts and expenses, or

- choose not to designate specific assets, which will mean that your personal representative will pay the debts and expenses as required by the laws of your state.

WHEN YOU NEED NOT WORRY—AND WHEN YOU SHOULD

Typically, you do not need to leave instructions about debts if:

- your debts and expenses are likely to be negligible—or to represent only a tiny fraction of a relatively large estate
- you are leaving all your property to your spouse or specify that it should be shared among a very few beneficiaries, without divvying it up in specific bequests. In this situation, your debts will be paid first and then the beneficiaries will receive what is left, or
- you know and approve of how your state law deals with debts and expenses.

But you may need to be concerned about how to cover your debts and death taxes when your willmaking plan involves dividing up your property among a number of beneficiaries.

And you need to plan more carefully if debts payable by your estate are likely to be large enough to cut significantly into bequests left to individuals and charitable institutions. The danger, of course, is that unless you plan carefully, the people whose bequests are used to pay debts and expenses may be the very people who you would have preferred to take your property free and clear.

Example: Ruth has $40,000 in a money market account and several valuable musical instruments, also worth $40,000. She makes a will leaving the money market account to her daughter and the instruments to her musician son, but does not specify how her debts and expenses should be paid. Due to medical bills and an unpaid personal loan from a friend, Ruth dies owing $35,000. After Ruth's death, her personal representative must follow state law which first requires that debts be paid out of the residuary estate. But because there is no residuary—all property is used up by specific bequests—a second rule applies that requires that debts be paid out of liquid assets. As a result, the personal representative pays the $35,000 out of the money market account, leaving the daughter with only $5,000. The son receives the $40,000 worth of musical instruments.

TIPS ON CHOOSING SPECIFIC ASSETS TO PAY DEBTS

If you select specific assets to pay your debts and expenses, here are some tips on what assets to choose.

Select liquid assets over nonliquid assets. Liquid assets are those easily converted into cash at full value—bank and deposit accounts, money market accounts, stocks and bonds. On the other hand, tangible assets such as motor vehicles, planes, jewelry, stamp and coin collections, electronic items and musical instruments must be sold to raise the necessary cash. Hurried sales seldom bring in anywhere near the full value, which means the net worth of your estate will also be reduced.

Example: Harry writes mystery books for a living. He has never produced a blockbuster but owns fifteen copyrights, which produce royalties of about $70,000 a year. During his life, Harry has traveled widely and collected artifacts from around the world. They have a value of $300,000 if sold carefully to knowledgeable collectors. Harry makes a will leaving his copyrights to his spouse and the artifacts to his children. He also designates that the artifacts should be used to pay his debts and expenses—which total $150,000 at death. Harry's personal representative, who is not a collector and has little time or inclination to sell the artifacts one by one, sells them in bulk for $140,000—less than half of their true value. To raise the extra $10,000, two of the copyrights are sold, again at less than their true value. As a result, Harry's children receive nothing and his spouse gets less than Harry intended.

Avoid designating property you have left to specific beneficiaries. It is important to review your specific bequests before designating assets to pay debts and expenses. If possible, designate liquid assets that have not been left to specific beneficiaries. Only as a last resort should you earmark a tangible item also left in a specific bequest for first use to pay debts and expenses.

One exception to this general recommendation occurs if you believe you are unlikely to owe much when you die, and that the expenses of probate will be low. Then, it makes sense for you to designate a substantial liquid asset left as a specific bequest to also pay debts and expenses.

1. Designating Specific Assets

One helpful approach to taking care of debts and expenses your estate owes is to designate one or more specific assets that your personal representative must use to pay them. If you designate a savings or money market account, for example, to be used for paying off your debts and expenses, and the amount in the account is sufficient to meet these obligations, the other bequests you make in your will not be affected by your estate's indebtedness.

Of course, if the source you specify is insufficient to pay all the bills, your personal representative will still face the problem of which property to use to make up the difference. For this reason, it is often wise to list several resources and specify the order in which they should be used. Also, make sure that they are worth more than what is likely to be required.

Example: Ella, a widow, makes a will that contains the following bequests:

- *My house at 1111 Soto Street in Albany, New York, to Hillary Bernette (The house has an outstanding mortgage of $50,000, for which Hillary will become responsible.)*
- *My coin collection (appraised at $30,000) to Stanley, Mark and Belinda Bernette*
- *My three antique chandeliers to Herbert Perkins*
- *The rest of my property to Denise Everread. Although not spelled out in the will, this property consists of a savings account ($26,000), a car ($5,000), a camera ($1,000) and stock ($7,000).*

  Using WillMaker, Ella specifies that her savings account and stock be used in the order listed to pay debts and expenses. When Ella dies, she owes $8,000; the expenses of probating her estate total $4,000. Following Ella's instructions, her personal representative would close the savings account, use $12,000 of it to pay debts and expenses, and turn the rest over to Denise along with the stock and camera.

Example: Now suppose Ella has only $6,000 in the savings account. When she dies, her personal representative, following the same instructions, would close the account ($6,000) and sell enough stock to make up the difference ($6,000). The remaining $1,000 worth of stock, the camera and the car would pass to Denise.

 Describe Property Consistently

Property designated both as a specific bequest and as a source for paying your debts should be described exactly the same in both instances to avoid confusion.

2. Not Specifying Assets

If you do not specify how you want your debts and expenses to be paid, your personal representative will be instructed by your will to follow your state's laws.

Some states require that debts and expenses be paid first out of property in your estate that does not pass under your will for some reason—for example, neither your residuary beneficiary nor alternate survive you—and next from the residuary of your estate. In other states, your debts and expenses must first be paid out of liquid assets such as bank accounts and securities, then from tangible personal property, and as a last resort, from real estate.

E. State and Federal Death Taxes

Before you concentrate on how you want your death taxes to be paid, consider whether you need to be concerned about these types of taxes at all. Most people do not.

Death taxes are taxes imposed on the property of a person who dies. Some people confuse probate avoidance devices, such as living trusts and joint tenancy, with schemes to save on death taxes. Unfortunately, avoiding probate does not reduce death taxes.

Death taxes are called by various names. The federal government, which imposes the stiffest taxes, calls them estate taxes. Some of the states that impose death taxes—half the states do not—call them inheritance taxes. In theory, these states tax the recipients of a deceased person's property rather than the property itself, but the reality is the same: the taxes are paid out of the dead person's estate.

Whether or not your estate will be likely to be required to pay death taxes depends on two factors:

- the value of your taxable estate—that is, your net estate minus any gifts or expenses that are tax-exempt, and

- the laws of the state in which you live.

COVERING YOUR DEBTS WITH INSURANCE

One way to deal with the problem of large debts and small assets is to purchase a life insurance policy in an amount large enough to pay your anticipated debts and expenses and have the proceeds made payable to your estate. You can then specify in your will that these proceeds should be used to pay your debts and expenses—with the rest going to your residuary beneficiary or a beneficiary named in a specific bequest.

But be careful. If large sums are involved, talk with an estate planner or accountant before adopting this sort of plan. Having insurance money paid to your estate subjects that amount to probate. A better alternative is often to provide that estate assets be sold, with the proceeds used to pay the debts. Then have the insurance proceeds made payable directly to your survivors free of probate.

1. Federal Estate Taxes

If the net worth of your estate will be less than $600,000, you will not be liable for federal taxes—assuming you have not made large gifts during your lifetime. Each person has a $600,000 personal exemption from federal estate taxes. If you are single and you are fairly certain your estate will not be larger than this amount, you need not worry about federal taxes, or about how to provide that they are paid after your death. If your estate exceeds $600,000, it will usually owe federal estate tax on your death, unless you make substantial tax-exempt gifts during your lifetime—including gifts to spouses, gifts for someone's education or medical costs and gifts to charity. (See Chapter 12, Section D.)

2. State Inheritance Taxes

Nevada is the only state with no death taxes. Half the states impose separate inheritance taxes on:

- all real estate owned in the state, and
- all other property owned by residents of the state, no matter where it is located.

The rest of the states impose only a pick-up tax, which means that the state is entitled to a part of any federal estate tax you pay, although no additional state tax is due.

However, state death taxes normally do not take a deep enough bite to cause serious concern unless your estate is very large. In fact, many states impose no significant death taxes. Among those that do, the taxes are technically imposed on the beneficiaries of the estate rather than on the estate itself. Still, your personal representative has an obligation to pay the taxes and will therefore deduct them from each bequest unless you specify differently in your will, as you can do when using

WillMaker. (For a list of states that impose death taxes, see Chapter 12, Section E.)

If the value of your estate is well below the federal and state tax range, and you have no reasonable expectation that your estate will grow to that level between the time you make your will and the time you die, skip the following discussion of your options for paying taxes. And, when asked by the WillMaker program your choice for paying death taxes, choose the third option: Don't specify.

If you are a relatively young, healthy person and your estate is only slightly larger than $600,000, you may want to adopt one of the WillMaker tax payment options now and worry about more sophisticated tax planning later. After all, by the time you die, federal and state tax rules may have changed many times.

 Getting Help With Large Estates

As you might imagine, financial planning experts have devised many creative ways to plan for paying estate and inheritance taxes. If your estate is large enough to warrant concern about possible federal estate and state inheritance taxes, it is large enough for you to afford a consultation with an accountant, estate planning specialist or lawyer specializing in estates and trusts. Again, the threshold at which you need to worry about taxes is normally at least $600,000, and often much higher if you plan to leave much of your property to your spouse. (See Chapter 12.)

F. Choosing How to Pay Death Taxes

WillMaker offers the following options for paying state and federal death taxes. You can:

- pay them from all property you own at death
- designate specific assets, or
- choose not to specify how your taxes will be paid, leaving that matter up to state law.

1. Paying Taxes From All Property You Own

For the purpose of computing estate and inheritance tax liability, your estate consists of all property you legally own at your death, whether it passes under the terms of your will or outside of your will—such as a joint tenancy, living trust, savings bank trust or life insurance policy. Because your estate's tax liability will be computed on the basis of all this property, you may wish to have the beneficiaries of the property share proportionately in the responsibility for paying the taxes.

Example: Julie Johanssen, a widow, owns a house (worth $500,000), stocks ($200,000), jewelry ($150,000) and investments as a limited partner in a number of rental properties ($300,000). To avoid probate, Julie puts the house in a living trust for her eldest son Warren, the stocks in a living trust for another son Alain, and uses her will to leave the jewelry to a daughter Penelope and the investments to her two surviving brothers, Sean and Ivan. She specifies that all beneficiaries of property in her taxable estate share in paying any estate and inheritance taxes.

When Julie dies, the net worth of her estate, which consists of all the property mentioned, is $1,150,000. Because this taxable estate is over $600,000, there is federal estate tax liability.

Each of Julie's beneficiaries will be responsible for paying a portion of this liability. Each portion will be measured by the proportion that beneficiary's inheritance has to the estate as a whole. Under this approach, Warren will be responsible for approximately 43% of the tax, Penelope for 13%, and so on. For Warren, this would mean a tax liability of $175,139. Penelope would owe $52,949.

2. Designating Specific Assets

As with payment of debts and expenses, it may be a good approach to designate one or more specific property items to satisfy the amount you owe in taxes. Again, if you designate a bank, brokerage or money market account to be used for paying taxes, and the amount in the account is adequate to meet these obligations, the other bequests you make in your will should not be affected.

Of course, if the resource you specify for payment of your estate and inheritance taxes is insufficient to cover the amount due, your personal representative will still face the problem of which property will be used to make up the difference. So, again, it is a good idea to list several resources which should be used to pay estate and inheritance taxes in the order listed.

Guidance for Selecting Specific Assets

If you do choose to select specific assets to be used to pay your taxes, follow the general rules set out in Section D1, above.

3. Not Specifying Method of Payment

If you choose this option, your will directs your personal representative to pay your death taxes as required by the laws of your state. As with your debts and expenses, your state law controls how your personal representative is to approach this issue if you do not establish your own plan. Some states leave the method of payment up to your personal representative, while others provide that all beneficiaries must share equitably in the tax burden. Depending on your financial and tax situation and the law of your state, more variables set in than can reasonably be covered here. If you are concerned about the possible legal repercussions of choosing this option, consider doing some cursory research of your state's law. (See Chapter 15, Section D.)

CHAPTER 9

Making It Legal: Final Steps

Once you have proceeded through all the WillMaker screens and responded to all the questions the program poses, you are nearly finished with the business of creating your will. There are just a few more steps you must take to make it legally effective so that the directions you expressed in it can be carried out after your death.

Note for Perfectionists: No Accents or Umlauts

WillMaker does not allow you to use special characters, such as an accent mark or an umlaut. You may be tempted to ink one in where your name, or the name of a beneficiary, carries the mark in question.

Do not do it. The fact that the character is missing may be displeasing to you, but it will have no adverse impact on your will's legality or effectiveness. Minor spelling errors, typos and even awkward wording in text that you enter also will not adversely affect the legality of your will.

A. Checking Your Will

Before you sign your will, take some time to scrutinize it and make sure it accurately expresses your wishes. You can do this either by calling it up on the screen or by printing out a draft copy. (Consult the User's Guide if you need additional guidance.) Or if you believe in the need for both a belt and suspenders, read both the screen and printed versions.

HAVING YOUR WILL CHECKED BY AN EXPERT

You may want to have your will checked by an attorney or tax expert. This makes good sense if you are left with nagging questions about the legal implications of your choices, or if you own a great deal of property or have a complicated idea of how you want to leave it. But keep in mind that you are your own best expert on what property you own, your relation to family members and friends and your own favorite charities—in short, most issues and decisions involved in making a will. Also, few attorneys support the self-help approach to making a will; you may be hard-pressed to find one who is cooperative. (See Chapter 15.)

B. Signing and Witnessing Requirements

To be valid, a will must be legally executed. This is not as bloody as it sounds. It means only that you must sign your will in front of witnesses. These witnesses must not only sign the will in your presence, but also in the presence of the other witnesses.

While state laws vary as to how many witnesses are required, three meets the minimum requirement of every state. Even if your state requires only two, it is preferable to have three witnesses for your will. That will ensure that there is one more person to establish that your signature is valid if it is later contested in court.

1. Requirements for Witnesses

There are a few legal requirements for witnesses. They need only be:

- adults—in most states, 18 or older
- of sound mind, and
- people who will not take any property under the will. Anyone to whom you leave property under your will, even as an alternate or residuary beneficiary, should not be a witness.

As a matter of common sense, the people you choose to be witnesses should be easily available when you die. While this bit of future history is impossible to foretell with certainty, it is usually best to choose witnesses who are in good health, younger than you are and who seem likely to remain in your geographic area. However, the witnesses do not have to be residents of your state.

2. Self-Proving Wills

For a will to be accepted by a probate court, the executor must show that the document really is the will of the person it purports to be—a process called proving the will. In the past, all wills were proved either by having one or two witnesses come into court to testify or swear in written, notarized statements called affidavits that they saw you sign your will.

Today, most states allow people to make their wills self-proving— that is, they can be admitted in probate court without the hassle of herding up witnesses to appear in court or sign affidavits. This is accomplished when the person making the will and the witnesses all appear before a Notary Public and sign an affidavit under oath, verifying that all necessary formalities for execution have been satisfied.

If you live in a state that offers the self-proving option, WillMaker automatically produces the correct affidavit for your state, with accompanying instructions. For the exception of New Hampshire, the self-proving affidavit is not part of your will, but a separate document. To use it, you and your witnesses must first sign the will as discussed above. Then, you and your witnesses must sign the self-proving affidavit in front of a Notary Public. This may be done any time after the will is signed, but obviously, it is easiest to do it while all your witnesses are gathered together to watch you sign your will. Most Notaries will charge at least a minimal amount for their services—and will require you and your witnesses to present some identification verifying that you are who you claim to be.

Many younger people—who are likely to make a number of wills before they die—decide not to make their wills self-proving, due to the initial trouble of getting a Notary at the signing. If you are one of these people, file the uncompleted affidavit and instructions in a safe place in case you change your mind later.

STATES WITHOUT STANDARD SELF-PROVING LAWS

The self-proving option is not available in the District of Columbia, Maryland, Ohio or Vermont. In these states, your personal representative will be required to prove your will.

In California, Michigan and Wisconsin, the self-proving feature does not require a separate affidavit. Instead, the fact that the witnesses sign the will under the oath printed above their signatures is sufficient to have the will admitted into probate, unless a challenge is mounted. There is no need to take further steps to make a California, Michigan or Wisconsin will self-proving.

3. Signing Procedure

You need not utter any magic words when signing your will and having it witnessed, but a few legal requirements suggest the best way to proceed.

- Gather all witnesses together in one place.

- Inform your witnesses that the papers you hold in your hand are your last will and testament. This is important, because the laws in many states specifically require that you acknowledge the document as your will before the witnesses sign it. The witnesses need not read your will, however, and there is no need for them to know its contents. If you want to ensure that the contents of the will stay confidential, you may cover all but the signature portion of your will with a separate sheet of paper while the witnesses sign.

- Initial each page of the will at the bottom on the lines provided. The purpose of initialing is to prevent anyone from challenging the will as invalid because changes were made to it by someone else.

- Sign the last page on the signature line while the witnesses watch. Use the same form of your name that appears in your WillMaker will. Again, this should be the form of the name you most commonly use to sign legal documents such as deeds, checks and loan applications.

- Ask each of the witnesses to initial the bottom of each page on a line there, then watch as they sign and fill in their addresses on the last page where indicated. Their initials act as evidence if anyone later claims you changed your will without going through the proper legal formalities.

C. Changing Your Will

Once you have signed your will and had it witnessed, it is extremely important that you do not alter it by inserting handwritten or typed additions or changes. Do not even correct misspellings. The laws of most states require that after a will is signed, any additions or changes to it, even clerical ones, must be made by following the same signing and witnessing requirements as for an original will.

Although it is legally possible to make handwritten corrections on your will before you sign it, that is a bad idea, since after your death, it will not be clear to the probate court that you made the corrections before the will was signed. The possibility that the changes were made later may throw the legality of the whole will into question.

If you want to make changes once your will has been signed and witnessed, there are two ways to accomplish it: You can either make a new will, or make a formal addition, called a codicil, to the existing one. Either approach requires a new round of signing and witnessing.

One of the great advantages of WillMaker is that you can conveniently keep up-to-date by simply making a new will. This does away with the need to tack in changes to the will in the form of a codicil and involves no need for additional gyrations. Codicils are not a good idea when using WillMaker because of the possibility of creating a conflict between the codicil and the original will. It is simpler and safer to make a new WillMaker will, sign it and have it witnessed.

MAKE SURE WITNESSES SIGN ON A PAGE WITH TEXT

If the final page of your will contains only spaces for the signatures of your witnesses, and no text of your will, it is remotely possible that after your death someone might claim that the witness page was illegally added later and that the will itself was not properly signed and witnessed.

To avoid this, change the number of lines printed per page by a line or two on the print set-up screen to alter the way the will prints out, so that either:

- some text of the will appears on the last page before the witness lines, or
- at least one of the witness lines appears on the next-to-last page.

(See the Users' Guide in this manual for instructions on how to do this.)

D. Storing Your Will

Once your will is properly signed and witnessed, your main consideration is that your personal representative can easily locate it at your death. Here are some suggestions.

- Store your printed and witnessed will in an envelope on which you have typed your name and the word "Will"—or use the preprinted envelope that comes with the WillMaker program.

- Place the envelope in a fireproof metal box, file cabinet or home safe. An alternative is to place the original copy of your will in a safe deposit box. But before doing that, learn the bank's policy about access to the box after your death. If, for instance, the safe deposit box is in your name alone, the box can probably be opened only by a person authorized by a court and, then, only in the presence of a bank employee. An inventory may even be required if any person enters the box or for state tax purposes. All of this takes time, and in the meantime, your document will be locked away from those who need access to it.

HELPING OTHERS FIND YOUR WILL

Your will should be easy to locate at your death. You want to spare your survivors the anxiety of having to search for your will when they are already likely to be dealing with the grief of losing you. Make sure your personal representative, and at least one other person you trust, know where to find your will.

E. Making Copies of Your Will

Some people are tempted to prepare more than one signed and witnessed original of their wills in case one is lost. While it is legal in most states to prepare and sign duplicate originals, it is never a good idea. Common sense tells you why: If you later want to change your will, it can be difficult to locate all the old copies to destroy them.

It can sometimes be a good idea, however, to make several unsigned copies of your current will. Give one to your proposed personal representative or executor. And, if it is appropriate, give other copies to your spouse, friends or children. In a close family, it can be a relief to everyone to learn your plans for distributing your property. But obviously, there are many good reasons why you may wish to keep the contents of your will strictly confidential until your death. If so, do not make any copies.

GIVING THE WILLMAKER DISK A GOOD HOME

Once you have printed out your will, you should make a copy of it in electronic form. Follow the instructions in the User's Guide on backing up your documents to a floppy disk. Find a safe, private place to store the disk so that you can use it to restore or update your will if that becomes necessary. Others should not have access to the disk without your permission.

As with other unsigned and unwitnessed copies, the copy of your will stored in your computer or on a floppy disk does not constitute a valid will. To be valid, a will must be printed out and formally signed and witnessed as discussed above.

CHAPTER 10

Updating Your Will

Your will is an extremely personal document. Your marital status, where you live, what kind and how much property you own and whether you have children are all examples of life choices that affect what you include in your will and what laws will be applied to enforce it.

Life wreaks havoc on even the best-laid plans. You may sell one house and buy another. You may divorce. You may have or adopt children. Eventually you will face the grief associated with the death of a loved one. Not all life changes require that you also change your will. However, significant ones often do. This chapter alerts you to changes that require you to make a new will.

A. When to Make a New Will

There are several occurrences that signal that you should make a new will.

1. Marrying or Divorcing

Suppose that after you use WillMaker to leave all or part of your property to your spouse, you get divorced. Under the law in many states, the divorce automatically cancels the bequest to the ex-spouse. The alternate beneficiary named for that bequest, or, if there is none, your residuary beneficiary, gets the property. In some states, however, your ex-spouse would still be entitled to take your property as directed in the will. If you remarry, state legal rules become even more murky.

Rather than deal with all these complexities, follow this simple rule: Make a new will if you marry, divorce or if you are separated and seriously considering divorce.

 Beware of State Laws on Spouse's Shares

If you leave your spouse out of your will because you are separated, and you die before you become divorced, it is possible that the spouse could claim a statutory share of your estate. (See Chapter 4, Section C2.) Consult a lawyer to find out how the laws of your state apply to this situation. (See Chapter 15.)

2. Getting or Losing Property

If you leave all your property in a lump to one or more people or organizations, there is no need to change your will if you acquire new items of property or get rid of existing ones—those individuals or organizations take all of your property at your death, without regard to what it is.

But if you have made specific bequests of property that you no longer own, it may be wise to make a new will. If you leave a specific item to someone—a particular Tiffany lamp, for example—but you no longer own the item when you die, the person named in your will to receive it is out of luck. He or she obviously cannot have the actual item, and is not entitled to receive another item or money in lieu of it.

The legal word for a bequest that fails to make it in this way is ademption. People who do not inherit the property in question are often heard to use an earthier term.

However, in some circumstances, if a specific item has merely changed form, the original beneficiary may still have a claim to it. Examples of this are:

- a promissory note that has been paid and for which the cash is still available, and

- a house which has been sold in exchange for a promissory note and deed of trust.

A problem similar to ademption occurs when there is not enough money to go around. For example, if you leave $50,000 each to your spouse and two children, but there is only $90,000 in your estate at your death, the gifts in the will must be reduced. In legal lingo, this is called an abatement. How property is abated under state law is often problematic.

You can avoid the vexatious legal problems of ademption and abatement if you adjust the type and amount of your bequests to reflect reality—a task that may require both diligence and the commitment to make a new will periodically.

3. Adding or Losing Children

Each time a child is born or legally adopted into your family, the new child should be named in the will—where you are asked to name your children—and provided for according to your wishes. If you do not do this, the child might later challenge your will in court, claiming that he or she was overlooked as an heir and is entitled to a substantial share of your property. (See Chapter 3, Section D.)

If any of your children die before you, and leave children, you should name those grandchildren in your will. If they are not mentioned in your will, they might later be legally entitled to claim a share of your estate. (See Chapter 3, Section E.)

4. Moving to a Different State

WillMaker applies several state-specific laws when it helps you create your will. These laws are especially important in two situations.

- If you have set up one form of management for young beneficiaries and then move to a different state, you may find when making a new will that WillMaker presents you with different management options. This is because some states have adopted the Uniform Transfers to Minors Act and others have not. If you want to see whether your new state offers different management options, see Chapter 6, Section D.

- If you are married and do not intend to leave all or most of your property to your spouse, review Chapter 4, Section C, that discusses the rules if you move from a community property state to a common law state or vice versa.

5. Losing Beneficiaries

If a beneficiary you have named to receive a significant amount of property dies before you, you should make a new will. It is especially important to do this if you named only one beneficiary for the bequest and did not name an alternate—or if the alternate you named is no longer your first choice to get the property.

6. Losing Guardians or Property Managers

The first choice or alternate named to serve as a personal guardian for your minor children or those you have named to manage their property may move away, become disabled, or simply turn out to be someone you consider unsuitable for the job. If so, you will probably want to make a new will naming somebody else.

7. Losing a Personal Representative

The personal representative or executor of your estate is responsible for making sure your will provisions are carried out. If you decide that the personal representative you named originally is no longer suitable—or if he or she dies before you do—you should make a new will in which you name another person for the job.

8. Losing Witnesses

The witnesses who sign your will are responsible for testifying that the signature on your will is valid and that you appeared capable of making a will when you did so. If two or more of your witnesses become unable to fulfill this function, you may want to make a new will with new witnesses—especially if you have some inkling that anyone is likely to contest your will after you die. But a new will is probably not necessary if you have made your will self-proving. (See Chapter 9, Section B2.)

B. How To Make a New Will

If you want to make a new will using WillMaker, a subsequent swoop through the program will proceed even more quickly than the first time through, since you will know what to expect and will likely be familiar with many of the legal concepts you had to learn the first time through.

If you review your will and wish to make changes in some of your answers, the program will automatically alert you to changes that may signal changes in the laws that apply to your individual situation. These include changes in:

- your marital status

- your state of residence

- the number of children you have, and

- your general approach to willmaking—from simple to complex, or vice versa.

If you make a new will, even if it only involves a few changes, you must follow the legal requirements for having it signed and witnessed just as if you were starting from scratch. If you choose to make your will self-proving, you must also complete a new affidavit.

In With the New, Out With the Old

As soon as you print, sign and have your new will witnessed, it will legally replace all wills you have made before it. But to avoid possible confusion, you should physically destroy all other original wills and any copies of them.

■

CHAPTER 11

Explanatory Letters

I n addition to the tasks that you can accomplish in a WillMaker will, you may also wish to:

- explain why bequests are being given to certain beneficiaries and not to others

- explain disparities in bequests

- express positive or negative sentiments about a beneficiary, or

- name someone to care for your pet after your death.

WillMaker does not allow you to do these things in your will for one important reason: The program has been written, tested and re-tested with painstaking attention to allowing you to make your own legal and unambiguous will.

If you add to your will general information, personal statements, or reasons for making or not making a bequest, you risk the possibility of producing a document with conflicting, confusing or possibly even illegal provisions.

Fortunately, there is a way you can have a final say about personal matters without seriously risking your will's legal integrity. You can write a letter to accompany your will expressing your thoughts to those who survive you.

Since what you put in the letter will not have legal effect as part of your will, there is little danger that your expressions will tread upon the time-tested legal language of the will or cause other problems later. In fact, if your will is ambiguous and your statement in the letter sheds some light on your intentions, judges may use the letter to help clarify your will. However, if your statements in the letter fully contradict provisions in your will, you may be guilty of creating interpretation problems after your death. For example, if you cut your daughter out of your will and also state in a letter attached to the will that she is your favorite child and that is why you are leaving her the family home, you are setting the stage for future confusion.

Keeping these cautions in mind, writing a letter to those who survive you to explain why you wrote your will as you did—and knowing they will read your reasoning at your death—can give you a great deal of peace of mind during life. It may also help explain potential slights and hurt feelings of surviving friends and family members. This chapter offers some guidance on how you can write clear letters that express your wishes without jeopardizing the legality of your will.

A. An Introduction for Your Letters

A formal introduction to the letter you leave can help make it clear that what you write is an expression of your sentiments and not intended as a will, an addition to or an interpretation of your will.

After the introduction, you are free to express your sentiments, keeping in mind that your estate may be held liable for any false, derogatory statements you make about an individual or organization.

One suggested introduction follows.

> To My Personal Representative:
>
> This letter expresses my feelings and reasons for certain decisions made in my will. It is not my will, nor do I intend it to be an interpretation of my will. My will, which was signed by me, dated and witnessed on _____ is the sole expression of my intentions concerning all my property, and other matters covered in it.
>
> Should anything I say in this letter conflict with, or seem to conflict with, any provision of my will, the will shall be followed.
>
> I request that my personal representative give a copy of this letter to each person named in my will to take property, or act as a guardian or custodian, and to anyone else my personal representative determines should receive a copy.

B. Expressing Sentiments and Explaining Choices

There is little that a manual such as this can say to guide highly personal expressions of the heart. What follows are some suggestions about things you might wish to cover.

1. Explaining Why Gifts Were Made

The WillMaker requirement that you must keep descriptions of property and beneficiaries short and succinct may leave you unsatisfied. You have thought hard and long about why you want a particular person to get particular property—and are constrained in your will to listing your wishes in a few bloodless words. You can remedy that by explaining the whys and wherefores of your will directives in a letter.

Example

[Introduction]

The gift of my fishing boat to my friend Hank is in remembrance of the many companionable days we enjoyed fishing together on the lake. Hank, I hope you're out there for many more years.

Example

[Introduction]

Julie, the reason I have given you the farm is that you love it as much as I do and I know you'll do your best to make sure it stays in the family. But please, if the time comes when personal or family concerns mean that it makes sense to sell it, do so with a light heart—and knowing that it's just what I would have done.

2. Explaining Disparities in Gifts

You may also wish to explain your reasons for leaving more property to one person than another. While it is certainly your prerogative to make or not bequests as you wish, you can also guess that in a number of family situations, unbalanced shares may cause hurt feelings or hostility after your death.

Ideally, you could call those involved together during your life, explaining to them why you plan to leave your property as you do. However, if you wish to keep your property plans private until after you die—or would find such a lifetime meeting too painful or otherwise impossible—you can cure the uncomfortability by attaching a letter of explanation to your will.

Example

[Introduction]

I love all my children equally. The reason I gave a smaller ownership share in the house to Tim than to my other children is that Tim received family funds to purchase his own home, so it is fair that my other two children receive more of my property now.

Example

[Introduction]

I am giving the bulk of my property to my son John for one reason: because of his health problems, he needs it more.

Ted and Ellen, I love you just as much, and I am extremely proud of the life choices you have made. But the truth is that you two can manage fine without a boost from me, and John cannot.

3. Expressing Positive or Negative Sentiments

Whatever your plans for leaving your property, you may wish to attach a letter to your will in which you clear your mind of some sentiments you formed during life. These may be positive—thanking a loved one for kind acts—or negative—explaining why you are leaving a person out of your will.

Example

[Introduction]

The reason I left $10,000 to my physician Dr. Buski is not only that she treated me competently over the years but that she was unfailingly gentle and attentive. I always appreciated that she made herself available—day or night—and took the time to explain my ailments and treatments to me.

Example

[Introduction]

I am leaving nothing to my brother Malcolm. I wish him no ill will. But over the years, he has decided to isolate himself from me and the rest of the family and I don't feel I owe him anything.

4. Providing Care for Your Pet

Legally, pets are property. Many pet owners, of course, disagree. They feel a true bond with their animals and want to make sure that when they die, their pets will get good care and a good home. The best way to do this is to make a formal arrangement. You cannot leave money or other property to your pet, either through a will or trust. Instead, the best legal approach is to use your will to leave your pet—and perhaps some money for the expenses of its care and feeding—to someone you trust to look out for it.

Make the bequest of pet and money in a specific bequest screen in your WillMaker will. Then attach a letter to your will explaining your wishes to the new owner, and include special instructions for the pet's care. Of course, make sure you get the new owner's welcome approval before making such a bequest.

Example

[Introduction]

I have left my dog Spot to my neighbor Belinda Mason, because she has been a willing and loving friend to him—grooming him willingly and well and taking him for walks when I was on vacation or unwell. I know that Belinda and her three children will provide a loving and happy home for Spot when I no longer can.

I request that Belinda continue to take Spot for his tri-annual check-ups with the veterinarian in town, Dr. Schuler, and have left her $2,000 to help cover the cost of that care.

FINDING A LOVING HOME FOR YOUR PET

It's often tough to find someone both willing and able to take care of your pet after you die. Responding to that need, a few programs have sprung up across the country to help assure people—especially older people—that their pets will have a loving home when they can no longer care for them.

After the San Francisco SPCA fought, successfully, to save a dog that was to be put to death after the death of its owner, the SPCA began a special service to find loving homes for the pets of deceased San Francisco SPCA members. The new owners are also entitled to free lifetime veterinary care for the pets at the SPCA's hospital.

The College of Veterinary Medicine at Texas A&M University takes in pets whose owners leave the college a $25,000 endowment. The interest on the money will go to support the Companion Animal Geriatric Center, which will provide a homey atmosphere and lifetime veterinary care for the animals.

The following sources can provide more information:

- San Francisco SPCA, 2500 16th Street, San Francisco, CA 94103; (415) 554-3000
- Companion Animal Geriatric Center, College of Veterinary Medicine, Texas A&M University, College Station, TX 77843; (409) 845-5051
- *Dog Law* by Mary Randolph (Nolo Press).

CHAPTER 12

Estate Planning

Preparing a basic will such as the one produced by WillMaker is the essential first step in planning any estate. More options are available, however, and may be especially appropriate for larger estates. This chapter provides a brief overview of what you might want to consider.

 Estate Planning Resources from Nolo Press

Nolo Press publishes many resources that can help you with estate planning. You may conclude that this makes our recommendation a little prejudiced, but we believe these are the best book and software products available, and offer a money-back guarantee if you do not agree. See the catalog at the back of this manual for more information.

- *Nolo's Living Trust*. A software package that shows users how to create their own living trust documents.

- *Plan Your Estate*. Shows how to prepare a complete estate plan without the expensive services of a lawyer. Considerable detail on federal estate taxes and simple strategies to avoid them.

- *Make Your Own Living Trust*. A step-by-step guide to living trusts—a popular probate avoidance device. Includes forms and instructions for setting up a living trust.

- *5 Ways to Avoid Probate*. A 60-minute audio cassette tape covering the five principal probate avoidance techniques—joint tenancy, savings account trusts, insurance, living trusts and naming a beneficiary for IRAs, Keoghs and 401K Plans.

- *Nolo's Personal RecordKeeper*. A software program that provides structure for a complete inventory of all your important legal, financial, personal and family records. Having accurate and complete records gets you organized, makes tax preparation easier and helps loved ones manage your affairs if you become incapacitated or die.

A. When You May Need More Than a Will

After using WillMaker to prepare a simple will, you may want to take another look at your situation and possibly do some additional estate planning to:

- avoid probate
- reduce or limit death taxes, or
- control how property left to one or more beneficiaries, such as a surviving spouse or a child, can be used.

Even though it is appropriate and wise to get your will done now, you may find that you will want to later revise it to take this additional planning into account.

These estate planning objectives are of interest primarily to people who own substantial property. Tax planning, especially, is the province of larger estates, because there are no federal estate taxes on the first $600,000 passed to other people. This assumes that the deceased person has not made certain gifts of valuable property during life. (See Section C.)

Planning to avoid probate or place controls on the future use of property can make sense even for estates of moderate size. But people who have little to leave their survivors will find there is little incentive to do anything beyond making a basic will.

Even people with larger estates should face a blunt truth: Estate planning benefits your inheritors, not you. And your survivors will not benefit from your time and trouble until you die, which may be many years from now. In the meantime, healthy people who expect to live for many more years often waste time, effort and money planning and replanning their estates every couple of years.

Although you will rarely find a high-priced lawyer or financial planner who will admit it, it makes sense for many relatively healthy people with moderate-sized estates to rely primarily on a basic will and maybe several other fairly easy-to-use probate avoidance devices such as holding title to their house in joint tenancy, but to postpone more involved types of estate planning such as establishing a living trust until they reach late middle age or face a life-threatening illness.

Deciding whether or not to plan to avoid probate involves at least three considerations:

- *Your age.* If you're under 60 and healthy, it often makes sense to prepare a will, adopt the easier types of probate avoidance devices such as joint tenancy or pay-on-death bank accounts and leave the more complicated estate planning until later. If you are truly wealthy, however, you may want to start more extensive planning earlier.

- *The size of your estate.* The bigger your estate, the bigger the potential probate cost and tax liability. And the more reason to plan to keep both at a minimum. Often with a large estate, it makes good sense to concentrate energy on seeing that major assets, such as real estate or business assets, are owned in a way that will avoid probate.

- *The type of property you own.* Some kinds of property are relatively easy to transfer directly to inheritors without a year's detour through probate—such as the bank balance in a pay-on-death account. Others are workier. For example, not only must a revocable living trust be created in the first place, but you must keep it up-to-date. This can require considerable time and trouble since to be effective, the trust must be the legal owner of your property when you die.

- *How much effort you are willing to expend.* Planning to avoid probate typically saves your inheritors 5% to 7% of the value of your estate and allows them to get the property you leave them more quickly. And as long as you do a good job, it makes no difference whether you do it 40 years or 40 days before you die. You must decide how early in your life you are willing to invest the time, trouble and expense necessary to achieve these benefits.

B. Planning to Avoid Probate

This section summarizes the principal ways to avoid probate. But first, you should understand what probate is and why you may want to avoid it.

1. Probate Defined

Probate is the legal process that includes filing a deceased person's will with a court, locating and gathering his or her assets, paying debts and death taxes and eventually distributing what is left as the will directs. With the exceptions noted below, property left by will must, by law, go through probate. If there is no will and no probate avoidance devices were used, property is distributed according to state law—and it still must go through probate. Fortunately, property left using other legal devices, including joint tenancy, revocable living trusts and pay-on-death beneficiary designations, is not required to go through probate. It can be transferred directly to the inheritors.

Small Estates May Be Exempt From Probate

Most states allow very small estates, usually in the $5,000 to $60,000 range, to pass to inheritors either free of probate or subject to a stream-lined, do-it-yourself probate process. This is true even if you make a will and do not adopt any probate avoidance devices. Some states also simplify or eliminate the normal probate process for property left by one spouse to the other.

2. Why Avoid Probate

Probate consists of a court process in which your executor submits your will and schedules of your debts and assets to a court which eventually approves their distribution. The process has many drawbacks and few advantages. It typically takes from nine to 18 months, and is usually costly, involving fees for attorneys, appraisers, accountants and the probate court. All these costs are paid from estate property—reducing the amount left for inheritors. Not surprisingly, the major money bite goes for lawyers. In some locales, hefty fees are charged even though most tasks are routine and farmed out to legal assistants. In many places, by sheer dint of custom, a probate lawyer's fees are typically a percentage of the estate's value, even if the work involves no more than transferring the property to a surviving spouse or dividing it among several children. Even worse, in a few states, the lawyer's fees consist of a percentage of the fair market value of the property that goes through probate, without subtracting what the deceased person owed on the property.

Beware of Doubletalk About Legal Fees

When quoting a fee for helping to probate an estate, lawyers often refer to the amount they will charge as the "standard statutory fee." That amount usually ranges from 5% to 7% of the total value of the estate. This percentage, listed in many state laws, is actually intended to be a cap on legal fees, and merely sets out the maximum that can be charged. Survivors can—and should—negotiate a lower legal fee if they wish to do so.

Example: If Harry, a resident of California, dies with a gross estate of $500,000—that is, the total value of everything he owns, without subtracting debts owed on the property—the maximum attorney's fees under that state's probate fee statute would be $11,500. The maximum fee is based on the $500,000 figure, even if Harry's house has a $200,000 mortgage on it. Court filing fees, property appraisals and other costs would typically add thousands more to the cost of settling the estate. And if the probate involves anything beyond preparing routine paperwork, it may cost even more.

The fundamental problem with probate is that most consumers receive little value for their money. In most situations, an executor of the will, or close relative if there is no will, could pay debts and taxes and transfer property to inheritors quickly and safely without probate court supervision—for much less than the typical probate lawyer's fee. Unless relatives are fighting over who gets what, or there are big claims against the estate, it is seldom necessary for a court to step in and supervise.

There is one advantage of probate. It sets a deadline by which creditors who have been properly notified of the probate proceeding must file formal claims against the estate. People worried about big claims—a person with a lot of debts or a professional who might face malpractice suits—sometimes find it valuable to know that this cut-off date will be imposed.

3. Avoiding Probate

There are several major ways to transfer property so that it avoids probate at your death:

- Pay-on-death accounts
- Gifts made during your life
- Life insurance
- Retirement accounts
- Joint tenancy
- Tenancy by the entirety
- Living trusts
- Pay-on-death government securities
- Pay-on-death securities accounts

a. Pay-on-death bank accounts

Banks and savings and loans allow you to name someone to receive, at your death, any money remaining in your account. No probate is required. To set up such an account, anyone with a checking, savings, or bank money market account or a certificate of deposit need only add a designation that the money be held in trust for a named beneficiary. Depending on local custom and state law, these accounts are called pay-on-death, savings bank or informal trust accounts.

A particularly attractive feature of such an account is that the person who establishes it retains complete control over the money until his or her death. Before that, the named beneficiary has no right to the money. The account owner can withdraw all the money or change the beneficiary any time before death.

Because it is so easy to set up, it makes sense for almost everyone with a substantial amount of money in the bank to use this technique— no matter their age or the size of their estate.

b. Gifts made during your life

Another simple way to keep property out of probate is to give property away during your life—even shortly before death. Anything you give away while you are alive is not part of your estate when you die, so it is not subject to probate. To make a legal gift, you must surrender ownership and control over the property. However, it is not enough to claim to give property away—for example, a valuable painting to our daughter—if for the rest of your life you hold onto it and continue to control it as if no gift had been made. (See Section D1.)

 Heed the Tax Laws

While gifts take property out of your estate for probate purposes, you should also become familiar with tax laws that may apply to such gifts. This is particularly important if your estate is likely to be worth $600,000 or more when you die. (See Section C.)

c. Life insurance

Americans have a tendency to over-insure their lives. Still, some life insurance can be useful, even essential, when a person wants to provide for children dependents who have disabilities. The proceeds of a life insurance policy pass to its beneficiaries free from probate as long as a specific beneficiary is named. Normally, all that is needed to collect the proceeds is a certified copy of the death certificate. However, if you designate your own estate as the policy beneficiary, as is occasionally done when the estate will need immediate cash to pay debts or taxes, the proceeds will be subject to probate.

d. Retirement accounts—IRAs, Keoghs and 401K plans

While retirement accounts were not designed as estate planning devices, they are currently used that way. Funds in a retirement account at death pass to the beneficiary designated in the account documents and are not subject to probate. Although the retiree must withdraw a minimum amount—the sum varies each year, based on the person's life expectancy—beginning at age $70\frac{1}{2}$, the rest can stay in the account. Knowing that it will avoid probate, many retirees withdraw the minimum amount allowable and instead use other funds to live on.

 Community Property Note

In community property states, one-half of the money put in a retirement account while a couple is married belongs to the surviving spouse, which may be an important consideration in fashioning an estate plan. (See Chapter 4, Section C1.)

e. Joint tenancy

Joint tenancy with right of survivorship can be an expedient probate avoidance technique for couples and co-owners of personal and real property who want the surviving owner to inherit their share. Couples who buy a house or other valuable property often take title in joint tenancy, so that when one of them dies, the other can get the property quickly and easily—and keep a significant portion of the estate out of probate. (See Chapter 4, Section B3.)

However, using joint tenancy as a probate avoidance technique is not a wise idea in a number of situations.

- Property transferred into joint tenancy with someone else cannot be called back if you change your mind. While the joint tenancy arrangement can often be converted to a tenancy in common, the other joint tenant will still own his or her share of the property. With a will, pay-on-death bank account, insurance policy or living trust, you are free to change your mind and give or leave the property to someone else. So unless you are making a transfer to someone you absolutely trust, taking on a joint property owner can be a mistake.

- Property transferred to a joint tenant belongs to the new joint tenant as soon as the transfer is made. The new owner can sell or give away the property, or it can be taken by his or her creditors or by the government to pay taxes. In short, your efforts to transfer property to avoid probate fees later can cause you serious problems now. So unless you are sure you will not need the property, giving part of it away can be mistake.

- Even if the original property owner is elderly and transfers the property into joint tenancy with a younger person, there is always the possibility that the younger person will die first and full ownership of the property will revert to the older one. If that individual does not make an updated plan for passing the property, it is likely to pass under the residuary clause of a will and end up in probate after all.

JOINT TENANCY IN COMMUNITY PROPERTY STATES

Community property states include Arizona, California, Idaho, Nevada, New Mexico, Texas, Washington and Wisconsin. Most married couples who live in states with community property laws prefer to take title to jointly-owned property as community property or as community property held in joint tenancy. The reason for this is that under federal estate tax rules, both shares of community property are automatically entitled to a stepped-up tax basis upon the death of either spouse. This can be a significant tax break. By contrast, only the deceased spouse's half of jointly-owned property that is not community property qualifies for a stepped-up tax basis.

Property held in the name of one spouse or in joint tenancy may legally be community property. If so, it will still qualify for a stepped-up tax basis. The problem is that when one spouse dies, the IRS presumes that property held in joint tenancy is not community property, and it is up to the surviving spouse to prove that it is.

In California and some other community property states, if the deceased person's share of community property is left to the surviving spouse, it qualifies for a quick and easy summary probate procedure that can be processed without a lawyer. Nevertheless, because some paperwork and delay is still involved, some estate planning experts recommend holding property in joint tenancy to avoid probate, while carefully documenting that it was purchased with community property funds or otherwise transferred to community property ownership, to qualify for the stepped-up tax basis.

f. Tenancy by the entirety

This type of ownership, now recognized in nearly half the states, operates the same as joint tenancy discussed above, but it is limited to married couples. (See Chapter 4, Section B4.)

g. Revocable living trusts

A revocable living trust is a legal entity you create by preparing and signing a document in which you specify who you want to receive certain property at your death. In that way, it operates similar to a will. Unlike a will, however, property subject to a living trust avoids the cost and delay of probate.

Revocable living trusts are extremely flexible. You can leave all of your property by living trust. Or, as commonly occurs, you can use a living trust to leave only some assets—leaving the remainder by will or one or more of the other probate avoidance techniques discussed in this chapter. Unlike wills, living trusts are not made public at your death.

These trusts are called living or sometimes inter vivos—Latin for "among the living"—because they are created while you are alive. They are called revocable because you can revoke or change them at any time, for any reason, before you die. During your lifetime, you still have control over all property transferred to your living trust and can do what you want with it—sell it, spend it, or give it away.

A living trust is a separate legal entity from the person who creates it. The trust can transfer property to inheritors only if ownership of the property is transferred to the trust's name in the first place. Ownership documents—the title to your house, your securities, and your motor vehicle title slip—must be officially changed to the trust's name or the trust will not control the property.

One drawback of a living trust is the relatively small hassle of transferring ownership of property to the trust and conducting future personal business in the name of the trust. In some state or localities, there may also be transfer taxes when you transfer property to the trust's name. Fortunately, there is no need to file a separate tax return for the trust. All transactions made by your living trust, such as the sale of property at a profit, are reported on your personal income tax return.

LIVING TRUST TECHNICALITIES

Living trusts are simple in concept. The person who establishes the trust—called either the settlor, grantor or creator—signs a trust document that contains these elements:

- A list of the property that is subject to the trust—for example, the house at 12 Marden Road, Purchase, New York, and brokerage account 1278 at Racafrax Co.
- The name of a trustee, who has power to manage the trust property. Normally, the person who establishes the trust names himself or herself as trustee.
- The names of the beneficiary or beneficiaries. These are the people who will receive the trust property at the creator's death.
- The name of the successor trustee who will take over when the person who set up the trust dies and turns the trust property over to the beneficiaries. In most living trusts, the successor trustee is also given the power to manage the trust property if the creator becomes disabled. The successor trustee is often one of the trust's principal beneficiaries.
- The terms of the trust. These give the creator power to buy and sell trust property and to amend or revoke the trust at any time.

 Self-Help for Living Trusts

You may be able to create a living trust without a lawyer's assistance by using the book: *Make Your Own Living Trust,* or software: Nolo's Living Trust, both published by Nolo Press. Order information is at the back of the manual.

WHO SHOULD HAVE A LIVING TRUST?

Despite its probate avoidance advantages compared with a will, a living trust is not the best choice for everyone. As noted earlier, the amount of energy you should expend on avoiding probate probably depends on your age, health, the amount of property involved and the workiness of a particular probate avoidance device. Here's a thumbnail outline of how to approach the problem sensibly.

Age 60 or under, in good health. Many people in this group conclude that they can get along fine for a while by using a will, coupled with some of the easier probate avoidance techniques, such as owning their house in joint tenancy or placing a pay-on-death designation on bank and retirement accounts. In this age group, with a normal life expectancy of at least 25 years, the time and trouble necessary to maintain a living trust for many years may be considerable.

Exception: Because probate fees inevitably increase with the size of the estate, people with estates worth more than $500,000 or so may conclude that placing a few of their most valuable assets in a living trust makes sense. For example, a business or real property not already held in joint tenancy could be transferred to a living trust while other assets are disposed of by a will.

Age 60 to 70. The older you get, the more sense it makes to plan to avoid probate on all or most of your estate. Especially if your estate is worth more than a few hundred thousand dollars, a revocable living trust is often the most comprehensive way to be sure that those you want to get your property will take it quickly and efficiently after your death.

Age 70 or over. Use a living trust for all or most valuable assets not covered by other probate avoidance devices.

Exception: Married couples in community property states such as California, whose property is all community property and who want the survivor to inherit everything, may conclude it is unnecessary to go through hoops to avoid probate. Community property left to a surviving spouse can already pass through a fast simplified probate procedure.

While both a living trust and a will both work to transfer property to your inheritors, a living trust cannot completely replace a will. Even if you use a living trust to pass all of your identifiable property, there are several reasons why you need a will, too:

- You can't nominate a personal guardian for minor children in a living trust—you need a will. (See Chapter 6, Section C.)

- A living trust works to pass only property you transfer to the trust's name. Property you may receive in the future, but do not have title to now, cannot be transferred at once by living trust— although you can add it to the living trust later if you are still alive. For example, if you have inherited property that is still tied up in probate, or you expect to receive money from the settlement of a lawsuit, you need a will in case something happens to you tomorrow. And because you cannot accurately predict what property you might receive shortly before death, it is advisable to back up a living trust with a will.

h. Pay-on-death government securities

You can hold U.S. Treasury Department Securities, or T-bills, in a pay-on-death account. The Treasury Department, or an investment advisor can provide the required form. In that form, you register ownership of your securities in your name, followed by "payable on death to [whomever you name as beneficiary]." If a minor or incompetent adult is beneficiary, that status must be stated on the registration.

i. Pay-on-death securities accounts

In a number of states, you can add a pay-on-death designation to individual securities (stocks and bonds) or broker accounts under the Uniform Transfers-on-Death Security Registration Act. The Act has been adopted in the following states:

Arkansas	Nebraska	Virginia
Colorado	New Mexico	Washington
Kansas	North Dakota	West Virginia
Minnesota	Ohio	Wisconsin
Missouri	Oregon	Wyoming
Montana		

In these states, if you register your stocks, bonds, stock bond accounts, mutual funds or other securities in a pay-on-death account form, the beneficiary or beneficiaries you designate will receive these securities after your death. No probate will be necessary. If you live in one of these states, a broker can provide the forms needed to name a beneficiary for your securities or security account.

If you do not live in a state that has adopted this law, and you want to avoid probate of securities or stock accounts, you have to use some other form acceptable to the institution involved—such as a living trust or joint tenancy—to transfer the account to your beneficiary. If you actually have possession of stock certificates, you must contact the transfer agent of the company in which you own stock.

C. Federal Estate Taxes

The old saying that the two things you cannot avoid are death and taxes has an interesting twist when it comes to federal estate taxes. All property you own at your death is taxed. Period. You are, however, entitled to an automatic tax credit, and many people will owe no federal estate taxes at all.

As a general rule, if you have never in your life made a gift of more than $10,000 to any one individual in any one year, you may own up to $600,000 when you die without owing one penny of federal estate tax. That is, the taxes on the first $600,000 of your estate are covered by the tax credit.

If you have made a gift of more than $10,000 to an individual within a year period, then the credit available to you when you die will be reduced by a particular amount, which means that your estate may be responsible for some tax even if your estate is not worth a full $600,000. The amount of tax will depend on the number of taxable gifts you have made and the amount that these gifts exceeded $10,000.

This section helps you estimate your federal estate tax liability, assuming you have not made any taxable gifts. If you need specialized information about what your estate tax liability is likely to be if you have made taxable gifts, consult an estate planning or tax expert. (See Chapter 15.)

Section D discusses what you can do to keep your tax bill to a minimum. Be aware that if an estate is large enough to be taxed, federal estate taxes are hefty. They begin at 37% for property valued between

$600,000 to $750,000 and increase gradually for larger estates—topping out at 55% for estates larger than $3,000,000.

 Gifts Made During Life

Gifts made during life—if worth over $10,000 per year per person and not made to a tax-exempt charity—count toward the $600,000 exempt amount. The federal government feared that if large gifts were not taxed at the same rate as property left at death, people with estates large enough to be taxed would simply give the bulk of their property away shortly before death.

The result of this fear is a unified system of estate and gift taxes. If you make a taxable gift during your life, you must file a gift tax return, but you do not pay tax then. Instead, the amount of the gift that exceeds $10,000 per person is subtracted from your $600,000.

Example: Clint gives his son Larry and daughter-in-law Glenda $30,000 for the downpayment on a house. Since $10,000 can be given to an individual each year free of any gift tax consequences, only $10,000 is taxable. But no gift tax is due. The $10,000 is subtracted from the $600,000 lifetime estate and gift tax exemption. Had John wanted to avoid tax altogether, he could have given Larry and Glenda $20,000 in one calendar year and $10,000 the next year.

TRUSTS THAT HELP DEFER ESTATE TAXES

There are a number of trust arrangements that may help lessen the estate tax bite—a particular concern for those who are likely to have estates worth $600,000 or more.

- *Charitable remainder trusts.* In a charitable remainder trust, the maker names an income beneficiary or beneficiaries, and a final beneficiary, which is always the charity. The income beneficiary receives a set payment from the trust or a set percentage of the worth of trust property for the term defined in the trust. Trust property is not included in the trustmaker's taxable estate, which means that the heirs get an estate tax break. The net value of the trust assets, as of the date they become solely owned by the charity—that is, when the income beneficiary's interest ends—is excluded from the taxable estate.

- *QTIP trusts.* A Qualified Terminable Interest Property or QTIP trust allows a married person to name the surviving spouse as the life beneficiary of the trust property. When the second spouse dies, the property passes to final beneficiaries named by the first spouse. When the first spouse dies, all the property in the trust is exempt from estate tax.

  However, property remaining in the QTIP trust when the second spouse dies is subject to estate tax. So taxes are postponed, not eliminated. The principal reason to use a QTIP is to avoid paying any estate tax when the first spouse dies, which makes more money available to the survivor. QTIPs are useful only if you and your spouse have a combined estate exceeding $600,000. And generally, QTIPs are not used unless a couple's combined estate exceeds 1.2 million.

- *QDOTs.* A Qualified Domestic Trust, or QDOT, is an option for a U.S. citizen married to a noncitizen. In a QDOT, when the citizen spouse dies, the federal estate tax that would otherwise be assessed on the property is deferred until the second spouse dies. This is an especially attractive arrangement if the noncitizen spouse is younger and likely to need a fair amount of lifetime income.

- *Widow's election trusts.* Occasionally, a married couple will consider using a Widow's Election trust, which enables the first spouse to die to name final beneficiaries for both spouses' estates. This type of trust is rare—and useful only if both agree that one spouse should control the disposition of both spouses' property. Estate taxes applied to the trust property of the first spouse to die are calculated according to a complex combination of actuarial tables and formulas.
- *Marital deduction trusts.* This type of trust has been largely replaced by QTIP trusts. On rare occasions, a couple will use a marital deduction trust—or A-B trust—which provides the estate tax postponement of a QTIP, but unlike a QTIP, permits the surviving spouse to name the final beneficiaries of this trust. No estate tax is assessed on property in the trust when the first spouse dies.

All of these trusts are discussed in detail in *Plan Your Estate* by Clifford and Jordan (Nolo Press).

1. Estimate the Value of Your Net Estate

Your net worth is all you own less all you owe—assets minus liabilities. If you are married or own property with another person, be careful to distinguish between your property and your spouse's or other owner's when computing your net worth. For example, if you and your spouse own a house in joint tenancy, include only half of your combined equity when computing your net worth.

Example: If you own a house worth $350,000 with a $100,000 mortgage, it is worth $250,000 for estate tax purposes. If you and your spouse or any other co-owner own the house in equal shares, your share is only $125,000.

MARITAL PROPERTY: WHO OWNS WHAT?

Here is a brief outline of marital property ownership laws. (See Chapter 4, Section C, for a more thorough explanation.)

Community Property States

Arizona	Nevada	Washington
California	New Mexico	Wisconsin
Idaho	Texas	

All property either spouse earns or acquires during marriage is community property, jointly owned by both, with several exceptions. The most important is that the gifts or inheritances of one spouse are that person's separately-owned property. All property acquired by one spouse before marriage is also separate property.

Other States

In all other states, the person whose name is on the title or other ownership document for a particular piece of property owns it for estate tax purposes. If both names are on the document, ownership is joint. Property with no title document belongs to the spouse who used his or her money to purchase it, unless it was a gift to the other person.

2. Deduct Estate Tax Exemptions

Federal law exempts certain property from estate tax, including:

- up to $600,000 left to any beneficiaries
- all property left to your spouse
- all property left to tax-exempt charitable organizations, and
- a few additional exemptions and credits—including amounts paid for last illness, burial and probate costs.

a. The $600,000 exemption

Property you own at your death worth up to $600,000 is exempt from federal estate tax. This is true no matter what type of property is involved, to whom you leave it and the legal device used to transfer it—will, living trust or joint tenancy.

Example: Bruce leaves his estate of $700,000 to his son—$100,000 is subject to federal estate tax. This is true whether he uses a will, a living trust or another transfer device.

b. Property left to a spouse

All property left to a surviving spouse, whether it's worth $10 or $10 million, is exempt from federal estate tax. In tax lingo, this exemption is called the marital deduction. Note, however, that this exemption does not apply if the surviving spouse is not a U.S. citizen.

Example: Sue has an estate valued at $6,600,000. She leaves $600,000 to her children and $6,000,000 to her husband. All of Sue's property is estate tax-exempt. The $6,000,000 is exempt as a result of the marital deduction, and the remaining $600,000 is exempt under the standard $600,000 exemption discussed above.

Often, however, you will not want to simply pile up all the money in the surviving spouse's estate because this often means an even higher tax liability when the survivor dies. Alternatives—including establishing a marital life estate trust—are discussed in Section D3, below.

 Unmarried Couples Note

There are no estate tax exemptions similar to the marital deduction for unmarried partners. However, the marital deduction is available for couples who entered into a common law marriage in one of the states that recognize this type of marriage. (See Chapter 3, Section C.) It is also available to people who marry very shortly before dying.

For a thorough discussion of the legal rights and responsibilities of unmarried couples, see *The Living Together Kit*, Warner and Ihara, and *A Legal Guide for Lesbian and Gay Couples*, Curry, Clifford and Leonard, both published by Nolo Press.

c. Charitable gift exemption

All bequests made to tax-exempt charitable organizations are exempt from federal estate taxes; they do not need to be subtracted from the $600,000 exemption. If you plan to make large charitable bequests to an organization, doublecheck its exemption status. The normal way an organization becomes a tax-exempt charity is by filing a request and receiving a favorable ruling from the IRS, under Internal Revenue Code Section 501(c)(3). Organizations that are active politically—a term not consistently defined by the IRS—are often not tax-exempt.

d. Other estate tax exemptions and credits

The other principal exemptions from federal estate tax and estate tax credits are:

- expenses of last illness, burial costs and probate costs, and

- a tax credit for money paid for state estate and inheritance taxes, and taxes imposed by foreign countries on property owned there. A few states have no estate or inheritance taxes. A second, larger group levies a small pick-up tax calculated to equal the maximum amount that can be credited against federal estate taxes. Other states, especially in the northeast, levy substantial death taxes on large estates. If your estate pays these, it will receive a small credit on your federal estate tax. (See Section D.)

3. Estimate Your Estate Tax

You are now ready to broadly estimate your tax liability, with the help of the table below. And the example that follows will help you understand how to estimate your tax.

First keep two points in mind.

- Your calculations will only be valid if you have made no taxable gifts during your life—gifts of more than $10,000 to an individual in any one year.

- The table indicates your estate tax liability in terms of the tax credit—so although the table shows your estate being taxed on every dollar, the estate will not be liable for any tax until the amount of property in your estate exceeds $600,000.

UNIFIED FEDERAL ESTATE AND GIFT TAX RATES

Column A	Column B	Column C	Column D
Net taxable estate over	Net taxable estate not over	Tax on amount in column A	Rate of tax on excess over amount in column A
$0	$10,000	$0	18 %
10,000	20,000	1,800	20
20,000	40,000	3,800	22
40,000	60,000	8,200	24
60,000	80,000	13,000	26
80,000	100,000	18,200	28
100,000	150,000	23,800	30
150,000	250,000	38,800	32
250,000	500,000	70,800	34
500,000	750,000	155,800	37
750,000	1,000,000	248,300	39
1,000,000	1,250,000	345,800	41
1,250,000	1,500,000	448,300	43
1,500,000	2,000,000	555,800	45
2,000,000	2,500,000	780,800	49
2,500,000	3,000,000	1,025,800	53
3,000,000	infinity		55

Example: Bernie, a resident of California, anticipates that after subtracting liabilities from assets and then subtracting exempt amounts, including charitable gifts and funeral costs, his estate's value is about $1.5 million. Bernie plans to leave $500,000 to his spouse and $1 million to his children and other beneficiaries. All property Bernie leaves to his spouse is exempt from federal estate tax because of the marital deduction. This means his net estate subject to tax is $1 million. Column C on the Estate Tax Chart reveals that the tax assessed on a $1 million estate is $345,800. Because $600,000 of that amount is not taxed, he subtracts $192,800—the tax assessed against a $600,000 estate. Bernie's estate will have to pay federal taxes of $153,000.

Bernie's estate would also be liable to pay state inheritance taxes. California takes some of the tax assessed by the federal government; it does not impose any extra tax.

Incidentally, Bernie is an excellent candidate to give money to his kids while he is still alive. By doing this, he can reduce the size of his estate and therefore the tax. (See Section D1.)

D. Reducing Federal Estate Taxes

Unfortunately, aside from leaving more money to your spouse or to charity, there are only a few major ways to lower estate taxes.

1. Give Away Property During Life

An excellent way to reduce your estate tax liability is to reduce the size of your estate by giving property to the same people or organizations you want to get it at your death. But, if you make large gifts—more than $10,000 per person or taxable organization per year—you accomplish nothing, because the amount of the gift over $10,000 is subtracted from your total $600,000 exemption. The key is to make a number of smaller gifts each year.

Annually, you can give away property worth $10,000 or less per person or any amount to a tax-exempt organization, tax-free. This means that a couple can give $20,000 a year tax-free to one person and $40,000 to another couple—or they can give a million dollars to their favorite tax-exempt organization.

Giving gifts to reduce estate tax liability works well for people who have enough property that they can afford to be generous. It is particularly advantageous for reasonably affluent people who have several children, grandchildren or other objects of their affection.

a. Gifts of appreciated property

Someone who inherits property gets a stepped-up tax basis in the property to its then-current market value. Because the tax basis is the number used to figure capital gains and losses, this means an inheritor who promptly sells property for its fair market value pays no capital gains tax. However, property given away keeps the giver's tax basis—purchase price plus any capital improvements. In the case of greatly appreciated property, a person who receives it by gift faces a much larger tax bill when it is sold than does someone who inherits it.

Example: Ellen gives a 100-acre parcel of undeveloped land to her son John shortly before she dies. Since Ellen's tax basis in the land at the time of *transfer was $100,000, this is now John's tax basis. If John sells the land for $500,000, he owes capital gains tax on $400,000. By contrast, had Ellen left John the property at death, his tax basis would have been stepped-up to $500,000, fair market value, and no tax would have been due had he sold it for that amount.*

b. Gifts of life insurance

Life insurance policies you own on your own life and give away at least three years before your death make good gifts from an estate planning vantage. Potential tax liability is assessed on the present value of the insurance policy, which is far less than the amount the policy will pay off at death. Indeed, in many instances, it will be less than the $10,000 annual tax exclusion for gifts.

To give away a life insurance policy, you must carefully follow fairly technical IRS rules, which should be available from your insurance company. Basically, you must make an irrevocable gift of the policy. If you keep the right to revoke the gift—that is, get the policy back—it will be taxed as part of your estate. If you prepay the entire policy with a single premium, giving it away creates no future payment problems. However, if you purchase a policy that requires annual premiums, the person you give it to must make future payments, which may mean you will want to make annual gifts large enough to cover the payments.

Example: Bert has an estate worth $1 million. He purchases three single-premium life insurance policies for $50,000 each and immediately transfers ownership of the policies to his three children. Tax will be assessed on $120,000—the $150,000 current value of the policies minus the $10,000 annual tax exemption for each gift. No gift tax need be paid at the time of transfer—the $120,000 is subtracted from the unified $600,000 estate and gift tax exemption, leaving $480,000 for use at death.

The policies pay off $200,000 each at Bert's death ten years later. Bert has transferred $600,000 to his children, but only $120,000 will be part of his taxable estate. Had he kept the policy because he wanted to borrow against it, or for some other reason, his estate would owe tax on the entire $600,000 of proceeds.

2. Generation-Skipping Trusts

Creating a generation-skipping trust for the benefit of your grandchildren will not reduce your own estate tax liability; it can, however, exempt up to $1 million from tax in the next generation. A generation-skipping trust, as the name indicates, leaves property in trust for beneficiaries two generations removed from the trust creator—normally, your grandchildren. For example, if you leave $1 million in trust for your grandchildren, with the income from the trust available to your children, that $1 million is excluded from your children's taxable estate when they die.

3. Marital Life Estate Trusts

Spouses who have a combined estate of more than $600,000 and who are both elderly should think twice before leaving large sums to one another. This is because the survivor's estate will have to pay a much larger estate tax than if the other spouse had left the property directly to the children or other beneficiaries. Instead of having two $600,000 exemptions as was the case when both spouses were alive, there is now only one.

One way to avoid this problem, and also provide some income for the surviving spouse, is for each spouse to leave the other property in a marital life estate trust—sometimes called a spousal trust or A-B trust.

With this kind of trust, the income goes to the survivor during his or her life, and the principal goes to named beneficiaries—often the children—when the second spouse dies. It allows a couple to take advantage of both $600,000 exemptions and to avoid needlessly increasing the size of your spouse's estate.

The main drawback of a marital life estate trust is that the surviving spouse's rights in it are limited. While the surviving spouse can, at the option of the trust creator, be given the right to spend trust principal for medical needs and other basic necessities, in most cases he or she receives only the income from the money or property placed in trust—or the use of the property if it is tangible, such as a house. He or she does not own it.

Another potential drawback to life estate trusts is that two generations have an interest in the property—the surviving spouse and the children. This fact alone can create stress between the generations. For instance, the children may come to believe that the surviving spouse is not properly caring for the property, depriving them of their inheritance. And the surviving spouse may come to believe that the children are just perched and waiting for their parent to die.

For a spouse who already has more than enough property, this is not a problem. However, marital life estate trusts are generally not desirable for younger couples because should one spouse die, the other spouse, who will likely live for many years, will want to own the property outright.

Example: Calvin and Phylo, husband and wife, are each in their mid-70s, and each has an estate worth $450,000. Calvin dies, leaving all his property to Phylo. Because of the marital deduction, no estate tax is assessed. Phylo dies the next year. Her estate consists of the entire $900,000 (plus any appreciation), which she leaves to the children. Because $600,000 can be left to anyone *free of estate tax, $300,000 of the money left to the children is subject to tax. Unfortunately, however, it is taxed at the hefty marginal rate of 39%.*

If Calvin and Phylo had each established a marital life estate trust, with the income to go to the survivor for life and the principal to the children at the survivor's death, there would be no estate tax liability.

E. State Death Taxes

About half the states impose death taxes on:

- all real estate owned in the state, no matter where the deceased lived, and

- all other property of state residents, no matter where it is located.

If you live in a state that does not impose death taxes—and do not own any real property in one that does—skip to Section F.

STATES WITHOUT DEATH TAXES

Note that many of the states below charge a small pick-up tax equal to the amount of the federal tax credit for state inheritance taxes, but the result is no net tax.

Alabama	Hawaii	Oregon
Alaska	Illinois	Texas
Arizona	Maine	Utah
Arkansas	Minnesota	Vermont
California	Missouri	Virginia
Colorado	Nevada	Washington
District of Columbia	New Mexico	West Virginia
Florida	North Dakota	Wyoming
Georgia		

1. What State Will Tax You

State death taxes are imposed on all those who reside in the state permanently. If you divide your time between states, you will probably want to establish your residence in the one with the lower tax rate. (See Chapter 3, Section B, for a discussion of legal residence.)

Example: James and Vivian, a retired couple, divide the year between Florida and their native New York. Florida effectively has no death taxes. New York imposes comparatively stiff taxes—with rates ranging from 2% for $50,000 or less to 21% for $100,000 or more. Other things being equal, it makes sense for them to officially reside in Florida. To establish this, they should scrupulously maintain all their major business contacts in Florida, including registered vehicles and bank accounts. In addition, they should vote there. And because real property is taxed in the state where it is located regardless of its owner's residence, they might consider selling any New York real property and renting there instead.

 Adjusting Your Tax State

Establishing residence in a no-tax state can sometimes be tricky if you also live in a high-tax one part of the year, because the high-tax state has an interest in concluding that you really reside there. If you find yourself in this situation and have a large estate, check your plan with a knowledgeable tax lawyer or accountant. (See Chapter 15.)

2. Estate Planning for State Death Taxes

In many instances, the bite taken out of estates by state death taxes is annoying, but relatively minor—especially when property is left to a spouse or children. But tax liability can be significant for property given to nonrelatives. For example, Nebraska imposes a 15% death tax rate if $25,000 is given to a friend, but only 1% if it is given to a spouse. It is probably rare that someone would change the amount of property left to a beneficiary because of the impact of state death taxes, but you should at least be aware of them.

 More on State Death Taxes

State death tax rules are summarized in *Plan Your Estate With a Living Trust*, by Clifford and Jordan (Nolo Press). More detailed information is available from your state tax officials.

F. Estate Planning to Control Property

Most people are content to leave their property to their inheritors outright, and not try to control what they do with it. However, there are times, especially for people with larger estates, when it can make sense to impose controls on what inheritors can do with property. The most common situations are discussed here.

1. Money Left to Minor Children and Young Adults

As discussed in Chapter 6, many people who leave property to minor children, either as first choice or alternate beneficiaries, want to delay the age at which the beneficiaries will receive the property.

2. Second or Subsequent Marriages

Some people enter into second, third or fourth marriages unencumbered by grand concerns about estate planning. If each spouse has enough property of his or her own to live comfortably, there may be no real need for them to merge property and the problems that often come attached to it. Their simplest solution to prevent thorny future battles may be to make a prenuptial agreement making it clear that separate property stays separate; then each can make an independent estate plan for that property.

But in many second or subsequent marriages, one or both spouses may feel truly conflicted about estate planning. On the one hand, a surviving spouse may really need additional income from, or the use of, the other spouse's property to live comfortably. On the other hand, children from a former marriage may believe they are entitled to inherit the property once a parent dies. Even if the children are not insistent, they may have financial needs and resent their inheritance being tied up while the other spouse lives. This situation—which can be dicey at the best of times—becomes even more complicated when a current spouse and children from a former marriage are estranged.

One possible solution is to set up a trust to try to balance the interests and needs of all concerned. Essentially, this type of trust imposes controls over your property after your death, so that the surviving spouse has some use of it, or income from it, but does not have unlimited rights to use it. By this control, you seek to ensure that most or all of the trust principal will remain intact for your children.

HOW A PROPERTY CONTROL TRUST WORKS

A common way to avert conflict between your children and present spouse over property you leave them is to create a property control trust.

This type of trust imposes restrictions and controls over the rights of the surviving spouse to the property placed in the trust. The surviving spouse is the life beneficiary of the trust, which means he or she receives benefits from the trust while living. However, the rights to use trust property, to receive trust income, or spend trust principal, are as limited as the grantor—the deceased spouse—determined they should be. These restrictions are expressly stated in the trust document.

A marital property control trust is in marked contrast to a marital life estate trust intended to save on estate tax, where the surviving spouse is usually granted the maximum rights to use and invade trust property allowed under IRS rules. The purpose of restricting the surviving spouse's rights in a marital property control trust is to protect the trust principal, so that it remains until the surviving spouse dies. Then, the trust property goes outright to the grantor's children from a prior marriage, or other final beneficiaries the grantor named.

Example: Lisi and Greg get married in their late 30s. Lisi has a child from a prior marriage; Greg has two children from his prior marriages. Lisi and Greg have a child together, Dory. Neither spouse has an immense estate: Lisi owns property worth $400,000, and Greg owns property worth $310,000. Together they own a house that cost $320,000. Each contributed half the downpayment for the house, and they share mortgage payments equally.

Each spouse creates a marital property control trust. The other spouse, as life beneficiary, has the rights:

- *to remain in the house for life*
- *to receive the income from any property placed in the trust, and*
- *to spend trust principal only for medical costs that cannot be paid for from other resources.*

Each spouse names the final beneficiaries for his or her trust. Lisi decides that her final beneficiaries are Dory and her daughter from her prior marriage, who will divide her trust's principal 50/50. Greg, who is not close to his children from his prior marriage, names them and Dory as his final beneficiaries. Dory will receive 60% of his trust property and the other two children will equally divide the remaining 40%.

3. Managerial Trusts

If a beneficiary will need long-term help with property management, you may want to establish a managerial trust that is carefully tailored to meet the complicated needs of the beneficiary.

 Consult an Expert

See a lawyer with experience in this area in your state for help in drafting a managerial trust. (See Chapter 15, Section B.)

a. Spendthrifts

If you want to leave property to a financially improvident adult in a way that prevents him or her from spending it all at once, a spendthrift trust, in which a trusted person or institution is empowered to dole out the money little by little, is a good idea.

b. People with disabilities

A person with a physical or mental disability may not be able to handle property, no matter what age. The solution is often to establish a trust with a reliable adult as trustee to manage the disabled person's trust property. This is similar in concept to a spendthrift trust, but a trust for a person with disabilities should be constructed to take full advantage of funds available from public sources.

c. Groups of beneficiaries

For a variety of reasons, someone may choose that the specific plan for how his or her estate is distributed should be determined after he or she dies instead of during life. The usual way to accomplish this is to create what is called a sprinkling trust, in legal parlance. Normally, the trust creator names the beneficiaries of the trust during life, but does not divide the property among them. That is done by the trustee, after the creator dies, under whatever general criteria the trust sets forth.

CHAPTER 13

Healthcare Directives

Nearly 80% of all Americans die in a hospital or other care facility. And doctors who work in them are generally charged with preserving a patient's life through whatever means are available. When a patient can no longer communicate and has little chance of recovering or leading a meaningful life, this guiding proposition of preserving life flies in the face of legitimate financial concerns and common sense. And most importantly, it often contradicts what the patient would have wished had he or she been able to express wishes.

Doctors' egos may be at play, too. For some of them, keeping a patient alive with tubes, machines and chemicals is preferable to "losing" him or her through a natural death.

Of course, the reverse may also be true: A person may be provided with less extensive care than he or she would like. For example, a doctor may be unwilling to try experimental treatments or maintain long-term treatments on a patient he or she feels has slim chances of recovery. And a doctor may have far different views of what is "proper" treatment than the patient slated to receive it.

The only way for patients to override a doctor's general duty, and the religious, philosophical and economic underpinnings of the healthcare institution, is to leave written instructions for the medical care they prefer in case they become unconscious or otherwise incapable of expressing those wishes.

A. What WillMaker Can Do

Using WillMaker, you can create a document that clearly expresses your preferences for your medical care. Prompted by the questions and choices in the program, you can specify what care you want provided or withheld if you are diagnosed to have a terminal illness or to be in a permanent coma. (See Section H.)

You can use WillMaker to create a document that will:

- specify that you do not want your life prolonged with medical treatments and procedures
- specify medical treatments and procedures that you want provided if you become unable to communicate your wishes, and
- appoint someone to be sure your wishes are carried out.

WillMaker also prints out a letter directed to your healthcare provider. This letter helps emphasize your choices and summarizes them so that they are quickly clear to all who glance through your medical file.

If you are currently under a doctor's care, or you are preparing your healthcare directives in anticipation of a hospitalization or other extensive medical treatment, it is a good idea to use the letter as a starting point for discussing your wishes with those involved in providing your care. The more you do to make your thoughts known and communicate them clearly to medical personnel involved in your care, the more likely they will be followed.

B. Legal History

Many assume that an individual's right to direct his or her own healthcare is a long-cherished legal principle. In fact, the first legal battles over patients' rights were fought during the last couple of decades. Not coincidentally, those battles coincided with dramatic advances in medical technology and equipment.

The first legal wranglings over healthcare were couched in terms of the Right To Die—cases that tested the bounds of what medical

treatment can be administered in the face of a patient's desire to die
naturally, free from artificial, life-prolonging machinery. Over time, the
Right To Die movement became a much broader movement, in which
supporters agitated for patients' rights to demand as well as reject
medical treatment.

1. Court Decisions

The first time the public became aware of the right to direct medical care
as a social issue was during the hard-fought legal battles over the life and
death of Karen Ann Quinlan. The 22-year-old Quinlan was admitted to a
New Jersey hospital after experiencing severe breathing difficulties. She
lost and never regained consciousness. Severely brain damaged, she
remained unresponsive, emaciated and in a fetal position—kept technically alive by round-the-clock nursing care, antibiotics, a respirator,
catheter and feeding tube.

Doctors pronounced that there was no hope of Quinlan's recovery,
but balked at her parents' repeated requests to remove the equipment
attached to her, claiming that would clash with "medical practices,
standards and traditions." Quinlan's family members persisted, claiming
the extensive medical procedures ran counter to what the patient would
have wanted. After several expensive, time-consuming and personally
wrenching appeals, the New Jersey Supreme Court held that the
patient's constitutional right to privacy mandated that her family could
enforce her right to refuse treatment on her behalf. (*Matter of Quinlan*,
355 A.2d 647 (1976).)

The 1976 *Quinlan* decision galvanized individuals who previously
felt completely powerless up against the medical establishment. From
1976 through 1988, over 60 cases were filed nationwide, claiming that
doctors should be legally bound to follow their patients' wishes for their
own medical treatment.

In 1990, the U.S. Supreme Court was asked to decide whether the U.S. Constitution grants individuals the right to have life-sustaining treatment withheld or withdrawn. The case arose when Nancy Cruzan, 30, was admitted to a Missouri hospital after suffering severe injuries in a car accident. Cruzan was diagnosed as permanently brain damaged and in a coma or persistent vegetative state. There was no hope of recovery. Her parents unsuccessfully pled with hospital officials to discontinue Cruzan's artificial food and water, which would eventually cause her death.

In a court challenge to the hospital's position, the parents pointed to evidence of Cruzan's own wishes—conversations in which she told friends that if she were sick or injured, she "would not wish to continue her life unless she could live at least halfway normally." The Supreme Court held that everyone retains a constitutional right to control his or her own medical care. It held that "clear and convincing" evidence of an individual's wishes about his or her own medical care should be followed—even if they conflict directly with the wishes of close family members. (*Cruzan v. Director, Missouri Dept. of Health*, 497 U.S. 261 (1990).)

2. State Legislation

In the wake of court decisions carving out individuals' rights to direct their own healthcare, people penned the first Living Wills—usually simply-worded requests that a person "be allowed to die with dignity." These missives met with a mixed reaction in the medical community. Some doctors welcomed the Living Wills as legal permission to honor their patients' preferences for specific kinds of medical care, free from the threat of lawsuits charging them with negligence or even as criminal accomplices in a patient's suicide. Other doctors, unsure about whether to enforce the directives—most of which directed that life support be withheld or withdrawn—sought advice from lawyers. Most of the lawyers worked on the hospital staffs—and most cautiously advised that the documents could be ignored if the doctor thought that was "in the patient's best interest."

Waves of activism in the late '60s and early '70s led to catalytic consumer lobbying efforts for legal recognition of individuals' rights to direct their medical care. In 1976, California became the first state to pass a law allowing individuals to write healthcare directives—documents informing doctors of the specific kind of medical care they want provided, withheld or withdrawn. By the end of the 1980s, most states had followed suit. And today, nearly every state has a law allowing some sort of directive.

3. Federal Law

A recent federal law, the Patient Self-Determination Act, has done much to increase the use and awareness of healthcare directives. The law, which became effective in December 1991, mandates that all facilities that receive Medicare or Medicaid must discuss healthcare directives with newly-admitted patients. When admitted to nearly any hospital, you should be given a written explanation of your state's law on healthcare directives, and an explanation of the hospital's policies in enforcing them. The law also directs healthcare facilities to record patients' healthcare directives as part of their medical records.

C. Putting Your Wishes in Writing

You will have the most thorough assurance that your preferences for medical care will be followed if you complete:

- specific written instructions—usually called a Declaration or Living Will—that describes the medical care you want if you can no longer express your wishes, and

- a written authorization—usually called a Healthcare Proxy or a Durable Power of Attorney for Healthcare—that names another person to supervise your wishes.

Using the WillMaker program, you can arrange for this full protection of your wishes.

1. Healthcare Directives

A healthcare directive, whether known as a Living Will, a Directive to Physicians or a Declaration, sets out a person's wishes about what life-prolonging treatment should be withheld or provided if the person becomes unable to communicate those wishes. A doctor who receives a properly signed and witnessed or notarized directive is under the duty either to honor its instructions, or to make sure the patient is transferred to the care of another doctor who will honor them.

In the early confusion about healthcare directives, people were concerned that doctors who followed them would risk being prosecuted for aiding in a suicide. Every law on healthcare directives now exempts from prosecution doctors who follow their dictates. And in fact, many laws now impose penalties on doctors who refuse to follow them.

Also, because healthcare directives sprung from the Right To Die movement, many people tend to think of them as documents appropriate only for directing that life-prolonging procedures should be withdrawn or withheld. However, these documents should more correctly be viewed as a way to direct doctors to provide you with whatever type of medical care you want, within reality and reason. For example, some people want to reinforce that they would like to receive all medical treatment that is available—and a healthcare directive is the proper place to specify that.

2. Who Can Make a Healthcare Directive

In most states, you must be 18 years old to make a valid document directing your healthcare; a few states allow parents to make healthcare directives for their minor children.

Every state law requires that the person making a healthcare directive be legally competent—that is, able to understand what the document means, what it contains and how it works. People with mental disabilities who cannot understand the contents of a healthcare document cannot make one that will be valid. People with physical disabilities may make valid healthcare documents; they can direct another to sign for them if they are unable to do so.

3. Naming Someone to Supervise Your Wishes

Using WillMaker, you can create a document authorizing a representative you name to supervise the wishes you set out in your healthcare directive. This document is usually called a Durable Power of Attorney for Healthcare or Healthcare Proxy. The person you name will be referred to as your agent, proxy or attorney-in-fact.

 If You Choose Not to Name a Proxy

Even if you do not know anyone you trust to name as your healthcare proxy or agent, it is still important to complete and finalize a healthcare directive recording your wishes. That way, your doctors will still be bound to follow your wishes.

If you do name a healthcare representative, WillMaker will provide users in most states with a separate document containing that authorization. In a few states—including Kentucky, Minnesota, Oklahoma, Oregon and South Carolina—the healthcare directive and the document appointing a healthcare representative will be combined in one document.

Giving Your Representative Additional Powers

A Durable Power of Attorney for Healthcare can be used to delegate decision-making in a number of additional situations. (See Section J.) If you need such a document, consult with an attorney who has experience in setting them up.

4. What Happens If You Have No Documents

If you have not completed either a formal document such as a healthcare directive to express your wishes, or a durable power of attorney to appoint someone to make healthcare decisions on your behalf, the doctors who attend you will use their own discretion in deciding what kind of medical care you will receive.

If there is a question about whether surgery or some other serious procedure is authorized, doctors will usually turn for guidance to a close relative—spouse, parent, child. Friends and unmarried partners, although they may be most familiar with your wishes for your medical treatment, are rarely consulted, or are purposefully left out of the decisionmaking process.

Problems arise where partners and family members disagree about what treatment is proper. The most common result is that emotions run high and irrational as family members and loved ones take sides in a strange version of the nurturing olympics, with both sides claiming they want the best care for the patient. In the most complicated scenarios, these battles over medical care wind up in court, where a judge, who usually has little medical knowledge and no familiarity with you, is called upon to decide the future of your treatment. Such battles—which are costly, time-consuming and painful to those involved—are unnecessary if you have the care and foresight to use a formal document to express your wishes for your healthcare.

5. The Documents You Produce Using WillMaker

State legislatures often jealously covet their power to control the specifics of what makes a document legal in their own state. And nowhere is this more evident than in the area of healthcare directives, where each state may impose its own requirements regarding the form of the document, whether it must be notarized, what can be included and even on the definitions of terminal illness and permanent coma.

The healthcare document you produce using WillMaker enables you to set out clear and effective directions for your medical care. If your state law requires you to use a specific form, your document will be in that format. However, in some instances, the directions that WillMaker produces as a result of your choices may go beyond what is addressed by your state law. For example, your state's law may be silent on whether individuals can direct their own healthcare if they become permanently comatose, or your state's law may specifically restrict you from having comfort care withheld, even though such care would prolong the dying process. However, if you indicate that you want to address these issues when using WillMaker, you can.

The reason that WillMaker lets you go beyond your state's law is that state strictures on your right to direct your own healthcare contradict what the U.S. Supreme Court held in the *Cruzan* case: that the Constitution guarantees every individual this right. The Court also ruled that if an individual has left "clear and convincing evidence" of his or her wishes for medical care, those wishes should be followed. While the *Cruzan* Court intimated that evidence of conversations about healthcare wishes might pass legal muster as an indication of a person's wishes, detailed written instructions are even better.

The document you print using WillMaker reflects your actual wishes rather than the constrictions of your state's law. If your choices are beyond or contrary to what your state law allows, your healthcare directive will call special attention to the fact. And it will state that the specific directions in the document you produce should be respected and followed in keeping with your constitutional right to direct your own healthcare.

On the off-chance that anyone later challenges your healthcare directive in a court because it goes beyond your state law, there is an additional legal failsafe. Your document contains a paragraph that allows the rest of your healthcare directive to be enforced as written even if any one of the directions you leave is found to be legally invalid.

D. The Basics of Your Healthcare Documents

The initial screens in this portion of WillMaker ask you to provide some basic identifying information.

1. Your Name

If you have already used WillMaker to prepare a will or final arrangements, your name should automatically appear on the screen that requests this information. Otherwise, enter your name in the same form that you use on other formal documents, such as your driver's license or bank accounts. This may or may not be the name that appears on your birth certificate. If you customarily use more than one name for business purposes, list all of them in your WillMaker answer, separated by "aka," which stands for "also known as."

There is room for you to list several names. But use your common sense. For purposes of your healthcare directive, your name is needed to identify you and to match you with your medical records. Be sure to include the name you have used on other medical documents such as prior hospital or doctor records.

2. Your State

You are asked to specify the state of your legal residence, sometimes called a domicile. This is the state where you make your home now and for the indefinite future. This information is important because it cues the WillMaker program to assemble and produce a healthcare directive that is specifically geared to the laws of your state.

If you divide up the year living in two or more states, you may not be sure which state is your legal residence. To decide, choose the state where you are the most rooted—that is, the state in which you:

- are registered to vote
- register your motor vehicles
- own valuable property—especially property with a title document, such as a house or car
- have checking, savings and other investment accounts, and
- maintain a business.

IF YOU MOVE OR SPEND TIME IN MORE THAN ONE STATE

Some people assume that once they have completed healthcare directives, those documents will be valid in every other state to which they may roam. Others who want to assure that their wishes will be followed fret that they may need to complete directives in all states in which they vacation or customarily spend time. The truth depends, somewhat confusingly, on what states are involved. However, as a general rule, people are safe in doing it right in their own state, even if their documents need to be used in another state.

The following states recognize healthcare directives that are written and signed in accord with laws of another state: Alaska, Arkansas, Colorado, Indiana, Kansas, Massachusetts, New York, Rhode Island, South Dakota and Vermont.

The following states recognize healthcare directives that are written and signed in accord with the laws of another state if they substantially comply with the laws of their own state: Hawaii and Montana.

Laws in the following states provide that they recognize healthcare directives that are written and signed in accord with laws of another state to the extent they are consistent with their own state's law: Arizona, Iowa, Maryland, Minnesota, New Hampshire, Oklahoma and Washington.

Laws in the following states specifically recognize healthcare directives that are written and signed in accord with either laws of their own state or the other state: California, Florida, Illinois, Maine, Nebraska, Nevada, New Jersey, North Dakota, Ohio, Tennessee, Virginia and West Virginia.

Laws in the following states are silent on the issue: Alabama, Connecticut, Delaware, District of Columbia, Georgia, Idaho, Kentucky, Michigan, Mississippi, Missouri, New Mexico, North Carolina, Oregon, Pennsylvania, South Carolina, Texas, Utah, Wisconsin and Wyoming.

3. Your Address

Healthcare directives in some states require that you fill in your address on them. If your state requires this information, the instructions that print out with your documents will indicate whether and where you must add it.

If an address is required, print the address of your residence—the place you live most of the year. Your address is just one additional piece of information that will help ensure that you are properly matched with your written directions for healthcare.

IT DOES NOT GET MORE PERSONAL THAN THIS

Be cautiously leery of those who try to convince you about the type of healthcare you should receive. For many people, the desire to direct what kind of medical care they want to receive is driven by a very specific event—watching a loved one die, having an unsatisfactory brush with the medical establishment, preparing for serious surgery.

Your ultimate decisions are likely to be influenced by many complicating factors: your medical history, your knowledge of other peoples' experiences with life-prolonging medical procedures, your religious beliefs. If you are having great difficulty in deciding about your preferences for medical care, take a few moments to figure out what's getting in your way. If you are unsure about the meaning or specifics of a particular medical treatment, turn to a doctor you trust for a more complete explanation. If the impediment is fear of sickness or death, talk over your feelings with family members and friends. (See Section Q.)

E. Life-Prolonging Medical Care

Healthcare directives in most states ask for your preferences about life-prolonging treatments or procedures. Many people who attempt to fill in the blanks on their state forms unaided by WillMaker or some sound medical advice are confounded by the question.

This section of the manual briefly discusses medical procedures that are most often deemed "life-prolonging." Ponderous as it seems, most people should at least read quickly through the definitions below so that they understand what the term life-prolonging means from a medical perspective. However, if you are firmly resolved to direct that all procedures be provided—or that all procedures be withheld—you will not need to deal with these definitions while preparing your healthcare directive, and you can skip directly to Section I.

Bear in mind that the types of medical procedures that are available will change over time. Technological advances mean that currently unfathomable procedures and treatments will become available and treatments that are now common will become obsolete. Also, the treatments that are available vary drastically with region, depending on the sophistication and funding levels of local medical facilities.

While putting together your healthcare directive, the best that you can do is to become familiar with the kinds of medical procedures that are most commonly administered to patients who are terminally ill or permanently comatose. The best that the WillMaker program can do is to provide you with clear definitions. Both of these feats will help you to produce the healthcare document that most accurately reflects your wishes.

Don't Let Indecision Stand in Your Way

If you have definite ideas about some medical treatments that you do or do not want provided, but are confused or steadfastly undecided about others, do not let that stop you from completing what you can in your healthcare directive. While using the WillMaker program, you can skip the answers to many of the specific questions asked; your document will print out with the response "no preference" where you have opted not to make a decision. You can always rewrite your documents later—and sign them and have them witnessed or notarized—if you change your mind.

1. Blood and Blood Products

Blood is composed of a pale yellow fluid called plasma. Within the plasma, red blood cells (erythrocytes), white blood cells (leukocytes), platelets and a variety of chemicals including hormones, proteins, carbohydrates and fats are suspended.

Partial or full blood transfusions may be recommended to combat diseases that impair the blood system, to foster healing after a blood loss or to replenish blood lost through surgery, disease or injury.

2. Cardio-Pulmonary Resuscitation (CPR)

Cardio-pulmonary resuscitation (CPR) is used when a person's heart or breathing has stopped. CPR includes applying physical pressure and using mouth-to-mouth resuscitation. Electrical shocks are also used if available. CPR is often accompanied by intravenous drugs used to normalize body systems. A final step in CPR is often attaching the patient to a respirator.

IN AN EMERGENCY: DNR ORDERS

In addition to the healthcare documents produced by WillMaker, you may want to secure a Do Not Resuscitate order, or DNR order. A DNR order documents the wish that you not be administered cardio-pulmonary resuscitation (CPR) and will alert emergency medical personnel to this wish. DNR orders were first used in hospital settings to alert hospital staff that CPR should be withheld from a patient, but now they are frequently used in situations where a person might require emergency care while outside of the hospital.

You may want to consider a DNR order if:
- you have a terminal illness
- you are at an increased risk for cardiac or respiratory arrest, or
- you have strong feelings against the use of CPR under any circumstances.

In most states, any adult may secure a DNR order. But some states, such as South Carolina and Utah, allow you to create an order only if you have been diagnosed as having a terminal illness.

Because emergency response teams must act quickly in a medical crisis, they often do not have the time to determine whether you have a valid healthcare directive explaining treatments you want provided or withheld. If they do not know your wishes, they must provide you with all possible life-saving measures. But if emergency care providers see that you have a valid DNR order—which is often made apparent by an easily identifiable bracelet, anklet, or necklace—they will not administer CPR.

If you ask to have CPR withheld, you will not be provided with:
- chest compression
- electric shock treatments to the chest
- tubes placed in the airway to assist breathing
- artificial ventilation, or
- cardiac drugs.

If you want to secure a DNR order, or if you would like to find out more about DNR orders, talk with a doctor. A doctor's signature is required to make the DNR valid—and in most states, he or she will obtain and complete the necessary paperwork. If the doctor does not have the form or other information you need, call the Health Department for your state and ask to speak with someone in the Division of Emergency Medical Services.

If you obtain a DNR order, discuss your decision with your family or other caretakers. They should know where your form is located—and who to call if you require emergency treatment. Even if you are wearing identification, such as a bracelet or necklace, keep your form in an obvious place. You might consider keeping it by your bedside, on the front of your refrigerator, in your wallet, or in your suitcase if you are traveling. If your DNR order is not apparent and immediately available, or if it has been altered in any way, CPR will most likely be performed.

3. Diagnostic Tests

Diagnostic tests are commonly used to evaluate urine, blood and other body fluids and to check on all bodily functions. Diagnostic tests can include X-rays and more sophisticated tests of brainwaves or other internal body systems. Some diagnostic tests, including surgery, can be expensive and invasive, producing pain and other side effects.

4. Dialysis

A dialysis machine is used to clean and add essential substances to the blood—through tubes placed in blood vessels or into the abdomen—when kidneys do not function properly. The entire cleansing process takes three or more hours and is performed on most dialysis patients from two to three times a week. With the portability of dialysis machines, it is often possible to have the procedure performed at home rather than in a hospital or other advanced care facility.

5. Drugs

The most common and most controversial drugs given to seriously ill or comatose patients are antibiotics—administered by mouth, through a feeding tube or by injection. Antibiotics are used to arrest and squelch infectious diseases. Patients in very weakened conditions may not respond even to massive doses of antibiotics.

Many healthcare providers argue that infectious diseases can actually be a benefit to those in advanced stages of an illness, since they may render a patient unconscious, and presumably not in pain, or help to speed up the dying process. Others contend that if an antibiotic can eliminate symptoms of an illness, it is almost always the proper medical treatment.

Drugs may also be used to eliminate or alleviate pain. While fashioning your healthcare directive using WillMaker, you can address your views on pain-relieving drugs in the portion of the program that deals with comfort care. (See Section F.)

6. Respirator

A mechanical respirator or a ventilator assists or takes over breathing for a patient by pumping air in and out of the lungs. These machines dispense a regulated amount of air into the lungs at a set rate—and periodically purge the lungs. Patients are connected to respirators either by a tube that goes through the mouth and throat into the lung or attaches directly through the lung surgically.

Respirators are often used to stabilize patients who are suffering from an acute trauma or breathing crisis. Once a patient has been attached to a respirator, most doctors will buck against removing the machinery unless there is clear written direction that this is what the patient would want.

7. Surgery

Surgical procedures such as amputation are often used to stem the spread of life-threatening infections or to keep vital organs functioning. Major surgery such as a heart bypass are also typically performed on patients who are terminally ill or comatose. You might want to consider the cost, time spent recovering from the invasive surgery and the ultimate prognosis in deciding whether to include surgery in your final medical treatment.

F. Comfort Care

The laws of most states assume that people want relief from pain and discomfort and specifically exclude pain-relieving procedures from definitions of life-prolonging treatments that may be withheld. If that was all there was to it, most people would agree with this approach and welcome the relief.

However, the issue of comfort care is fraught with controversy. Medical experts disagree on whether a patient who is comatose or close to death from a terminal illness can feel pain, so they also debate whether such patients benefit from pain control medications. There is also disagreement over whether administering drugs to make a person comfortable or alleviate pain will also have the effect of prolonging the person's life. An additional complication in some cases is that high doses of pain control drugs can impair respiration—and so such drugs sometimes hasten death in a seriously ill patient.

WillMaker allows you to state whether you want comfort care withheld or provided. If your state's law does not permit it to be withheld, but that is your wish, your healthcare directive will assert your right to have it withheld under the U.S. Constitution. (See Section B.)

G. Artificially-Administered Food and Water

If you are close to death from a terminal condition or in a permanent coma and cannot communicate to others your preferences for your own healthcare, it is also likely that you will not be able to voluntarily take in water or food through your mouth. The medical solution to this is to provide you with food and water—as a mix of nutrients and fluids—through tubes inserted in a vein, into your stomach through your nose, or directly into your stomach through a surgical incision, depending on your condition.

Intravenous feeding, where fluids are introduced through a vein in an arm or a leg, is a short-term procedure. Tube feeding through the nose (nasogastric tube), through the stomach (gastrostomy tube), intestines (jejunostomy tube) or largest vein, the vena cava (total parenteral nutrition) can be carried on indefinitely.

Controversies over artificially-administered food and water still rage because medical experts disagree about whether its purpose is to sustain life or to cure an illness. The state laws governing healthcare directives reflect this controversy. A few states specify that artificial feeding—also called nutrition and hydration—cannot be rejected; some states allow people to specify the circumstances under which they would want feeding; other state laws are silent on the topic.

WillMaker allows you to state whether you want artificially-administered food and water withheld or provided. If your state's law does not permit food and water to be withheld, but that is your wish, your healthcare directive will assert your right to have it withheld under the U.S. Constitution. (See Section B.)

H. Directing Healthcare for Different Situations

Despite drastic technological advances in medicine, much about physical symptoms and effects remains uncharted. For example, medical experts disagree over whether comatose patients can feel pain, and over whether some treatments are universally effective.

People who have strong feelings about what medical care they want to receive are usually guided by personal experience rather than a greater knowledge of current medical capabilities or future advances. For example, if you have watched a grandparent suffer a prolonged death while hooked to a respirator, you may opt not to have a respirator as part of your medical care. If a friend who was diagnosed as terminally ill was much improved by a newly-developed antibiotic, you may adamantly demand that drugs be administered to you, no matter what the medical prognosis.

WillMaker allows you to specify that you should receive different kinds of medical care when you are in a permanent coma and when you are diagnosed to be close to death from a terminal condition. This flexibility is built in to accommodate healthcare wishes stemming from personal preference and experience, while balancing the unknowns of medicine.

For example, medical personnel usually give those diagnosed to be terminally ill a short time to live—less than six months or so. Some people feel that the best medical care under such a prognosis would be to have as much pain and suffering alleviated as possible through drugs and IVs, without any heroic medical maneuvers, such as invasive surgery or additional painful diagnostic tests.

However, patients often prove doctors wrong. Those diagnosed to die of a terminal illness within a few months sometimes stabilize or improve and live on for many years. If you opt to direct that no life-prolonging treatments be provided, you gamble that your condition will not improve—a gamble you must weigh against your own definitions of life.

Comatose patients face even less certain futures. Many comatose patients are kept alive for many years with some mechanical assistance to keep breathing, circulation and other vital bodily functions operating. While most long-term coma patients never recover, there are, of course, instances of miraculous awakenings.

There is no general rule, no strict legal guidance, to offer on this topic. People fashioning documents to direct their healthcare in the case of a coma will likely be guided by their own very personal definitions of quality of life. Some hold out hope for the possibility of some medical cure for their condition—and direct that all possible medical treatments be administered to them if they become comatose. Others feel strongly that life in a coma would completely lack meaning for them—and direct that all medical procedures, including food and water, be discontinued. And still others walk the middle ground, opting to direct that only the minimum—food and water and pain-alleviating drugs—be administered to them if they become comatose.

If you are having a difficult time making this choice, you may get good guidance by discussing the matter with a doctor you trust, or with another experienced healthcare worker.

1. Close to Death From a Terminal Condition

Generally, a terminal condition is any disease or injury from which doctors believe there is no chance of recovery and from which death is likely to occur within a short time—such as the final stages of cancer or AIDS.

State laws on healthcare directives define terminal condition slightly differently, but commonly refer to it as "incurable," "hopeless" or "irreversible." Many state laws explain in addition that a patient who is terminally ill will die unless artificially supported through life-sustaining procedures.

Most states require that one or two physicians verify that the patient has a terminal condition before the documents directing healthcare will go into effect. In some states, this verification must be in writing.

2. Permanently Comatose

A coma is a state of unconsciousness caused by various medical conditions, head traumas or other body injuries.

While comatose people appear to go through sleep cycles and to respond to some noises and physical stimulation, medical experts disagree over whether a person in a coma is capable of experiencing pain or discomfort. Most comatose people do not require mechanical assistance with breathing or circulation, but must be provided food and water through artificial means—usually through tubes inserted in the veins or stomach—if the condition persists.

Generally, people who become comatose either regain consciousness within a short time or enter a permanent coma or a persistent vegetative state in which it is uncertain whether consciousness will ever be regained. They may be kept alive for many months or even years. Medical personnel usually declare that a person who remains in a persistent vegetative state for many months without change has passed into a terminal condition.

ASSISTED SUICIDE: A LESSON FROM DR. DEATH

Behind closed doors, many doctors acknowledge that they have helped seriously ill patients end their own lives—many of them tacitly writing large prescriptions for Seconal or other drugs, ostensibly to help patients with sleeping problems. But most won't discuss the issue openly.

Jack Kevorkian, a doctor practicing in Michigan, was the first to buck the silence—loudly. In June 1990, Kevorkian took part in the first in a series of physician-assisted suicides. He met with Janet Adkins, a 54-year-old Oregon schoolteacher suffering from Alzheimer's Disease, and agreed to help her end her life. First he videotaped a conversation between them in which Adkins lamented the diminishing quality of her life, her inability to read or play the piano. Adkins agreed she would take ultimate control of the final act—which would, she said, allow her to "get out with dignity."

The next morning Kevorkian led Adkins to a red van outside a public park, where he attached her to an intravenous drip connected to three vials—in the first, saline solution; in the second, Thiopental, to induce unconsciousness; and in the third, Potassium Chloride, to cause the heart to stop. Adkins was found dead hours later.

The well-orchestrated event earned Kevorkian a blaze of media attention—and the nickname Dr. Death. Patients, family members and doctors alternately pronounced his tactics humane and unconscionable. Polls taken at the time showed that 45% of all doctors and 53% of the general public strongly supported the idea of physician-assisted suicide. But opponents questioned the real dignity in dying alone, in a rusting VW bus.

Doctor-assisted suicide is a crime in the grand majority of the states. But legislation is pending in several states that would allow voters to consider the desirability of allowing doctor-assisted lethal injections for incurably ill patients. A number of states have recently established commissions to study and make recommendations on the issue.

To this day, most of the furor on legality still focuses on Kevorkian, whose license to practice medicine has been suspended and reinstated, and who has, after assisting in many deaths since Adkins, been charged with murder. In April 1995, the U.S. Supreme Court refused to hear Kevorkian's appeal of a Michigan court order banning his work, leaving the legal picture of doctor-assisted suicide incomplete.

I. Choosing a Healthcare Proxy

By taking the time and making the effort to draw up documents to direct your healthcare if you become unable to do so, you have already done much to assure that your wishes will be followed. The next desirable step is to discuss those wishes with a doctor if you have one—and with patient administrators if you anticipate being admitted to a hospital. In most cases, medical personnel and relatives faced with difficult decisions about continuing or discontinuing another's medical care are relieved and delighted to take direction from the person by following the healthcare documents.

Occasionally, however, and especially if your wishes for your healthcare are different than what your doctors or close relatives want for you, problems can arise in getting the documents enforced. For this reason, it is best to name a person—usually called a healthcare proxy or attorney-in-fact—to reinforce that the wishes you have expressed are followed to the letter. That way, there will be someone to lobby on your behalf to get your wishes enforced, to make sure medical personnel know of your wishes, to argue with them if need be, to enforce your healthcare directives in court if necessary.

1. Guidance in Choosing a Proxy

The person you name as your healthcare proxy should be someone you trust—and someone with whom you feel confident discussing your wishes. While your proxy need not agree with your wishes for your medical care, you should believe that he or she respects your right to get the kind of medical care you want.

The person you appoint to oversee your healthcare wishes could be a spouse or partner, relative or close friend. Keep in mind your proxy may have to fight to assert your wishes in the face of a medical establishment hard to budge from its position—and against the wishes of family members who may be driven by their own beliefs and interests, rather than yours. If you foresee the possibility of a conflict in enforcing your wishes, be sure to choose a proxy who is strong-willed and assertive.

While you need not name someone who lives in the same state as you do, proximity should be one factor you consider. If you languish long with a protracted illness, the reality is that the person you name may be called upon to spend weeks or months near your bedside, making sure medical personnel abide by your wishes for your medical treatment.

 Do Not Choose Medical Personnel

You should not choose your doctor, or an employee of a hospital or nursing home where you are receiving treatment. In fact, the laws in many states prevent you from naming such a person. In a few instances, this legal constraint may frustrate your wishes. For example, you may wish to name your spouse or partner as your representative, but if he or she also works as a hospital employee, that alone may bar you from naming that person in some states. If the laws in your state ban your first choice, you may have to name another person to serve instead. (See the chart in Section I2, for more on your state's law on healthcare proxy restrictions.)

2. State Requirements for Proxies

A number of states have strict bans against allowing some people to serve as your healthcare proxy. Attending physicians and other healthcare providers are those commonly banned from serving. Some states presume that the motivations of such people may be clouded by self-interest. For example, an attending physician may be motivated to provide every medical procedure available—to try every heroic or experimental treatment—even if that flies in the face of a patient's wishes.

Consult the listing below for the specifics of your state's law on proxy requirements and restrictions before you select a proxy.

STATE PROXY REQUIREMENTS

ALABAMA

No requirements.

ALASKA

No requirements.

ARIZONA

Your healthcare representative must be at least 18 years old.

ARKANSAS

Your healthcare representative must be at least 18 years old.

CALIFORNIA

Your healthcare representative may not be:
- your treating healthcare provider
- an employee of your treating healthcare provider, unless the employee is related to you or you and the employee both work for your treating healthcare provider
- an operator of a community care facility
- an employee of the operator of the community care facility, unless the employee is related to you or you and the employee both work at the community care facility
- an operator of a residential care facility for the elderly
- an employee of the operator of the residential care facility for the elderly, unless the employee is related to you or you and the employee both work at the residential care facility, or
- your conservator.

COLORADO

No requirements.

CONNECTICUT

If, when you appoint your healthcare representative, you are a patient or a resident of, or have applied for admission to, a hospital, home for the aged, rest home with nursing supervision or chronic and convalescent nursing home, your healthcare representative may not be:
- an operator, unless the operator is related to you by blood, marriage or adoption
- an administrator, unless the administrator is related to you by blood, marriage or adoption, or
- an employee, unless the employee is related to you by blood, marriage or adoption.

In any case, your healthcare representative may not be:
- a witness to the document appointing him or her as your healthcare representative
- your attending physician, or
- an employee of a government agency which is financially responsible for your medical care—unless that person is related to you by blood, marriage or adoption.

DELAWARE

No requirements.

DISTRICT OF COLUMBIA

Your healthcare representative may not be your healthcare provider.

FLORIDA

Your healthcare representative may not be a witness to the document naming your healthcare representative.

GEORGIA

Your healthcare representative may not be your healthcare provider if your healthcare provider is directly or indirectly involved in the medical treatment given to you under your durable power of attorney for healthcare.

HAWAII

Your healthcare representative may not be your treating physician.

IDAHO

Your healthcare representative may not be:
- under the age of 18
- a witness to your durable power of attorney for healthcare
- your treating healthcare provider
- an employee of your healthcare provider, unless the employee is related to you
- an operator of a community care facility, or
- an employee of an operator of a community care facility, unless the employee is related to you.

ILLINOIS

Your healthcare representative may not be a healthcare provider.

INDIANA

No requirements.

IOWA

Your healthcare representative may not be:
- your healthcare provider, or
- an employee of your healthcare provider, unless these individuals are related to you by blood, marriage or adoption—limited to parents, children, siblings, grandchildren, grandparents, uncles, aunts, nephews, nieces and great-grandchildren.

KANSAS

Your healthcare representative may not be:
- your treating healthcare provider
- an employee of your treating healthcare provider, or
- an employee, owner, director or officer of a healthcare facility unless:
  - related to you by blood, marriage or adoption, or
  - a member of the same community of people to which you belong who have vowed to lead a religious life and who conduct or assist in conducting religious services and actually and regularly engage in religious, charitable or educational activities or the performance of healthcare services.

KENTUCKY

Your healthcare representative may not be an employee, owner, director or officer of a healthcare facility where you are a resident or patient, unless
- they are related to you more closely than first cousins, once removed, or
- a member of the same religious order.

MAINE

Your healthcare representative may not be an owner, operator or employee of a residential long-term healthcare institution in which you are receiving care, unless he or she is related to you.

MARYLAND

Your healthcare representative may not be an owner, operator, or employee of a healthcare facility where you are receiving treatment unless he or she would qualify as your surrogate decisionmaker under Maryland law.

MASSACHUSETTS

Your healthcare representative may not be an operator, administrator or employee of a facility where you are a patient or resident or have applied for admission, unless the operator, administrator or employee is related to you by blood, marriage, or adoption.

MICHIGAN

No requirements.

MINNESOTA

Your healthcare representative may not be your treating healthcare provider or an employee of your treating healthcare provider, unless he or she is related to you by blood, marriage, registered domestic partnership, or adoption.

MISSISSIPPI

Your healthcare representative may not be:
- a treating healthcare provider, or
- an employee of a treating healthcare provider.

MISSOURI

Your healthcare representative may not be:
- your attending physician, or
- an employee of the healthcare facility where you live, unless
  - you and your healthcare representative are related as parents, children, siblings, grandparent, or grandchildren, or

- you and your healthcare representative are members of the same community of people who have vowed to lead a religious life and who conduct or assist in conducting religious services and actually and regularly engage in religious, charitable or educational activities or the performance of healthcare services.

MONTANA

No requirements.

NEBRASKA

Your healthcare representative may not be:
- under the age of 19, unless he or she is married
- a witness to your durable power of attorney for healthcare
- your attending physician
- an employee of your attending physician, unless the employee is related to you by blood, marriage or adoption
- a person unrelated to you by blood, marriage or adoption who is an owner, operator, or employee of a healthcare provider of which you are a patient or resident, or
- a person unrelated to you by blood, marriage or adoption who is presently serving as an healthcare representative for ten or more people.

NEVADA

Your healthcare representative may not be:
- your healthcare provider
- an employee of your healthcare provider
- an operator of a healthcare facility, or
- an employee of a healthcare facility, unless they are your spouse, legal guardian or next of kin.

NEW HAMPSHIRE

Your healthcare representative may not be:
- your healthcare provider
- an employee of your healthcare provider, unless the employee is related to you
- your residential care provider, or
- an employee of your residential care provider, unless the employee is related to you.

NEW JERSEY

Your healthcare representative may not be:
- under the age of 18, or
- an operator, administrator or employee of a healthcare institution in which you are a patient or resident, unless the operator, administrator or employee is related to you by blood, marriage or adoption, or, in the case of a physician, is not your attending physician.

NEW MEXICO

No requirements.

NEW YORK

Your healthcare representative may not be:
- under the age of 18, unless he or she is the parent of a child, or married.
- your attending physician
- presently appointed healthcare representative for ten or more other people, unless he or she is your spouse, child, parent, brother, sister or grandparent
- an operator, administrator or employee of a hospital if, at the time of the appointment, you are a patient or resident of, or have applied for admission to, such hospital. This restriction shall not apply to:
  - an operator, administrator, or employee of a hospital who is related to you by blood, marriage or adoption, or
  - a physician, who is not your attending physician, except that no physician affiliated with a mental hygiene facility or a psychiatric unit of a general hospital may serve as agent for you if you are living in or being treated by such facility or unit unless the physician is related to you by blood, marriage or adoption.

NORTH CAROLINA

Your healthcare agent may not be:
- under the age of 18, or
- providing healthcare to you for compensation.

NORTH DAKOTA

Your healthcare representative may not be:
- your healthcare provider
- an employee of your healthcare provider, unless the employee is related to you
- your long-term care services provider, or
- an employee of your long-term care services provider, unless the employee is related to you.

OHIO

Your healthcare representative may not be:
- under the age of 18
- your attending physician
- an administrator of any nursing home in which you are receiving care
- an employee or agent of your attending physician, or
- an employee or agent of any healthcare facility in which you are being treated, except that you may appoint any of the above employees or agents if they are 18 years of age or older and are members of the same religious order as you.

OKLAHOMA

Your healthcare representative must be at least 18 years old.

OREGON

Your healthcare representative may not be:
- under the age of 18
- your attending physician or an employee of your attending physician, unless the physician or employee is related to you by blood, marriage or adoption, or
- an owner, operator or employee of a healthcare facility in which you are patient or resident, unless related to you by blood, marriage or adoption—or appointed before you were admitted to the facility.

PENNSYLVANIA

No requirements.

RHODE ISLAND

Your healthcare representative may not be:
- your treating healthcare provider
- an employee of your treating healthcare provider, unless the employee is related to you
- an operator of a community care facility, or
- an employee of an operator of a community care facility, unless the employee is related to you.

SOUTH CAROLINA

Your healthcare representative may not be:
- under the age of 18
- your healthcare provider at the time you execute your healthcare power of attorney, unless he or she is related to you
- a spouse or employee of your healthcare provider, unless he or she is related to you, or
- an employee of the nursing care facility where you live.

SOUTH DAKOTA

No requirements.

TENNESSEE

Your healthcare representative may not be:
- your treating healthcare provider
- an employee of your treating healthcare provider, unless he or she is related to you by blood, marriage or adoption
- an operator of a healthcare institution, unless he or she is related to you by blood, marriage or adoption
- an employee of an operator of a healthcare institution, unless he or she is related to you by blood, marriage or adoption, or
- your conservator.

TEXAS

Your healthcare representative may not be:
- your healthcare provider
- an employee of your healthcare provider, unless the employee is related to you
- your residential care provider, or
- an employee of your residential care provider, unless the employee is related to you.

UTAH

Your healthcare representative must be at least 18 years old.

VERMONT

Your healthcare representative may not be:
- under the age of 18
- your healthcare provider
- an employee of your healthcare provider, unless he or she is related to you
- your residential care provider, or
- an employee of your residential care provider, unless he or she is related to you.

VIRGINIA

Your healthcare representative must be at least 18 years old.

WASHINGTON

Your healthcare representative may not be:
- any of your physicians
- your physicians' employees
- owners, administrators or employees of the healthcare facility where you live or receive care.

WEST VIRGINIA

Your healthcare representative may not be:
- your treating healthcare provider or an employee of your treating healthcare provider, unless he or she is related to you
- an operator of a healthcare facility serving you, or
- an employee of an operator of a healthcare facility, unless he or she is related to you.

WISCONSIN

Your healthcare representative may not be:
- your healthcare provider or the spouse or employee of your healthcare provider unless he or she is related to you, or
- an employee or spouse of an employee of the healthcare facility in which you are a patient, unless he or she is related to you.

WYOMING

Your healthcare representative may not be:
- your treating healthcare provider
- an employee of your treating healthcare provider, unless he or she is related to you by blood, marriage or adoption, or
- an operator of a community care facility or residential care facility, unless he or she is related to you by blood, marriage or adoption.

3. Choosing an Alternate

Do not choose as an alternate someone who may be disqualified by state law from serving in your state. (See Section 12, above.)

A BAD IDEA: NAMING MORE THAN ONE REPRESENTATIVE

Name only one person as your representative, even if you know of two or more people who are suitable candidates and who agree to undertake the job together. There may be problems, brought on by passing time and human nature, with naming people to share the job. In the critical time during which your representatives will be overseeing your wishes, they could disagree or suffer a change of heart, rendering them ineffective as lobbyists on your behalf.

If you know of two people you would like to name as your representatives, it is better to name only one person for the job—and name the other as an alternate to take over in case your first choice is unable to act when needed.

4. If You Do Not Name a Representative

Naming a healthcare representative is an optional part of making out your directives for your healthcare. If you do not know of anyone you trust to oversee your medical care, skip this part of the program. It is better not to name anyone than to name someone who is not comfortable with the directions you leave—or who is not likely to assert your wishes strongly.

Medical personnel are still technically bound to follow your written wishes for your healthcare—or to find someone who will care for you in the way you have directed. It is far better to put your wishes for final healthcare in writing than to let the lack of a representative stand in the way. If you do not name a healthcare proxy, redouble your efforts to discuss your wishes for medical care with a doctor or patient representative likely to be involved in providing that care.

J. Broader Durable Powers of Attorney

The durable power of attorney you produce with WillMaker gives the person you name the limited authority to supervise and enforce your written wishes for the type of medical care you wish to receive.

The power of attorney that prints out specifically gives the person you name as your healthcare proxy the authority to:

- review your medical records
- grant releases to medical personnel
- take any legal action necessary to ensure your wishes are followed
- hire and fire medical personnel such as homecare providers and attending physicians, and
- visit you in a hospital or other healthcare facility.

This should allow your proxy to do everything needed to make sure your healthcare wishes are carried out as written—and if they are not, to get you transferred to another facility or to the care of another doctor who will enforce them.

1. Possible Additional Powers

Be aware that most states allow you to prepare Durable Powers of Attorney for Healthcare that delegate much broader authority than the one produced for you by the WillMaker program. Such powers of attorney may authorize your proxy to make healthcare decisions for you even if you are not terminally ill or permanently comatose, but, for example, you have an ongoing medical condition such as Alzheimer's disease that renders you incompetent. Because that type of durable power of attorney must be closely tailored to your needs and the abilities of your proxy—and must often be revised to meet changing medical conditions—you need the help of an experienced attorney or other estate planning expert to fashion one. (See Chapter 15.)

2. Durable Powers of Attorney for Finances

Another type of durable power of attorney—called a Durable Power of Attorney for Finances—can be used to give a person you trust the legal authority to handle many of your financial matters if you become unable to do so. People who are facing illness, injury or old age are particularly good candidates for this type of document.

The person you name in a Durable Power of Attorney for Finances, who is usually called an attorney-in-fact, can be given broad authority to handle your finances and investments. Powers commonly given an attorney-in-fact include the authority to:

- use your assets to pay for expenses for you and your family, including food, mortgage, education, cars and medical expenses
- buy, sell and maintain real estate and other property
- collect benefits from Social Security, Medicare or military service
- invest your money in stocks, bonds and mutual funds
- handle transactions with banks and other financial institutions
- handle insurance policies
- file and pay your taxes, and
- operate your small business.

If you need a Durable Power of Attorney for Finances, go to the nearest law library to obtain the proper form for your state, or consult an experienced attorney for help. (See Chapter 15.)

3. Why Separate Documents Are Required

Although the WillMaker program does not provide for the option, some state laws allow people to draw up a single durable power of attorney in which one person is named to oversee both healthcare and financial matters. While this sounds like a logical and simple solution to planning for possible incapacity, it is usually not a good idea, for a number of reasons.

- Most forms for durable powers of attorney that combine medical and financial matters do not allow you to include many specific details about how you would like to direct your medical care.

- Each of these types of durable power of attorney will be used for a very different purpose and must be presented to different people and organizations—often at different times.

- If you use two separate documents, you do not have to show your medical wishes to people who are concerned only with your finances—and vice versa.

- It is essential for the documents delegating authority for your healthcare and finances to be kept current to reflect your changing wishes, adjustments in your money matters—even advances in medical technology. Having a single document that controls both finances and healthcare makes it unwieldy to update any of your wishes.

YOU CONTROL YOUR HEALTHCARE IF YOU ARE ABLE

Most people know it is a good idea to complete a healthcare directive. But some run smack into a psychological roadblock. They are worried that they may experience a change of heart or mind later—and that they will receive more or less medical care than they would want in a particular situation.

There are two soothing axioms for such people to keep in mind.

First, the directions set out in your written healthcare directive will only be followed if you later become unable to communicate your wishes about the treatment. If, for example, you indicate in a healthcare directive that you do not wish to have water provided, healthcare providers will not deny you a glass of water as long as you are able to communicate your wishes for one.

Second, you can change or revoke your written healthcare wishes at any time in the future. If you find that your document no longer accurately expresses your wishes for your medical care, you can easily draw up and finalize a new document which does reflect your wishes. (See Section M.)

K. When Your Documents Take Effect

Your healthcare directive takes effect when three things happen:

- You are diagnosed to be close to death from a terminal condition or to be permanently comatose

- You cannot communicate your own wishes for your medical care—orally, in writing or through gestures, and

- The medical personnel attending you are notified of your written directions for your medical care.

In most instances, you can ensure that your directive becomes part of your medical record when you are admitted to a hospital or other care facility. But to ensure that your wishes will be followed if your need for care arises unexpectedly or while you are out of your home state or country, it is best to give copies of your completed documents to several people. (See Section N.)

L. How Pregnancy May Affect Your Directions

There is one limited situation in which a patient's specific directions about healthcare might be challenged or ignored: when the patient is pregnant. Many states specifically restrict the effect of healthcare documents if a woman is pregnant, stating that wishes that life support be withdrawn or removed will not be honored.

These state restrictions have rankled many supporters of women's rights and have become legally suspect since the U.S. Supreme Court set out and reaffirmed that women have a constitutionally-protected right to choose whether or not to bear children. In 1973, the Court in the case of *Roe v. Wade* (401 U.S. 113), overturned a restrictive Texas anti-abortion law, with a tersely delineated holding. The Court held that:

- during the first trimester of pregnancy, states may not intervene to regulate pregnancy

- during the second trimester, states may set up restrictions only to protect a woman's health, and

- during the third trimester, or at the point of viability, when a fetus "presumably has the capability of meaningful life outside the mother's womb," states can intervene to protect it.

Several states fashioning or refining their healthcare directives took a cue from this holding about when a state might legally claim it has a right to limit individuals' rights to direct their healthcare. They wrote into their legislation the condition that a healthcare directive will not take effect "if your doctors believe the fetus can be brought to term while you are receiving life-sustaining procedures."

Other state attempts to control your choices about healthcare before a fetus is viable would most certainly be held unconstitutional. However, it is good to be aware of the restrictions that may exist in your state for pregnant women's healthcare directives. (See the chart below.)

WillMaker allows all women for whom pregnancy may be possible to specify that their healthcare directions:

- be given no effect during the course of a pregnancy, or

- be carried out as written.

If you specify that your healthcare directives be given no effect, the decision for appropriate care will be left to the discretion of your healthcare providers. They are most likely to be conservative and administer whatever life-prolonging procedures are available—particularly if the fetus is at least four or five months old and potentially viable and unharmed by your condition.

If you choose that your healthcare directions be carried out as written if you are pregnant, beware that you may meet some resistance from the medical establishment. This is particularly true if you have directed that life-prolonging treatment, comfort care or food and water should be withheld. And you are more apt to run into resistance the more advanced your pregnancy becomes. If you are into the second trimester—fourth through sixth months—doctors are likely to administer all medical care they deem necessary to keep you and the fetus alive.

By the third trimester of a pregnancy—seventh through ninth months—it may be practically impossible to overcome a state's proscription against withholding life-prolonging medical care. And doctors who balk at enforcing your contrary wishes have some legal support for ignoring you and administering all available care. Since the *Roe* decision discussed above, they can argue that while individuals may have the right to direct their own healthcare, they have no right to direct that care for another living being—arguably, a fetus six months old or older.

If you are pregnant or anticipate becoming pregnant and have strong feelings about overcoming your state's strictures—that is, you live in a state that renders your directive completely ineffective if you are pregnant, but you wish to have it enforced—it is especially important for you to name a proxy to lobby on your behalf. Discuss your wishes and alert your proxy to any differences between your wishes and your state law. It would also be wise to write a brief explanation of your thoughts and understanding on this specific issue and attach it to your healthcare directive.

STATE LAWS ON PREGNANCY AND HEALTHCARE DIRECTIVES

"No Effect" means that the law in your state does not allow your document directing healthcare to take effect when you are pregnant.

"To Term" means that the law in your state will not allow your document directing healthcare to take effect if you are pregnant and your doctors believe the fetus could be brought to term while you are receiving life-sustaining treatment.

"No Statute" means that your state does not have any law about pregnancy and your healthcare document.

State	No Effect	To Term	No Statute
Alabama	•		
Alaska		•	
Arizona	You may indicate whether or not you want your healthcare directions to be carried out in the event of your pregnancy.		
Arkansas		•	
California	•		
Colorado		•	
Connecticut	•		
Delaware	•		
District of Columbia			•
Florida	If you are pregnant, life-prolonging procedures will be provided unless you have expressly indicated that your healthcare surrogate may authorize that life-prolonging procedures may be withheld if you are pregnant, or if your healthcare surrogate obtains court approval for withholding life-prolonging procedures.		
Georgia	If you are pregnant, life-sustaining procedures will be provided unless the fetus could not develop to the point of live birth and you expressly indicate that you want your healthcare instructions to be carried out.		
Hawaii	•		

State	No Effect	To Term	No Statute
Idaho	•		
Illinois		•	
Indiana	•		
Iowa		•	
Kansas	•		
Kentucky	•		
Maine			•
Maryland	You may indicate whether or not you want your healthcare directions to be carried out in the event of your pregnancy.		
Massachusetts			•
Michigan	Your healthcare representative cannot make any medical decision to withhold or withdraw treatment that would result in your death if you are pregnant.		
Minnesota		•	
Mississippi	•		
Missouri	•		
Montana		•	
Nebraska	•		
Nevada		•	
New Hampshire	•		
New Jersey	If you are pregnant when diagnosed to be terminally ill and near death or permanently comatose, your express wishes as to your care during pregnancy, if written in your Advance Directive, will be carried out.		
New Mexico			•
New York			•
North Carolina			•

State	No Effect	To Term	No Statute
North Dakota		If you are pregnant, life-sustaining procedures will be provided unless the fetus could not develop to the point of live birth with continued application of those life-sustaining procedures, or your doctors conclude that prolonging your life would cause you unreasonable pain or prolong severe pain that cannot be alleviated by medication.	
Ohio		•	
Oklahoma	•		
Oregon			•
Pennsylvania		If you are pregnant, life-sustaining procedures will be provided unless the fetus could not develop to the point of live birth with continued application of those life-sustaining procedures, or your doctors conclude that prolonging your life would cause you unreasonable pain or prolong severe pain that cannot be alleviated by medication.	
Rhode Island		•	
South Carolina	•		
South Dakota		If you are pregnant, life-sustaining procedures will be provided unless the fetus could not develop to the point of live birth with continued application of those life-sustaining procedures, or your doctors conclude that prolonging your life would cause you unreasonable pain or prolong severe pain that cannot be alleviated by medication.	
Tennessee			•
Texas	•		
Utah	•		
Vermont			•
Virginia			•
Washington			•
West Virginia			•
Wisconsin	•		
Wyoming	•		

WHERE TO GO FOR MORE HELP

Awareness of healthcare directives has skyrocketed in the past few years. This rapid-fire education was aided substantially by the 1991 Patient Self-Determination Act, which requires admitting room personnel in most healthcare facilities to discuss medical directives with patients and note whether they have one in effect. This familiarity has meant not only that many more people have healthcare directives, but that doctors are more likely to recognize and enforce them. But because hospital admission time may not be the best time to learn about your options in directing healthcare or to reflect on your wishes, it is a better idea to become informed and complete your documents in a less stressful time and place.

A side benefit of healthcare directives' increased popularity is that there are a growing number of places you can turn if you need more assistance in completing your healthcare directive or have specific questions about it.

Local senior centers may be good resources for help. Many of them have trained healthcare staff on hand who will be willing to discuss your healthcare options.

The patient representative at a local hospital may also be a good person to contact for help. If you have a regular physician, by all means discuss your concerns with him or her.

Local special interest groups and clinics may provide help in filling out healthcare directives—particularly organizations set up to meet the needs of the severely ill such as AIDS groups or cancer organizations. Check your telephone book for a local listing—or call one of the group's hotlines for more information or a possible referral.

There are also a number of seminars offered. Beware of groups that offer such seminars for a hefty fee, however. Hospitals and senior centers often provide them free of charge.

M. Making It Legal: Final Steps

By proceeding through this portion of the WillMaker program and answering all the questions you can about your future healthcare, you have put the hard parts behind you. You have overcome the twin evils of procrastination and death-avoidance to assert your right to keep control over your own healthcare.

However, there are still a few technical requirements with which you must comply before the documents that print out will be considered legally valid and binding. WillMaker provides detailed, state-specific instructions that will print out with each of your document. But first, review the documents and make sure they are accurate.

1. Signing Your Documents

Every state law requires that you sign your documents—or direct another person to sign them for you—as a way of verifying that you understand them and that they contain your true wishes.

But do not sign them immediately. Every state law also has a requirement that you sign your documents in the presence of witnesses or a notary public—sometimes both. The purpose of this additional formality is so that there is at least one other person who can attest that you were of sound mind and of legal age when you made the documents. (See Section C2.)

2. Having Your Documents Witnessed and Notarized

In some states, you may have your documents notarized instead of witnessed. In others, you will be required to have both witnesses and a notary sign your document. The chart below lists the witnessing and notarizing requirements for your state. Note that a few states have different requirements for your document directing your healthcare and your document naming a proxy.

Witnessing. Many states require that two witnesses see you sign your healthcare documents and that they verify in writing that you appeared to be of sound mind and signed the documents without anyone else influencing your decision.

Each state's qualifications for these witnesses are slightly different. In many states, for example, a spouse, other close relative or any person who would inherit property from you, is not allowed to act as a witness for the document directing healthcare. And many states prohibit your attending physician from being a witness.

The purpose of the laws restricting who can witness your documents is to avoid any appearance or possibility that another person was acting against your wishes in encouraging specific medical care. States that prevent close relatives or potential inheritors from being witnesses, for example, justify their restrictions by noting that these people may be subject to ulterior influences. Some people, anxious to hold on to any sign of life, may urge that all possible medical treatments be administered, no matter what little hope they offer for a cure. Others, driven by fears of bankruptcy or dreams of riches, may encourage that no additional treatment be administered. Either course may not be what an individual patient would want.

If your state has restrictions on who may serve as witnesses to your healthcare documents, those restrictions are listed below in Section M3 and will also be noted on your documents, just before the witness signature lines.

Notarizing. A Notary Public is an individual who is certified to verify signatures on documents. You can locate one by looking in the telephone book; most banks, insurance and title companies also have a Notary on staff. Most will charge a small fee for notarizing your documents.

The chart below, as well as the instructions accompanying your documents will tell you if your state requires that your documents be notarized.

If you do go to a Notary, bring with you some identification that will help prove that you are who you say you are.

STATE WITNESSING AND NOTARIZING REQUIREMENTS

"Witnesses" means witnesses are required to finalize your healthcare document; the number of required witnesses is noted.

"Notarization" means that your document will need to be notarized.

"Witnesses or Notarization" means that you may either have your document witnessed or notarized and that you are not required to have both procedures performed.

"Witnesses and Notarization" means that you must have your document witnessed and notarized.

"Witnesses/Optional Notarization" means that you must have your document witnessed, but you need not have it notarized.

State	Document Appointing Healthcare Representative	Healthcare Directive
Alabama	2 Witnesses or Notarization	2 Witnesses
Alaska	Notarization	2 Witnesses or Notarization
Arizona	1 Witness or Notarization	1 Witness or Notarization
Arkansas	2 Witnesses or Notarization	2 Witnesses
California	2 Witnesses	2 Witnesses
Colorado	Notarization	2 Witnesses/Optional Notarization
Connecticut	2 Witnesses/Optional Notarization	2 Witnesses
Delaware	2 Witnesses or Notarization	2 Witnesses
District of Columbia	2 Witnesses	2 Witnesses

State	Document Appointing Healthcare Representative	Healthcare Directive
Florida	2 Witnesses	2 Witnesses
Georgia	2 Witnesses	2 Witnesses
Hawaii	2 Witnesses and Notarization	2 Witnesses and Notarization
Idaho	2 Witnesses or Notarization	2 Witnesses
Illinois	1 Witness	2 Witnesses
Indiana	1 Witness and Notarization	2 Witnesses
Iowa	2 Witnesses or Notarization	2 Witnesses or Notarization
Kansas	2 Witnesses or Notarization	2 Witnesses or Notarization
Kentucky	SINGLE DOCUMENT—2 Witnesses or Notarization	
Maine	2 Witnesses	2 Witnesses
Maryland	2 Witnesses	2 Witnesses
Massachusetts	2 Witnesses	2 Witnesses
Michigan	2 Witnesses	2 Witnesses
Minnesota	SINGLE DOCUMENT—2 Witnesses or Notarization	
Mississippi	2 Witnesses or Notarization	2 Witnesses
Missouri	Notarization	2 Witnesses
Montana	Notarization	2 Witnesses
Nebraska	Notarization	2 Witnesses or Notarization
Nevada	2 Witnesses or Notarization	2 Witnesses
New Hampshire	2 Witnesses/Optional Notarization	2 Witnesses and Notarization
New Jersey	2 Witnesses or Notarization	2 Witnesses or Notarization
New Mexico	Notarization	2 Witnesses
New York	2 Witnesses	2 Witnesses
North Carolina	2 Witnesses and Notarization	2 Witnesses and Notarization
North Dakota	2 Witnesses	2 Witnesses
Ohio	2 Witnesses or Notarization	2 Witnesses
Oklahoma	SINGLE DOCUMENT—2 Witnesses	
Oregon	SINGLE DOCUMENT—2 Witnesses	
Pennsylvania	2 Witnesses or Notarization	2 Witnesses
Rhode Island	2 Witnesses	2 Witnesses
South Carolina	SINGLE DOCUMENT—2 Witnesses and Notarization	
South Dakota	2 Witnesses or Notarization	2 Witnesses/Optional Notarization
Tennessee	2 Witnesses and Notarization	2 Witnesses/Optional Notarization
Texas	2 Witnesses	2 Witnesses
Utah	Notarization	2 Witnesses
Vermont	2 Witnesses	2 Witnesses
Virginia	2 Witnesses	2 Witnesses
Washington	2 Witnesses or Notarization	2 Witnesses
West Virginia	2 Witnesses and Notarization	2 Witnesses and Notarization
Wisconsin	2 Witnesses	2 Witnesses
Wyoming	2 Witnesses or Notarization	2 Witnesses

3. Who May Serve As a Witness

Most states that require healthcare documents to be witnessed prohibit certain people from serving as witnesses. The qualifications for witnesses in your state are set out below. They are also listed in your healthcare documents just above where the witnesses sign. In many instances, these qualifications are written in legalese—by your state's legislature—and may be hard to interpret. See Section M4 for a glossary that provides brief definitions of common terms used in setting out these qualifications.

State Witness Requirements

ALABAMA

DOCUMENT APPOINTING HEALTHCARE REPRESENTATIVE
Neither of your witnesses may be:
- under the age of 18, or
- your healthcare representative.

HEALTHCARE DIRECTIVE
Neither of your witnesses may be:
- under the age of 19
- the person who signed your Declaration for you, if you were unable to sign it yourself
- related to you by blood or marriage
- entitled to any portion of your estate by operation of law or under your will, or
- directly financially responsible for your medical care.

ALASKA

DOCUMENT APPOINTING HEALTHCARE REPRESENTATIVE
No witnesses
HEALTHCARE DIRECTIVE
Neither of your witnesses may be:
- under the age of 18, or
- related to you by blood or marriage.

ARIZONA

DOCUMENT APPOINTING HEALTHCARE REPRESENTATIVE
Your witness may not be:
- your healthcare representative
- any person involved in providing your healthcare
- related to you by blood, marriage or adoption, or
- entitled to any part of your estate by operation of law or under your will.
HEALTHCARE DIRECTIVE
No requirements.

ARKANSAS

DOCUMENT APPOINTING HEALTHCARE REPRESENTATIVE
Your witnesses must be at least 18 years old.
HEALTHCARE DIRECTIVE
No requirements.

CALIFORNIA

DOCUMENT APPOINTING HEALTHCARE REPRESENTATIVE
Neither of your witnesses may be:
- your healthcare representative
- your healthcare provider
- an employee of your healthcare provider
- the operator of a community care facility
- an employee of an operator of a community care facility
- the operator of a residential care facility for the elderly, or
- an employee of an operator of a residential care facility for the elderly.
In addition, one of your witnesses must not be related to you by blood, marriage or adoption, and must not be entitled to any part of your estate by operation of law or under your will.
HEALTHCARE DIRECTIVE
Neither of your witnesses may be:
- your healthcare provider
- an employee of your healthcare provider
- the operator of a community care facility
- an employee of an operator of a community care facility
- the operator of a residential care facility for the elderly, or
- an employee of an operator of a residential care facility for the elderly.
In addition, one of your witnesses must not be entitled to any part of your estate by operation of law or under your will.

COLORADO

DOCUMENT APPOINTING HEALTHCARE REPRESENTATIVE
No witnesses
HEALTHCARE DIRECTIVE
Neither of your witnesses may be:
- your attending physician
- any other physician
- an employee of your attending physician
- an employee of a healthcare facility where you are a patient
- a person with a claim against your estate, or
- a person entitled to any part of your estate by operation of law or under your will.

CONNECTICUT

DOCUMENT APPOINTING HEALTHCARE REPRESENTATIVE
Your witnesses must be at least 18 years old.
HEALTHCARE DIRECTIVE
No requirements.

DELAWARE

DOCUMENT APPOINTING HEALTHCARE REPRESENTATIVE
Your witnesses must be at least 18 years old.
HEALTHCARE DIRECTIVE
Neither of your witnesses may be:
- related to you by blood or marriage
- an employee of a hospital or other healthcare facility where you are a patient
- a person directly financially responsible for your medical care
- a person with a claim against your estate, or
- a person entitled to any part of your estate by operation of law or under your will.

DISTRICT OF COLUMBIA

DOCUMENT APPOINTING HEALTHCARE REPRESENTATIVE
Neither of your witnesses may be:
- your healthcare representative
- your healthcare provider, or
- an employee of your healthcare provider.
HEALTHCARE DIRECTIVE
Neither of your witnesses may be:
- under the age of 18
- related to you by blood or marriage
- your attending physician
- an employee of your attending physician

- an employee of a healthcare facility where you are a patient
- the person who signed your Declaration for you, if your were unable to sign it yourself
- a person entitled to any part of your estate by operation of law or under your will, or
- a person directly financially responsible for your medical care.

FLORIDA

DOCUMENT APPOINTING HEALTHCARE REPRESENTATIVE
Your witnesses must be at least 18 years old. In addition, one of your witnesses must not be related to you by blood or marriage.
HEALTHCARE DIRECTIVE
One of your witnesses must not be related to you by blood or marriage.

GEORGIA

DOCUMENT APPOINTING HEALTHCARE REPRESENTATIVE
Your witnesses must be at least 18 years old.
HEALTHCARE DIRECTIVE
Neither of your witnesses may be:
- under the age of 18
- related to you by blood or marriage
- your attending physician
- an employee of your attending physician
- an employee of a hospital or skilled nursing facility where you are a patient
- a person who is directly financially responsible for your medical care
- a person with a claim against your estate, or
- a person entitled to any part of your estate by operation of law or under your will.

HAWAII

DOCUMENT APPOINTING HEALTHCARE REPRESENTATIVE
Neither of your witnesses may be:
- under the age of 18
- related to you by blood, marriage or adoption
- your attending physician
- an employee of your attending physician, or
- an employee of a healthcare facility where you are a patient.
HEALTHCARE DIRECTIVE
Neither of your witnesses may be:
- under the age of 18
- related to you by blood, marriage or adoption
- your attending physician
- an employee of your attending physician, or
- an employee of a healthcare facility where you are a patient.

IDAHO

DOCUMENT APPOINTING HEALTHCARE REPRESENTATIVE
Neither of your witnesses may be:
- under the age of 18
- your healthcare representative
- a healthcare provider
- an employee of a healthcare provider
- the operator of a community care facility, or
- an employee of an operator of a community care facility.

In addition, one of your witnesses must not be related to you by blood, marriage or adoption, and must not be entitled to any part of your estate by operation of law or under your will.
HEALTHCARE DIRECTIVE
No requirements.

ILLINOIS

DOCUMENT APPOINTING HEALTHCARE REPRESENTATIVE
Your witness must be at least 18 years old.
HEALTHCARE DIRECTIVE
Neither of your witnesses may be:
- under the age of 18
- the person who signed your Declaration for you, if you were unable to sign it yourself
- a person entitled to any part of your estate by operation of law or under your will, or
- a person directly financially responsible for your medical care.

INDIANA

DOCUMENT APPOINTING HEALTHCARE REPRESENTATIVE
Your witness must be at least 18 years old.
HEALTHCARE DIRECTIVE
Neither of your witnesses may be:
- under the age of 18
- your parent, spouse or child
- a person entitled to any part of your estate, or
- a person directly financially responsible for your medical care.

IOWA

DOCUMENT APPOINTING HEALTHCARE REPRESENTATIVE
Neither of your witnesses may be:
- under the age of 18
- your healthcare provider, or
- an employee of your healthcare provider.

In addition, one of your witnesses must not be related to you by blood, marriage or adoption within the third degree of consanguinity.
HEALTHCARE DIRECTIVE
Neither of your witnesses may be:
• under the age of 18
• your healthcare provider, or
• an employee of your healthcare provider.
In addition, one of your witnesses must not be related to you by blood, marriage or adoption within the third degree of consanguinity.

KANSAS

DOCUMENT APPOINTING HEALTHCARE REPRESENTATIVE
Neither of your witnesses may be:
• under the age of 18
• related to you by blood, marriage or adoption
• entitled to any part of your estate by operation of law or under your will, or
• directly financially responsible for your healthcare.
HEALTHCARE DIRECTIVE
Neither of your witnesses may be:
• under the age of 18
• the person who signed your Declaration for you, if you were unable to sign it yourself
• related to you by blood or marriage
• entitled to any part of your estate by operation of law or under your will, or
• directly financially responsible for your healthcare.

KENTUCKY

Neither of your witnesses may be:
• related to you by blood
• your beneficiary by operation of Kentucky law
• your attending physician
• an employee of a healthcare facility where you are a patient, or
• directly financially responsible for your healthcare.

MAINE

DOCUMENT APPOINTING HEALTHCARE REPRESENTATIVE
Your witnesses must be at least 18 years old.
HEALTHCARE DIRECTIVE
No requirements.

MARYLAND

DOCUMENT APPOINTING HEALTHCARE REPRESENTATIVE
Neither of your witnesses may be:
• under the age of 18, or
• your healthcare representative.
In addition, one of your witnesses must not be entitled to any part of your estate or any financial benefit by reason of your death.
HEALTHCARE DIRECTIVE
One of your witnesses must not be entitled to any part of your estate or any financial benefit by reason of your death.

MASSACHUSETTS

DOCUMENT APPOINTING HEALTHCARE REPRESENTATIVE
Neither of your witnesses may be:
• under the age of 18, or
• your healthcare representative.
HEALTHCARE DIRECTIVE
No requirements.

MICHIGAN

DOCUMENT APPOINTING HEALTHCARE REPRESENTATIVE
Neither of your witnesses may be:
• under the age of 18
• your healthcare representative
• your spouse, parent, child, grandchild or sibling
• your healthcare provider
• an employee of your life or health insurance provider
• an employee of a healthcare facility where you are a patient
• an employee of a home for the aged where you live, or
• your presumptive heir or known devisee.
HEALTHCARE DIRECTIVE
No requirements.

MINNESOTA

Neither of your witnesses may be:
• your healthcare representative, or
• entitled to any part of your estate by operation of law or under your will.

MISSISSIPPI

DOCUMENT APPOINTING HEALTHCARE REPRESENTATIVE
Neither of your witnesses may be:
- under the age of 18
- your healthcare representative
- related to you by blood, marriage or adoption
- a healthcare provider
- an employee of a healthcare provider or facility, or
- a person entitled to any part of your estate by operation of law or under your will.

HEALTHCARE DIRECTIVE
Neither of your witnesses may be:
- related to you by blood or marriage
- your attending physician
- an employee of your attending physician
- a person with a claim against your estate, or
- a person entitled to any part of your estate by operation of law or under your will.

MISSOURI

DOCUMENT APPOINTING HEALTHCARE REPRESENTATIVE
No Witnesses.
HEALTHCARE DIRECTIVE
Neither of your witnesses may be:
- under the age of 18, or
- the person who signed your Declaration for you, if you were unable to sign it yourself.

MONTANA

DOCUMENT APPOINTING HEALTHCARE REPRESENTATIVE
No Witnesses.
HEALTHCARE DIRECTIVE
No requirements.

NEBRASKA

DOCUMENT APPOINTING HEALTHCARE REPRESENTATIVE
Neither of your witnesses may be:
- your healthcare representative
- your attending physician
- your spouse, parent, child, grandchild or sibling
- your presumptive heir or known devisee, or
- an employee of your life or health insurance provider.

In addition, one of your witnesses must not be an administrator or employee of your healthcare provider.
HEALTHCARE DIRECTIVE
No requirements.

NEVADA

DOCUMENT APPOINTING HEALTHCARE REPRESENTATIVE
Neither of your witnesses may be:
- under the age of 18
- your healthcare representative
- a healthcare provider
- an employee of a healthcare provider
- the operator of a healthcare facility, or
- an employee of the operator of a healthcare facility.

In addition, one of your witnesses must not be related to you by blood, marriage or adoption and must not be entitled to any part of your estate by operation of law or under your will.
HEALTHCARE DIRECTIVE
No requirements.

NEW HAMPSHIRE

DOCUMENT APPOINTING HEALTHCARE REPRESENTATIVE
Your witnesses must be at least 18 years old.
HEALTHCARE DIRECTIVE
Neither of your witnesses may be:
- your spouse
- your heir at law
- your attending physician
- any person acting under the direction or control of the attending physician, or
- a person with a claim against your estate.

If you are a resident of a healthcare facility or a patient in a hospital, no more than one witness may be the healthcare provider or the provider's employee.

NEW JERSEY

DOCUMENT APPOINTING HEALTHCARE REPRESENTATIVE
Your witnesses must be at least 18 years old.
HEALTHCARE DIRECTIVE
Neither of your witnesses may be:
- under the age of 18, or
- your healthcare representative.

NEW MEXICO

DOCUMENT APPOINTING HEALTHCARE REPRESENTATIVE
No witnesses.
HEALTHCARE DIRECTIVE
No requirements.

NEW YORK

DOCUMENT APPOINTING HEALTHCARE REPRESENTATIVE
Neither of your witnesses may be:
- under the age of 18, or
- your healthcare representative.

HEALTHCARE DIRECTIVE
No requirements.

NORTH CAROLINA

DOCUMENT APPOINTING HEALTHCARE REPRESENTATIVE
Neither of your witnesses may be:
- under the age of 18
- related to you by blood or marriage
- an employee of your life or health insurance provider
- an employee of a healthcare facility that is treating you
- an employee of a nursing or group home where you reside
- your heir or beneficiary under your will, or
- a person with a claim against you.

HEALTHCARE DIRECTIVE
Neither of your witnesses may be:
- related to you by blood or marriage
- your attending physician
- an employee of your attending physician
- an employee of a healthcare facility where you are a patient
- an employee of a nursing or group home where you reside
- a person entitled to any part of your estate by operation of law or under your will, or
- a person with a claim against you.

NORTH DAKOTA

DOCUMENT APPOINTING HEALTHCARE REPRESENTATIVE
Neither of your witnesses may be:
- under the age of 18
- your spouse
- your healthcare representative
- a healthcare provider
- an employee of a healthcare provider
- the operator of a long-term care facility
- an employee of an operator of a long-term care facility
- a person entitled to any part of your estate upon your death, or
- a person with a claim against your estate.

HEALTHCARE DIRECTIVE
Neither of your witnesses may be:
- related to you by blood or marriage
- your attending physician
- a person with a claim against your estate
- a person entitled to any part of your estate upon your death, or
- a person directly financially responsible for your medical care.

OHIO

DOCUMENT APPOINTING A HEALTHCARE REPRESENTATIVE
Neither of your witnesses may be:
- under the age of 18
- related to you by blood, marriage or adoption
- a physician with or an employee of a healthcare facility that is treating you
- a person with a claim against you, or
- your heir or beneficiary under your will.

HEALTHCARE DIRECTIVE
Neither of your witnesses may be:
- related to you by blood, marriage or adoption
- a physician
- an employee or agent of a physician or healthcare facility, or
- a person who is entitled to benefit in any way from your death.

OKLAHOMA

Neither of your witnesses may be:
- under the age of 18
- a person with an interest in your estate, or
- a person named to inherit property in your will or other estate planning document.

OREGON

Neither of your witnesses may be:
- your healthcare representative or alternative representative .
- related to you by blood, marriage or adoption
- your attending physician
- an owner, operator, or employee of a healthcare facility where you are a resident, or
- a person entitled to any part of your estate upon your death.

PENNSYLVANIA

DOCUMENT APPOINTING HEALTHCARE REPRESENTATIVE
Your witnesses must be at least 18 years old.
HEALTHCARE DIRECTIVE
Neither of your witnesses may be:
- under the age of 18, or
- the person who signed your Declaration for you, if you were unable to sign it yourself.

RHODE ISLAND

DOCUMENT APPOINTING HEALTHCARE REPRESENTATIVE
Neither of your witnesses may be:
- under the age of 18
- your healthcare representative
- a healthcare provider
- an employee of a healthcare provider
- the operator of a community care facility, or
- an employee of an operator of a community care facility.

In addition, one of your witnesses must not be related to you by blood, marriage or adoption, and must not be entitled to any part of your estate by operation of law or under your will.
HEALTHCARE DIRECTIVE
Your witnesses may not be related to you by blood or marriage.

SOUTH CAROLINA

Neither of your witnesses may be:
- related to you by blood, marriage or adoption
- your attending physician
- an employee of your attending physician
- a person directly financially responsible for your medical care
- a person entitled to any part of your estate by operation of law or under your will
- a beneficiary of your life insurance policy, or
- a person who has a claim against your estate

No more than one of your witnesses may be an employee of a healthcare facility where you are a patient. If you are in a hospital or nursing care facility when you sign your declaration, at least one of your witnesses must be an ombudsman designated by the state.

SOUTH DAKOTA

DOCUMENT APPOINTING HEALTHCARE REPRESENTATIVE
Your witnesses must be at least 18 years old.
HEALTHCARE DIRECTIVE
Your witnesses must be at least 18 years old.

TENNESSEE

DOCUMENT APPOINTING HEALTHCARE REPRESENTATIVE
Neither of your witnesses may be:
- your healthcare representative
- related to you by blood, marriage or adoption
- a healthcare provider
- an employee of a healthcare provider
- the operator of a healthcare institution
- an employee of a healthcare institution
- a person who has a claim against your estate, or
- your heir or beneficiary under a will or by operation of law.

HEALTHCARE DIRECTIVE
Neither of your witnesses may be:
- related to you by blood or marriage
- your attending physician
- an employee of your attending physician
- an employee of a healthcare facility where you are a patient
- a person with a claim against your estate, or
- a person entitled to any part of your estate by operation of law or under your will.

TEXAS

DOCUMENT APPOINTING HEALTHCARE REPRESENTATIVE
Neither of your witnesses may be:
- your healthcare representative
- related to you by blood, marriage or adoption
- your health or residential care provider
- an employee of your health or residential care provider
- the operator of a healthcare facility
- the employee of an operator of a healthcare facility
- your creditor or any other person with a claim against you, or
- a person entitled to any part of your estate by operation of law or under your will.

HEALTHCARE DIRECTIVE
Neither of your witnesses may be:
- related to you by blood or marriage
- your attending physician
- an employee of your attending physician
- a patient in a healthcare facility where your are a patient
- a person with a claim against your estate, or
- a person entitled to any part of your estate upon your death.

Your witnesses may be employees of a healthcare facility where you are a patient only if they are not involved in providing direct care to you and not involved in the financial affairs of the facility.

UTAH

DOCUMENT APPOINTING HEALTHCARE REPRESENTATIVE
No witnesses.
HEALTHCARE DIRECTIVE
Neither of your witnesses may be:
- under the age of 18
- the person who signed your Directive for you, if you were unable to sign it yourself
- related to you by blood or marriage
- a person entitled to any part of your estate by operation of law or under your will
- a person directly financially responsible for your medical care, or
- an agent of a healthcare facility where you are a patient.

VERMONT

DOCUMENT APPOINTING HEALTHCARE REPRESENTATIVE
Neither of your witnesses may be:
- under the age of 18
- your healthcare representative
- your spouse
- your health or residential care provider
- an employee of your health or residential care provider
- your heir or a beneficiary under your will, or
- your creditor or any other person with a claim against you.
HEALTHCARE DIRECTIVE
Neither of your witnesses may be:
- your spouse
- your heir
- your attending physician
- an employee of your attending physician, or
- a person with a claim against your estate.

VIRGINIA

DOCUMENT APPOINTING HEALTHCARE REPRESENTATIVE
Neither of your witnesses may be:
- under the age of 18
- related to you by blood, or
- your spouse.
HEALTHCARE DIRECTIVE
Neither of your witnesses may be your spouse or blood relative.

WASHINGTON

DOCUMENT APPOINTING HEALTHCARE REPRESENTATIVE
No requirements.
HEALTHCARE DIRECTIVE
Neither of your witnesses may be:
- related to you by blood or marriage
- your attending physician
- an employee of your attending physician
- an employee of a healthcare facility where you are a patient, or
- a person entitled to any part of your estate by operation of law or under your will.

WEST VIRGINIA

DOCUMENT APPOINTING HEALTHCARE REPRESENTATIVE
Neither of your witnesses may be:
- under the age of 18
- your healthcare representative or successor representative
- the person who signed your document, if you were unable to sign it yourself
- related to you by blood or marriage
- your attending physician
- a person directly financially responsible for your medical care, or
- a person entitled to any part of your estate by operation of law or under your will.
HEALTHCARE DIRECTIVE
Neither of your witnesses may be:
- under the age of 18
- your healthcare representative or successor representative
- the person who signed your Living Will, if you were unable to sign it yourself
- related to you by blood or marriage
- your attending physician
- a person directly financially responsible for your medical care, or
- a person entitled to any part of your estate by operation of law or under your will.

WISCONSIN

DOCUMENT APPOINTING HEALTHCARE REPRESENTATIVE
Neither of your witnesses may be:
- under the age of 18
- your healthcare representative
- related to you by blood, marriage or adoption
- your healthcare provider
- an employee of your healthcare provider, other than a chaplain or a social worker
- an employee of an inpatient healthcare facility where you are a patient, other than a chaplain or a social worker
- a person directly financially responsible for your medical care, or

- a person with a claim against your estate.

HEALTHCARE DIRECTIVE

Neither of your witnesses may be:

- related to you by blood, marriage or adoption
- your healthcare provider
- an employee of your healthcare provider, other than a chaplain or a social worker
- an employee of an inpatient healthcare facility where you are a patient, other than a chaplain or a social worker
- a person directly financially responsible for your medical care, or
- a person who has a claim against your estate.

WYOMING

DOCUMENT APPOINTING HEALTHCARE REPRESENTATIVE

Neither of your witnesses may be:

- under the age of 18
- your healthcare representative
- a healthcare provider
- an employee of a healthcare provider
- the operator of a community care facility, or
- the employee of an operator of a community care facility.

In addition, one of your witnesses must not be related to you by blood, marriage or adoption, and must not be entitled to any part of your estate by operation of law or under your will.

HEALTHCARE DIRECTIVE

Neither of your witnesses may be:

- the person who signed your Declaration for you if you were unable to sign it yourself
- related to you by blood or marriage
- directly financially responsible for your medical care, or
- entitled to any part of your estate by operation of law or under your will.

4. Glossary of Witnessing Terms

If you have read the requirements for witnesses in your state in the preceding section, and are up against a particularly obtuse legislature that has included words that do not faintly ring bells for you, this section provides brief definitions of the terms that most commonly occur.

Beneficiary. Any person who is entitled to receive property belonging to a deceased person.

Beneficiary of a will. Any person or organization named in a will to receive property, either as a first choice or if the first choice as beneficiary does not survive the person making the will.

Claim against the estate. Any right that a person has to receive property from a person's estate. This may arise under a will or living trust, from a contract or because of a legal liability that the deceased owes to the person.

Codicil. An amendment to a will, prepared with the same formality as is required for the will.

Devisee. A person who has been named to receive property in a will.

Domicile. The state where the person makes his or her home.

Duress. Threats of physical or other harm used to coerce a person to act against his or her free will. In will contests, the concern is that someone is using threats and pressure that cause a person to write a will that does not reflect true wishes for how property should be divided and distributed.

Heir at law. Any person who qualifies to inherit property from a person on the basis of his or her relationship with that person. Usually, heirs at law are spouses, children, parents, brothers and sisters. However, if none of these people exist, an heir at law might be a niece, nephew or even a distant cousin.

Inchoate claim. A claim against a person's estate that does not yet exist but might if certain conditions occur. For instance, a person named as an alternate beneficiary in a will has an inchoate claim against the estate—conditional upon the first choice beneficiary not surviving the person making the will.

Inherit by operation of law. When a person dies owning property that has not been distributed in a will or by some other legal device such as a living trust, the property will be distributed according to the laws of the state where the person died—that is, by operation of law. These laws—commonly referred to as the "laws of intestate succession"—usually cause the property to be distributed first to a spouse and children and then to parents, brothers and sisters.

Intestate succession. Rules that a state uses to decide what should happen to the property of a deceased individual if the property has not be left in a will or other legal device—such as a living trust. While the rules are slightly different for every state, the property will go first to a spouse and children, and if none survive, then to brothers and sisters and parents.

Known devisee. Any person who either is entitled to inherit property from a person under the state's law or who has been named to inherit the property in a will or living trust.

Lawful heirs. Anyone who is entitled to inherit property from a deceased person under the state's laws of intestate succession.

Legatee. A person who has been named to receive property in a will.

Presumptive heir. Any person who either is entitled to inherit property from a person under the state's law or who has been named to inherit the property in a will or living trust.

Rules of descent and distribution. Rules that a state uses to decide what should happen to the property of a deceased individual if the property has not been left in a will or other legal device—such as a living trust.

While the rules are slightly different for every state, the property will go first to a spouse or children, and if there are not any, then to brothers and sisters and parents.

Testamentary instrument. A document that describes who is to receive property upon the death of the person making the document and that goes into effect when the document maker dies.

Undue influence. Any improper or wrongful constraint or persuasion that overcomes the free will of another. In will contests, this is similar to duress, but the wrongdoer is more likely to be in some position of authority over the willmaker.

N. Making and Distributing Copies

Ideally, you should make an effort to make your wishes for your future healthcare widely known. Keep a copy of your healthcare directive, and give other copies to:

- any physician with whom you now consult regularly
- the proxy you named in your directive
- the office of the hospital or other care facility in which you are likely to receive treatment
- the patient representative of your HMO or insurance plan
- close relatives, particularly immediate family members—a spouse, children, siblings, and
- trusted friends.

Some people are hesitant to discuss the particulars of their medical care with other people, feeling that it is an intensely private issue. However, in the case of healthcare directives, you must weigh this yen for privacy against the need for the documents to be effective. Your carefully-reasoned medical directive will simply be wasted words unless you make sure it gets into the hands of the people who need to know about it.

At a minimum, give copies of your signed and completed healthcare directive to the doctors or medical facility most likely to be treating you and to any proxy you have named.

 Keep Your Documents Together

If you have named a healthcare representative or proxy, he or she will need to have a copy of your healthcare directive to learn the specific details of your medical care directions. And hospital personnel will need to see a copy of the Durable Power of Attorney for Healthcare that authorizes your agent to supervise your wishes, to get copies of your medical records and to hire and fire medical personnel.

O. Keeping Your Documents Up to Date

Review your healthcare documents occasionally—at least once a year—to make sure they still accurately reflect your wishes for your medical care. Advances in technology and changes in health are two changes in course that prompt many people to change their minds about the kind of healthcare they want.

In addition, you should consider making new documents if:

- you move to another state (see Section D2 for more information on this point)

- you made and finalized a healthcare directive many years ago, because your state's law controlling them have probably changed substantially, and

- the proxy or representative you named to supervise your wishes becomes unable to do so.

P. Revoking Your Documents

If you have a change of mind and wish to revoke or cancel your healthcare directive, you can do so at any time. The safest, most direct and most common sense way to cancel your document is to destroy it physically—by burning it up or tearing it into pieces. Be sure to contact all those who have copies of your document and ask that the copies be returned so you can destroy them, too.

Q. Expressing Additional Concerns

After using WillMaker, review your healthcare directive to make sure it is the best possible expression of your tangible wishes for medical care. If you feel frustrated that your documents do not address a vital concern you have, there are several additional steps you can take.

PUTTING TIME LIMITS ON LIFE-PROLONGING TREATMENT

A number of people are guided by the feeling that they would like to have invasive life-prolonging care such as CPR and respirators for a limited but specific time—three to six months, for example. After that time elapses without medical improvement they would like to dictate that they be allowed to die naturally, without medical intervention of any kind. Such wishes—which require a subjective judgment to assess medical improvement and require a firm hand to impose time limits in treatment—do not fit easily on conventional healthcare directives.

If you want to put specific time limits on the medical treatments and procedures that may be administered to you, conventional healthcare directives may not be your best route. In such cases, it may be best to discuss your thoughts with medical personnel. Then see an experienced lawyer to help craft a specialized durable power of attorney for healthcare, in which you name another person to enforce your specific directions. (See Chapter 15.)

1. Talking With Doctors

There is no substitute for talking over your medical care wishes with the doctors who will be likely to provide your care. Unfortunately, this task is made more difficult by reality. Few people have the luxury of cultivating a meaningful relationship with any individual doctor. Soaring costs of medical care and cutbacks in insurance coverage have made many people miserly about making medical appointments. And many now depend for medical care on monolithic medical centers, in which it is sheer happenstance if you see the same healthcare provider more than once. Most of us die in the hands of medical personnel who are strangers to us.

However, if you do have a regular doctor, or if you are approaching surgery or some other drastic medical event and have been assigned to a specialist, talk over your directive with him or her. If you have other, more subjective concerns about your medical condition, such as the effects of certain treatments or the probability of carrying on certain life activities, discuss those, too.

2. Talking With Family Members and Friends

It is also best to discuss your healthcare directives and other medical care concerns with family members and close friends who are likely to oversee or witness your care. Unfortunately, this urging, too, is sometimes frustrated by reality. Families these days are often flung far across the map. And even those who remain geographically close often stray from the Ozzie and Harriet ideal of familial harmony.

Still, those who make the effort to discuss the hard topic of what kind of medical care they want if incapacitated usually find the effort worth the price. Not only do those involved get peace of mind in knowing true wishes, the knowledge can often be a bridge to closer relationships. If the topic seems too difficult to broach, consider using a relevant book or magazine article, television show or film as a catalyst for discussion.

3. Writing a Letter Expressing Other Wishes

WillMaker produces a healthcare directive that is a straightforward and unambiguous expression of wishes about medical care. For most people, this provides the best framework and the most effective way to convey their thoughts to the medical establishment that will ultimately provide the care.

But for some people, medical directives—no matter how specifically they address wishes about respirators and surgery—do not reach the heart of their concerns: money available for care, dying with dignity, quality of life, the well-being of those who care for them. These more worldly worries may be a far stronger pull than possible differences in the medical care they might receive if stricken by a coma or terminal illness. For them, their wishes sound simple, and the pieces of paper comprising healthcare directives seem unfulfilling.

Your true concerns may reflect a number of motivations and fears. For example, you may feel strongly that you would not want:

- to have a spouse become bankrupt spending money on your medical care

- to have your life prolonged by medical intervention if you become unable to live at home, or

- to have life-saving surgery performed if you were never able to walk or talk again.

These are all valid human concerns that do not fit neatly on the lines of your medical directives. If such concerns are paramount in your mind when thinking about the type or duration of medical care you would want, write them in a letter that you attach to your healthcare directives. And because it is not uncommon for such thoughts to change over time, you can update this letter as your need arises. Again, it is best to talk over these thoughts with your doctors and loved ones, if possible. Your letter may help introduce your wishes—and emphasize to others that your feelings are important to you.

■

CHAPTER 14

Final Arrangements

Most people avoid the subject of death—and are especially uncomfortable thinking about their own mortality. You, too, may be tempted to leave the details of your final arrangements for what happens to your body after death to those who survive you.

But, as discussed in this chapter, there are two good reasons not to do this: care and cost.

A. Making Final Arrangements in Advance

Anyone who has lost a loved one knows how agonizing it can be to decide what he or she would have wanted as a commemoration. And most people have attended funerals or other after-death services that seem uniquely unsuited to the person who has died.

Letting your survivors know what kind of disposition and ceremonies you envision saves them the pain of making such decisions at what is likely to be a difficult time for them.

And many family members and friends have found that an open discussion of preferences for final arrangements is a grand relief—especially if a person is elderly or in poor health and death is likely to occur soon.

Planning some of these details in advance can also help save money. For many people, after-death goods and services are the third most costly expense—just after a home and a car. Advance planning, with some wise comparison shopping, can help ensure that costs will be controlled or kept to a minimum.

Without some direction, your survivors are most likely to choose the most expensive goods and services available, to assuage their own feelings of guilt or grief or due to coercion by funeral industry providers.

The best way to prevent this from happening is to leave a written instruction of your preferences with as much detail as you are able to give.

A WILL IS NOT THE WAY

Many people think of a will as the proper document in which to specify final instructions for whether they want to be buried or cremated and whether they wish to have any ceremonies held after they die.

In fact, a will should be reserved only for directions on how to divide and distribute your property, and, if you wish, may include your preferences for who should get care and custody of your minor children after you die.

But a will is a singularly poor place to express your death and burial preferences for one simple reason: Your will probably will not be located and read until several weeks after you die—long after the time such final arrangements must occur.

---

1. The Legal Effect of Your Document

In most cases, your arrangements will be carried out as written.

However, if a dispute arises among your loved ones—for example, between your partner or spouse and other relatives—the funeral industry personnel involved are usually bound to follow any written instructions the deceased person has left. The grandest sticking points arise when the deceased person has not provided in advance for payment of the arrangements. (See Section C2.)

Court battles over preferences for body or funeral ceremonies almost never arise, primarily because of the lack of time and the prohibitive cost of litigation.

ATTACHING A LETTER OF EXPLANATION

The document you produce using WillMaker will set out the details of what you want to occur after your death. Depending on your responses while using the WillMaker program, your instructions may be as sparse or as detailed as you wish.

In addition to the specifics of body disposition and ceremonies, some people may want to explain their choices or leave some final message to their survivors. An excellent way to do this is to write a letter and attach it to the Final Arrangements document that WillMaker produces. (See Chapter 11.)

2. What Happens If There Is No Document

If you die without leaving written instructions about your preferences, the person who has the right to control how your remains will be disposed of are determined by state law. In most states, the right—and the liability for paying for the reasonable costs of a disposition—is with the following people, in order:

- surviving spouse
- surviving child or children
- surviving parent or parents
- the next of kin, and
- the public administrator, who is appointed by a court.

Most disputes arise where there is more than one person—three children, for example—who disagree over a fundamental decision, such as whether the body of a parent should be buried or cremated. As mentioned, such disputes can be avoided if you are willing to do some planning—and put your wishes in writing.

IF YOU HAVE ALREADY MADE SOME FINAL ARRANGEMENTS

Those who have already made arrangements for burial or cremation may wonder whether it is necessary to use this portion of the WillMaker program. It would be wise to do so. It will only take a few minutes—and the program may direct your attention to one or more issues that you have not already addressed in your previous arrangements.

In addition, WillMaker produces a document that allows you to organize your thoughts and directions for your final disposition. This may be essential for your survivors who want to see that your wishes are carried out as written. Also, the program prompts you to describe two very common types of arrangements that you may have made:

- donation of one or more organs, and
- donation of your body to a medical institution.

Setting out these arrangements in writing will help assure that the donations are carried out.

B. The Basics of Your Final Arrangements

This portion of the WillMaker program allows you to state your preferences on the following specific issues:

- the name of the mortuary or other institution that will handle your burial or cremation

- whether you wish to be embalmed

- the type of casket or container in which you will be buried or cremated, including whether you want it present at any after-death ceremony

- the details of any ceremony you want before the burial or cremation, including specific clothing and jewelry in which you want your body to be attired

- who your pallbearers will be

- how you will be transported to the cemetery and gravesite

- where your remains will be buried, stored or scattered

- the details of any ceremony you want to accompany your burial, interment or scattering

- the details of any marker you want to show where your remains are buried or interred

- any epitaph you wish placed on your burial marker, and

- the details of any ceremony you want held after you are buried or cremated.

ATTEND TO AS MANY DETAILS AS POSSIBLE

This portion of WillMaker covers a wide variety of after-death details—from specifics of body disposition to the type and tenor of ceremonies you wish to be held. The questions posed to you are intended as a structure so that you can leave the most complete instructions possible.

For people who have very simple plans, many of these questions will not be relevant. And a number of other people may simply be stumped or undecided about some aspects of the instructions they wish to leave.

In the Final Arrangements portion of WillMaker, you need only respond to those questions you wish to answer. While it behooves you and your survivors for you to be as specific as you can in your instructions, the document produced can be as sketchy or complete as you wish. If there is an issue you do not wish to address, simply skip the questions that pertain to it.

C. Help with Your Final Arrangements

There are a number of places you can turn to for help in planning your Final Arrangements.

1. Mortuaries

Most mortuaries or funeral homes are equipped to handle many of the details related to disposing of a person's remains. These include:

- collecting the body from the place of death
- storing the body until it is buried or cremated
- making burial arrangements with a cemetery
- conducting ceremonies related to the burial
- preparing the body for burial, and
- arranging to have the body transported for burial.

2. Memorial or Funeral Societies

Choosing the institution to handle your burial is probably the most important final arrangement that you can make, from an economic standpoint. For this reason, many people join memorial or funeral societies, which help them find local mortuaries that will deal honestly with their heirs and charge prices that accurately reflect the value of their services.

Society members are free to choose whatever final arrangement they wish. Most societies, however, emphasize simple, dignified arrangements over the costly, elaborate services often promoted by the funeral industry.

While the services offered by each society differ, most societies distribute literature and information on options and legal controls on final arrangements.

Members receive a prearrangement form upon joining, which allows them to plan for the goods and services they want—and to get them for a predetermined cost. The society also serves as a watchdog—making sure that individuals get and pay for only the services they have specified.

The cost for joining and getting these organizations is low—usually from $20 to $40 for a lifetime membership, although some societies charge a small renewal fee periodically.

To find a funeral or memorial society nearest you, look in the Yellow Pages of your telephone book under Funeral Information & Advisory Services, or contact the Continental Association of Funeral and Memorial Societies, (800) 458-5563, for additional information.

3. Finding a Mortuary on Your Own

If you are not a member of a funeral or memorial society, then it is important that you find the institution that best meets your needs in terms of style, proximity and cost.

This has become somewhat easier than it used to be, since the Federal Trade Commission (FTC) passed regulations to stem the tide of abuses by the funeral industry. Under the FTC Funeral Rule, those who provide death goods and services must give price lists to consumers who visit a funeral home—and must disclose prices and other information to those who ask for it over the phone.

The law also enables consumers to select and purchase only the goods and services they want, and clamps down on untoward practices such as false or unclear advertising.

However, there is a loophole. Under the law, mortuaries are free to tack on a nebulously referred to as Professional Services or Overhead. If the cost of such services seems out of line with what is being promised, consumers should negotiate to lower it. Charges for other common mortuary services, such as limousine and chapel services, may also be negotiable.

BEWARE OF PREPAYMENT PLANS

Shopping around for the most suitable and affordable funeral goods and services is a wise consumer idea. However, be extremely cautious about paying in advance—or prepaying—for them.

While there are a number of legal controls on how the funeral industry can handle and invest funds earmarked for future services, there are many reported abuses of mismanaged and stolen funds. A great many other abuses go unreported by family members too embarrassed or too grief-stricken to complain.

There are additional pitfalls. When mortuaries go out of business, the consumer who has prepaid is often left without funds and without recourse. Also, many individuals who move to a new locale during their lifetimes are dismayed to find that their prepayment funds are nonrefundable—or that there is a substantial financial penalty for withdrawing or transferring them. In addition, money paid now may not cover inflated costs of the future—meaning that survivors will be left to cover the substantially inflated costs.

If you are interested in setting aside a fund of money to pay for your final arrangements, a more prudent approach for most people is to set up a Totten Trust—a trust or savings plan earmarked to pay for your final arrangements—with a bank or savings institution. Most financial institutions will do so for a very slight charge. And the trust funds are easily transferred or withdrawn if need be and you have complete control over the money during your life.

4. Survivors Caring for the Dead

There is a growing trend in America for people to revert to caring for their own dead, from preparing to burying the deceased person—doing an end-run around all funeral industry personnel.

Despite a monied funeral industry lobby, most states do allow individuals to act completely on their own. But those who do so must be armed with information on what is and what is not allowed. For example, most states have laws that regulate the depth of a site for a body burial.

In addition, the laws in several states—including Louisiana, Massachusetts, Michigan, Nebraska, New Hampshire, New Jersey and New York—specifically require that a funeral director must handle the disposition of a deceased person.

If you are considering directing that a family member or friend handle your disposition independently, consult a local funeral or memorial society for information on what restrictions may apply. In addition, a book entitled *Caring for Your Own Dead* by Lisa Carlson (Upper Access Publishers, Vermont) includes a state-by-state synopsis of relevant statutes and a discussion of other concerns for those who wish to bury their own dead.

D. Body and Organ Donations

There is a growing trend for people to donate their bodies or organs for medical research or transplant after they die.

1. Whole Body Donations

Most medical schools need donations of whole bodies for medical research and instruction—and shortages may be especially acute at osteopathic and chiropractic schools. The reason they are called whole body donations is that the donation will be rejected if any of the organs have been removed.

After using a donated body for study or instruction, a medical institution will usually cremate it—and bury or scatter the cremains in a specified plot. However, the remains or cremains can be returned to family members for burial—usually within a year or two. Those who want the body or cremains returned to a friend or family members for the final disposition should specify this when arranging for the donation.

No medical institution is allowed to buy a body, but there is usually little or no expense to the survivors when a body is donated. When a death occurs, most medical schools will pay to transport the body, as well as pay for any final disposition. Ask the nearest medical institution that accepts body donations whether it has specific arrangements for transporting and disposing of bodies to avoid any unexpected charges.

Body donations are usually arranged with a particular institution while the donor is living, but some institutions will accept the donation at death with the written permission of the next of kin.

There are currently medical schools in every state except for Alaska, Delaware, Idaho, Montana and Wyoming. The medical schools in Arizona, Nebraska, Nevada, South Carolina and Wisconsin have the strictest rules about enrolling in body donation programs before death.

If you live in a state with no medical school or one that has very strict requirements for whole body donations, you may find out more about your body donation options from the National Anatomical Service, which operates 24-hour phone services out of New York (718) 948-2401 and St. Louis (314) 726-9079.

YOUR DONATION MAY BE REJECTED

Even if you have arranged in advance to donate your body to a medical institution, the institution may reject the donation if:

- you have also donated one or more of your organs and these are taken at your death
- the institution's current supply exceeds its demand and there are no facilities for storage
- you die during surgery, or
- your body is unsuitable for study because it is extremely obese, or you have died due to a number of diseases that render it unacceptable according to the institution.

---

2. How to Make Whole Body Donations

Whole body donations must usually be made while you are alive, although some medical schools will accept a cadaver through arrangements made after death.

The best place to contact to arrange a whole body donation is the nearest medical school. Or call the National Anatomical Service at (800) 727-0700 for additional information on body donation.

3. Organ Donations

As medical technology has made successful organ and tissue transplants cheaper, easier and safer, organs and tissues are in great demand.

Among the organs and tissues now commonly being transplanted are:

- corneas
- hearts
- livers
- kidneys
- bone and bone marrow
- tendons, ligaments, connective tissue
- skin
- pancreas, and
- lungs.

Tissues and corneas can be taken from almost anyone—and are often used for research and study. However, there are far greater problems with donating major organs such as hearts and livers. For example, while there are tens of thousands of people now on waiting lists to receive kidneys alone, only about 1% of all people who die are suitable kidney donors.

4. How to Arrange for Organ Donations

The principal method for donating organs is by indicating your intent to do so on a uniform donor card. Once signed, this card identifies you to medical personnel as a potential organ donor.

You can get a donor card or form from most hospitals, the county or state office of the National Kidney Foundation or a community eye bank.

In most states, you can also obtain an organ donation card from the local Department of Motor Vehicles. Depending on where you live, you can check a box, affix a stamp or seal, or attach a separate card to your license, indicating your wish to donate one or more organs.

If you fill out an organ donor card, make sure you tell family members you have done so.

Even if you have not signed a card or other document indicating your intent to donate your organs, your next of kin can approve a donation at the time of your death. And conversely, even if you have indicated an intent to donate your organs, an objection by your next of kin will often defeat your intention; medical personnel will usually not proceed in the face of an objection from relatives. The best safeguard is to discuss your wishes with close friends and relatives, emphasizing your strong feelings about donating your body for research or teaching.

WHEN ORGANS ARE REMOVED

Major organs for transplantation must be taken from a donor who is in reasonably good health—and must be removed while the donor's heart is still beating, but he or she is brain-dead. In reality, nearly all suitable donors of major organs are short-term patients who have been hospitalized and who have received artificial respiration.

Some people fear that agreeing to donate an organ will mean that they run the risk of being declared dead prematurely while eager doctors rush to remove their organs.

There is a strong safeguard against this possibility. Before any organ is removed from a donor, two doctors who are not involved in the transplantation must declare that the patient is "irretrievably deceased"—with an ultimate diagnosis of being brain-dead. From that time on, the cadaver must be maintained on a respirator to keep blood flowing through the organ.

TELL OTHER PEOPLE ABOUT YOUR WISHES

For organ donations to be successful, several people must know about the arrangement before you die. These people are your doctors, personnel at the hospital or other healthcare facility where you die, and the people who your doctors or the institution are likely to contact if there are any questions about the donation. These might be your spouse, other close relatives or the people you have named to supervise your healthcare in a durable power of attorney or other document. At a minimum, it is essential that you notify your spouse and closest relatives about your wishes for organ donation.

5. Laws on Organ Donations

In most states, if a deceased person has not left explicit instructions about donating an organ, a coroner must make a reasonable search for a deceased's person's next of kin or get the express consent of the next of kin before an organ may be removed for donation.

However, many states have recently passed laws that specify that a coroner may authorize that certain organs, body parts or tissues be removed from a body as long as certain conditions are met.

Under these laws, you become an automatic organ donor when you die and need not take any action while you are alive. But usually one or more of the following conditions must be satisfied first:

- There must be a request for the organ by a qualified recipient.

- The removal must not interfere with a pending investigation or autopsy of the body.

- The deceased person must have died under circumstances that already require an inquest by the state medical examiner. Inquests are typically required in deaths with no known cause, deaths when people are not attended by a physician, deaths from diseases that may be a threat to the public health and deaths that appear suspicious, unusual or unnatural.

- The deceased's facial appearance must not be altered in the process of becoming a donor.

- The coroner must not be aware of any objections from the next of kin.

The following are states that have some such form of presumed consent to organ donation.

State	Organ
Arizona	corneas
Arkansas	pituitary gland
California	pituitary gland, corneas
Colorado	pituitary gland, corneas
Connecticut	pituitary gland, corneas
Delaware	corneas
District of Columbia	corneas, aortic and pulmonary heart valves
Florida	corneas
Georgia	eyes, corneas
Illinois	corneas
Indiana	corneas
Iowa	corneas
Kentucky	corneas
Maryland	corneas
Massachusetts	corneas
Michigan	pituitary gland, corneas
Minnesota	pituitary gland
Mississippi	pituitary gland, corneas, other body tissues
Missouri	pituitary gland
Montana	any body part
Nebraska	eyes, pituitary gland

New Hampshire	corneas
New York	pituitary gland, corneas
North Carolina	corneas
Ohio	pituitary gland, corneas
Oklahoma	pituitary gland, corneas
Pennsylvania	corneas
Tennessee	pituitary gland, corneas
Texas	any body part
Vermont	pituitary gland
Virginia	pituitary gland
Washington	corneas
West Virginia	corneas

E. Burial or Cremation

When using WillMaker, you are asked to decide whether:

- your whole body, minus any organs you have donated, is to be buried in the ground or other place, or

- your body is to be cremated and whether the remains, called cremains, should be buried, stored or scattered.

This choice must be made even if you have arranged to have some organs or your entire body donated to a medical institution. Even if one or more of your organs is accepted for donation, the rest of your body must be disposed of or buried.

Whether you choose cremation or burial, your choice will likely be guided by a number of personal preferences—which may include religion, community custom, family tradition and cost.

Even if you have arranged to have your entire body donated, there is the possibility that donation may be rejected because of the condition of your body or simply because it is not needed. Also, after the medical institution has finished using the body for teaching or research, it must be disposed of or buried—usually, between one to two years after it is accepted for donation.

1. Body Burial

While cremation is gaining popularity as an option, most bodies in the U.S. are buried. Contrary to popular misconception, embalming prior to burial is not usually required by law. However, a number of other substantial charges may be added for:

- getting and processing the death certificate
- transporting the body
- opening and closing a grave
- burial vaults, required by most cemeteries
- the cost of a casket, and
- additional handling and service charges paid to funeral industry personnel.

2. Cremation

When a body is cremated, it is heated intensely—1,800 degrees Fahrenheit or higher—in an ovenlike device called a retort, until it is reduced to several pounds of ash and some fragments of bones, called cremains. The entire process usually takes from two to three hours.

Larger bone fragments within the cremains are usually pulverized before being gathered. They can then be placed in an urn or other container to be buried, stored or scattered. The cost of cremation varies widely, but usually runs from $100 to $500—substantially less than embalming and full body burial. The costs differ depending on your locale.

However, a number of other substantial charges may be added for:

- getting and processing the death certificate
- a certificate releasing the body for cremation, issued by a medical examiner or coroner in some locales
- transporting the body
- disposing of the cremains
- the cost of a casket or container, and
- additional handling and service charges paid to funeral industry personnel.

In addition, most cremation facilities require that a pacemaker be removed before a body is cremated, since the devices can explode and damage the cremation chamber—and there is usually a charge for the removal operation.

CREMATION WITNESSES

In recent years, some mortuaries and crematoriums have been disciplined for mixing the remains of the bodies they cremate, in violation of state laws.

While this may not bother some people, others are horrified at the thought of having their remains mixed with those of other people or animals and want to do everything possible to prevent this. One way is to appoint someone to witness the cremation, which forces the mortuary or crematorium to be scrupulous about not mixing cremains and bodies.

Not all mortuaries and crematoriums cooperate to allow this witnessing. If this concerns you, check with the mortuary or crematorium you have selected. If it does not allow witnesses—and witnesses are what you want—select a different institution.

F. Embalming

Embalming is a process in which the blood is drained and replacement fluids are pumped into the body to temporarily retard its disintegration.

1. About Embalming

Embalming has a rich history in the United States. Originally considered barbaric and paganistic, the process first gained popularity during the Civil War, when bodies of the war dead were transported over long distances through tough travel arrangements. When the war ended, embalming was promoted, mostly by those who performed the service, as a hygienic means of preserving the body.

While it has now become a common procedure, embalming is rarely necessary; refrigeration serves the same purpose.

2. When Embalming Is Required

There is a popular misconception that embalming is always required by law after death. In fact, it is legally required only in some states and only in a few instances, such as:

- when a body will be transported by plane or train from one country or state to another

- where there is a relatively long time—usually a week or more—between the death and burial or cremation, and

- in some cases, where the death occurred because of a communicable disease.

3. What Happens If Your Body Is Not Embalmed

If you choose not to be embalmed, that should have no effect on your final arrangements. Your body will be refrigerated until the time of burial, and, if you choose, you can have a funeral or other service with an open casket.

The only effect of not being embalmed will be that if you opt to be buried, your body will decompose within days instead of weeks.

4. The Cost of Embalming

The cost of embalming ranges from about $100 to $500, depending on your location and on the individual setting the rate of the charges.

Refrigeration is usually less costly, involving a daily charge of about $10 to $30, depending on the facility. Some facilities will provide refrigeration free of charge.

G. Caskets

The container in which your body will be buried is called a casket or coffin. This item has been subject to more controversy in recent years than any other aspect of the funeral industry, because it traditionally carries the biggest mark-up of all funeral goods and services.

Anyone who has been asked to choose a casket for a deceased loved one knows the complex feelings that this choice engenders—often a mix of pride and guilt tempered by the reality of affordability. The sales personnel are well aware of their customers' vulnerabilities and some do their best to sell the most expensive models. Lower-priced caskets are often displayed in the dingy, out-of-the-way corners of a funeral home's showroom.

Most funeral establishments now also carry caskets that may be rented and lined with inexpensive liners during viewing of the body instead of purchased for use. However, these too, are generally relegated to far-off, poorly-lit corners—or the funeral director may fail to mention this option to grieving family members.

While they are rare, there are some independent casketmakers or artisans who specialize in making low-cost or uniquely-styled caskets. To locate an independent casketmaker, check the Yellow Pages of your telephone book under Funeral Information and Advisory Services, or a similar heading. Your local funeral or memorial society may also provide guidance on how to find a local independent casketmaker.

THE HIGH COST OF CASKETS

Those in the funeral industry mark up the cost of caskets substantially, pricing them from hundreds to many thousands of dollars. The price differentials are usually based on the type of material used for the lining and exterior of the container and the type of hardware used for the handles and clasps. They range from $200 for a simple wooden casket to $20,000 for an elaborate engraved container with goldleaf decorations.

Caskets for children should be priced considerably below adult models.

Most state laws require that caskets displayed in a showroom for potential purchase must be tagged with prices, a description of their composition and identifying model numbers. If an establishment uses a catalog to show the caskets it offers for sale or order, the same information must be included there. These laws allow individuals who have decided on a particular type or model of casket to comparison shop for the best price.

H. Ceremonies

Death often involves at least one ceremony and sometimes more. The most common is the funeral, which occurs just prior to burial—although smaller informal ceremonies, often called wakes or visitations, are also commonly held the night before burial occurs. The specific details of a funeral or wake can vary enormously, depending on community custom and the religious, cultural and personal backgrounds of the deceased and his or her survivors.

1. Pre-Burial Ceremonies

There are two good reasons to describe your wishes for a ceremony to be held before your body is buried. The first is that the ceremony is an indirect last way for your survivors—your friends and family members—to say goodbye to you, to comfort one another and to continue the grieving process.

The second is that the more details you arrange while you are alive, the fewer decisions will be left for your survivors at a time when decisions are likely to be hard for them to make.

a. Common elements of pre-burial ceremonies

Some concerns you may wish to address when planning a pre-burial ceremony are:

- where the ceremony should be held

- who should be invited

- whether clergy should be invited to participate, along with specific names of clergy you would like

- any specific music you would like played, along with the names of the musicians or singers you would like to perform it

- preferences for a eulogy, and the name of the person or people you would like to speak

- whether you want your body to be present in a casket at the ceremony, and if so, whether you would like the casket open or closed

- any specific clothing or jewelry in which you wish to be attired, and

- whether you want to direct survivors to send flowers or memorial donations.

MAKING THE CHOICE

Most people will want at least one ceremony held after they die but before they are buried, even if it is simple and informal. However, there may be reasons why a pre-burial ceremony is not appropriate. One may be that you live far from most of your friends and family members, and they would have to drop everything and attend a pre-burial ceremony at a great personal cost.

Since burial typically occurs within a few days of death, attending ceremonies held before burial can be very disruptive. For this reason, many people opt not to have a funeral, but instead prefer a memorial ceremony, usually held days or weeks after the burial, that is more accessible to more people.

2. Pre-Cremation Ceremonies

The most common of these ceremonies is the funeral, which occurs just prior to burial—although smaller informal ceremonies, often called wakes or visitations are also commonly held before cremation occurs.

The specific details of a funeral or wake can vary enormously, depending on community custom and the religious, cultural and personal backgrounds of the deceased and his or her survivors.

a. Common elements of pre-cremation ceremonies

While people who choose cremation over body burial are often predisposed to direct that any ceremonies held be low on frills, you are free to direct your pre-cremation ceremony to be as simple or as elaborate as you like.

Some concerns you may wish to address when planning a pre-cremation ceremony are:

- where the ceremony should be held

- who should be invited

- whether clergy should be invited to participate, along with specific names of clergy you would like

- any specific music you would like played, along with the names of the musicians or singers you would like to perform it

- preferences for a eulogy, and the name of the person or people you would like to speak

- whether you want your cremains present at the ceremony, either in a casket or other container, or whether you would like a picture displayed, instead, and

- whether you want to direct survivors to send flowers or memorial donations.

3. Informal Get-Togethers

Some people wish to direct that an unstructured gathering of friends and family be held before their bodies are buried or cremated, usually in an informal setting such as a home or perhaps a favorite restaurant or club. This is a common choice for people who have not adhered to a specific religion during their lifetimes—and for those who are not strongly tied to family or community traditions.

a. Common elements of informal get-togethers

There are few common elements to more informal after-death ceremonies, which range from the austere to the zany. These ceremonies are most dependent upon the whims and wishes of the deceased person. If you want some sort of informal ceremony held after your death, at a minimum, you may wish to consider:

- where the ceremony should be held

- who should be invited

- any specific music you would like played, along with the names of the musicians or singers you would like to perform it

- preferences for a eulogy, and the name of the person or people you would like to speak, and

- whether you want to direct survivors to send flowers or memorial donations.

There are a great number of additional details you can specify, of course. Some people have directed the survivors who attend to wear bright colored clothing, to bring their favorite pets, to read a favorite poem.

4. Funerals

A traditional funeral is a brief ceremony, most often held in a funeral home chapel or a church. The body is usually present—either in an open or a closed casket. Beyond that, there are no absolutes or requirements about what constitutes a funeral. If the deceased person adhered to a particular religion, funerals often include a brief mass, blessing or prayer service.

In some traditions, only family members attend the funeral, while friends and the general public are invited to attend other scheduled ceremonies. In other locales and traditions, this is reversed—and the funeral is the less private event.

Some concerns you may wish to address when planning a funeral are:

- where the ceremony should be held

- who should be invited

- whether clergy should be invited to participate, along with specific names of clergy you would like

- any specific music you would like played, along with the names of the musicians or singers you would like to perform it

- preferences for a eulogy, and the name of the person or people you would like to speak

- whether you want your body or cremains present at the ceremony, either in a casket or other container, or whether you would like a picture displayed, instead, and

- whether you want to direct survivors to send flowers or memorial donations.

a. Pallbearers

In some funeral ceremonies, the casket is carried to and from the place where the ceremony is held—and sometimes again carried from a transportation vehicle to a burial site. The people who carry the casket are termed pallbearers. If you envision a ceremony in which your casket will be carried, you can name here people you would wish to serve as pallbearers.

The number of pallbearers usually ranges from four to eight, but you can name as many or as few as you wish here.

b. Transportation to grave

You may have a preference about the type of vehicle that will carry your body to the cemetery and gravesite from the place where the funeral ceremony is held. This might be a horse-drawn carriage, a favorite antique car or a stretch limousine.

If you have selected a mortuary to handle some of your arrangements, it may have only one type of vehicle available. If the vehicle customarily provided is not what you would want for yourself, check to be sure the mortuary is flexible about that—and be sure that it will not add its transportation charge to your costs. If this is an important issue for you, check with the mortuary you selected earlier and, if their arrangements about transportation are not satisfactory, shop for another mortuary.

5. Commitment Ceremonies

In addition to or instead of holding a ceremony prior to burial, it is common to hold a brief ceremony at the gravesite at which a religious leader or relative or family friend says a few prayers or words of farewell.

If this is something you want, and have an idea of who should be there, who should speak and what they should say, describe those details.

6. Memorial Ceremonies

A memorial ceremony is an informal ceremony held to commemorate someone who has died. It usually takes place some time after burial or cremation, so the body is not usually present. Memorial ceremonies may be held anywhere—a mortuary, religious building, a home, outside or even a restaurant.

Because memorial ceremonies are not structured or dominated by those in the funeral industry, there is more opportunity to tailor them to the deceased person's personality than a traditional funeral. Memorial ceremonies are more often the choice of those who wish to have an economic, simple after-death commemoration.

While traditional professionals—funeral directors, grief counselors, clergy—may be involved in memorial ceremonies, they are not the people to consult for objective advice. Many will advocate that traditional funerals—traditionally more costly and less personalized—are most effective in helping survivors through the mourning process. The truth is that most survivors are likely to take the greatest comfort in attending a ceremony that reflects the wishes and personality of the deceased person.

I. Final Disposition of Your Body

Your directions for the final disposition of your body will turn on your initial decision of whether you opt for a body burial or cremation.

1. Body Burial

If you have a decided upon a cemetery in which you wish to be buried, describe it here. If you have purchased a gravesite in advance, describe it—and attach any pertinent documents to the Final Arrangements document that will print out when you are finished using this portion of WillMaker.

If you have not purchased a gravesite, but you have a preference as to the part of the cemetery you want to be buried in, state that preference here. There is no guarantee that it will be available to you when you die, but your survivors will know what you had in mind.

2. Scattering Cremains

Many people wish to have their cremated remains, or cremains, scattered over some area that has special significance for them—a garden, look-out point or the ocean.

California is the only state that has specific legal controls over the disposition of cremains. That law was passed after a commercial scattering firm was discovered to have mishandled cremains and consistently overcharged for its services. In California, cremains may be scattered at sea after being removed from their container; however, a verified statement must be filed nearest the point where the scattering occurred. Also in California, cremains may be buried, but may not be scattered on land.

Wisconsin law requires that cremains must be scattered or buried within 60 days after the body is cremated.

A CAVEAT ON SCATTERING SERVICES

Most people opt to have family members or friends conduct the scattering in private, in their own time and style.

However, there are some commercial firms that arrange to transport and scatter cremains over land or sea. Beware when dealing with such groups. While several masquerade as nonprofit groups by appending the term Society to their names and charging a membership fee, they are in the business for profit.

If you do decide to hire one of these services, make sure you understand their pricing structures in advance. Also, attach a copy of any written agreement you may enter to the Final Arrangements that print out when you are finished using this portion of the WillMaker program.

Contact your local funeral or memorial society—or contact the Continental Association of Funeral and Memorial Societies, (800) 458-5563, for additional information.

3. Placing Cremains in a Container

Crematories will usually arrange to return cremains to a family member or friends in a small, inexpensive plastic or cardboard container. The cremains may then be shipped, buried or placed in a niche above ground in a columbarium.

Some people opt to purchase a special container, usually called an urn, in which to store or bury cremains. There are no legal controls on the size, shape or type of urn that may be used, although a number of columbariums and cemeteries impose restrictions due to space if the cremains will be interred or buried.

Urns may be purchased from funeral homes, usually at a substantial mark-up. A small number of artists now also craft low-cost or specialized urns for cremains. Look in the Yellow Pages under Funeral

Information and Services or a similar heading, or contact the local funeral or memorial society for more information on alternatives for containers for cremains.

4. Burying Cremains

Cremains can be buried in the ground. While there are some legal controls in some states on where the burial may take place—such as that they must be buried a specified distance from a residence—most of these controls are part of local zoning ordinances.

If you wish to have a family member or friend bury your cremains independently, it is a good idea to first check local zoning ordinances to see whether burial is permitted on the site you have chosen. Contact the local funeral or memorial society for more information on local rules about burying cremains.

Cremains can also be buried in a cemetery, either in a special urn garden or in a plot. It is not necessary to place the cremains in an urn before burial, although some places may require a plot liner to prevent the earth from sinking over time.

J. Markers and Headstones

It has become an American tradition—and a requirement in many traditional cemeteries and columbariums—that a marker or headstone be placed to indicate where the remains of the deceased have finally been placed.

1. Crypt Markers

If you have chosen to have your cremains placed in a crypt or drawer in a columbarium, you may wish to have a marker identifying where they are. Depending on the location, you may be restricted to a marker of a certain type or size.

For instance, if your cremains are placed or interred in a columbarium, you may be limited to a plaque of specific dimensions and of a specific style.

2. Cemetery Markers

Many people want the place they are buried to be identified by a marker. Often this consists of an upright block of stone with words engraved on it. Some tend toward the elaborate—including sculptures and detailed etchings. However, many cemeteries require that all grave markers be flush with the ground to facilitate mowing—or may have other restrictions according to either aesthetic or land quality controls.

If you have identified a cemetery where you wish to be buried, check whether it has any restrictions on burial markers. Then, within those constraints, identify the marker you want for your grave.

K. Epitaphs

Perhaps the most entertaining aspect of making final arrangements is choosing the words that you wish to appear on your burial marker. These words are known as your epitaph. Your epitaph can be extremely simple, stating only the years you were born and died—or it can reflect your personality by including a witty saying, favorite phrase or poem.

L. Choosing Someone to Oversee Your Wishes

If you have definite ideas about who should carry out your wishes as you have stated them, name the person.

If you do not name anyone, it is likely that your closest relatives will become responsible.

If you name someone to handle this responsibility, make sure that he or she has a copy of the document that sets out your wishes and agrees to carry them out as you express them.

It is always a good idea to pick an alternate person to carry out your wishes, in case your first choice is unable or unwilling to perform this role when the time comes.

THE IMPORTANCE OF ATTACHING OTHER DOCUMENTS

Many people make burial or cremation arrangements while they are still alive, through a local funeral or memorial society or directly with funeral industry providers. These arrangements may consist of:

- buying a burial plot
- contracting for a specific or similar type of casket, and
- indicating that cremation or burial is preferred.

If you have made any such arrangements, you should have documents that specify them. Attach copies of those documents to the Final Arrangements document you create using this part of WillMaker.

CHAPTER 15

Experts and Legal Research

Experience has shown that most WillMaker users do not need help from a lawyer or other expert. The issues involved in making a basic will are normally straightforward and easy to understand.

The same goes for basic estate planning to avoid probate and save on estate taxes. Legal questions can arise, however, for which you will want to see an expert—especially if you have a very large estate, if you must plan for an incapacitated minor or if you have to deal with the assets of a small business.

A. Consulting an Expert

The first question in deciding if you want to consult an expert is what type of help you need.

Here are a few suggestions.

- A financial planner is probably your best bet if you want to integrate estate planning into the rest of your life, including your retirement. A planner can help advise you about a number of variables such as how much you are saving, the most suitable type of investments given your age and family structure, expected retirement income and insurance needs.

- A certified public accountant (CPA) is most appropriate if you are primarily concerned about determining federal and state death tax liability. If you conclude that you will need a trust or other legal document drafted, this may mean you will also need to consult an attorney. But it is usually best, and less expensive, to start with a CPA.

WHEN A LAWYER MAY BE NEEDED

A lawyer's help is most appropriate if:

- You want to learn more about a specific area of your state's laws when fashioning your will.
- Your estate is likely to be in the $600,000 range or more and will be subject to a substantial federal estate tax unless you engage in tax planning.
- You want to establish a trust, other than a simple trust for your children or others.
- You want to give a gift with complex shared ownership, such as a marital life estate.
- You own a part of a small business and have questions as to the rights of surviving owners and your ownership share.
- You must make arrangements for long-term care of a beneficiary—for example, to create a trust for a disadvantaged child.
- You fear someone will contest your will—for example, on grounds of fraud, undue influence or incompetence.
- You wish to disinherit, or substantially disinherit, your spouse.

B. Finding a Lawyer

Finding a competent lawyer who charges a reasonable fee and respects your efforts to prepare your own will may not be easy. Many lawyers will instinctively react with barely-disguised hostility if you voice a desire to be involved in making your own decisions about drafting your will. But like all generalizations, this one has exceptions. Lawyers who will work willingly and well with people who want to be actively involved in their own legal lives do exist.

Here are some suggestions on how to find one.

1. Friends and Business Associates

Almost anyone running a small business has a relationship with a lawyer. Ask around to find someone you know who has been satisfied with a lawyer's services. If that lawyer does not handle estate planning, he or she will likely know one who does. And because of the continuing relationship with your friend, the lawyer making the referral has an incentive to recommend someone who is competent. These days, most urban areas have a number of lawyers who specialize in estate planning, so if you want a specialist, you do not need to settle for a friend of a friend who does an occasional will.

Also ask people you know in any political or social organization in which you are involved. They may know of a competent lawyer whose attitudes are similar to yours. Senior citizen centers and other groups that advise and assist older people are particularly likely to have a list of local lawyers who specialize in wills and estate planning and who are generally regarded as competent and caring.

2. Group Legal Plans

Some unions, employers and consumer action organizations offer group legal plans to their members or employees, who can obtain comprehensive legal assistance free or for low rates. If you are a member of such a plan, check with it first. Your problem may be covered free of charge. But if the plan gives you only a slight reduction in a lawyer's fee, as many do, keep in mind that you may be referred to a lawyer whose main virtue is the willingness to reduce fees in exchange for a high volume of referrals.

3. Prepaid Legal Plans

Prepaid legal plans are sold by companies such as Bank of America and Amway, and are often offered to credit card holders or sold door-to-door. They typically offer the subscriber the right to have simple questions answered, letters written or a straightforward will drafted. Often, the will that comes with the plan is less sophisticated than WillMaker's, so there is little reason to consult one of these plans merely to draft a simple will. The basic fee in most plans will rarely cover more sophisticated estate planning, but of course, plan lawyers will usually be happy to sell you their time and expertise.

Unfortunately, there is no guarantee that the lawyers available through these plans are of the best caliber. In fact, competent, busy lawyers rarely join these plans because they already have enough business. As with any consumer transaction, if you do go the prepaid route, check out the plan and the credentials of the lawyer to whom you are referred—before signing up.

Whenever you avail yourself of any service offered by these prepaid insurance plans, be forewarned: The lawyer you see receives at most $2 or $3 for dealing with you, and may have agreed to this minimal amount in the hope of finding clients who will pay for extra legal services not covered by the monthly premium. For example, some plans that offer a will for no charge beyond the original membership fee charge hundreds of dollars extra if you want to include a simple children's trust such as the one included in the WillMaker will. So, if the plan lawyer recommends an expensive legal procedure rather than a simple will or probate avoidance device such as a living trust, get a second opinion.

4. Law Clinics

Law clinics such as Hyatt Legal Services and Jacoby & Meyers loudly advertise their low initial consultation fees. This generally means that a basic consultation is cheap—often about $20. Anything beyond that is not so cheap. Generally, the rates are about the same as those charged by the average lawyer in general practice.

What is not advertised is that most clinics have extremely high turnover and, as a result, it is usually impossible to form a long-term relationship with a lawyer. This may be fine if you want a simple question answered. However, if you want a lawyer to help you draft a fairly complicated estate plan and then be available over the years to redraft it a number of times as your needs change, a legal clinic is probably a poor choice.

5. Attorney Referral Services

Most county bar associations maintain referral services that will give you the name of an attorney who practices in your area. Usually you can get a referral to an attorney who claims to specialize in wills and estate planning and who will give you an initial consultation for a low fee. A problem with these services is that they usually provide minimal screening for the attorneys listed, which means those who participate may not be the most experienced or competent. It may be possible to find a skilled estate planning specialist following this approach, but be sure to take the time to check out the credentials and experience of the person to whom you are referred.

6. Classified Ads

Check the classified ads under Attorneys. There are quite a few attorneys around who are no longer interested in handling court-contested matters but do provide consultations at relatively low rates. This could be just what you need—especially if yours is a fairly basic question.

C. Managing a Lawyer

Once you have concluded on the basis of a reliable referral that a particular lawyer is probably competent, your next job is to check his or her attitude. People who use self-help tools such as WillMaker typically expect professionals to help educate them to make their own informed decisions—not to treat them as a traditional, obedient client. Such a match may be difficult to find.

Most important, be sure you have settled your fee arrangement—in writing—at the start of your relationship. Depending on where you live, generally, fees of $100 to $150 per hour are reasonable for a general practice lawyer. Experienced specialists are likely to charge closer to $200 per hour. In addition to the hourly fee, get a clear, written commitment from the lawyer concerning how many hours it is likely to take to resolve your problem.

Finally, ask the lawyer several specific questions about your problem. Pay attention to whether you get clear, concise answers. If not, try someone else. If the lawyer acts wise but says little except to ask that the problem be placed in his or her hands—for a substantial fee, of course—watch out. You are either dealing with someone who does not know the answer and will not admit it—a common complication—or someone who finds it impossible to let go of the Me Expert, You Plebeian philosophy—even more common.

 Get It In Writing

Most disagreements between lawyers and clients involve fees, so be sure to get all the details involving money in writing—including the per hour billing rate or other fee arrangement, the frequency of billing and how the attorney will handle any funds you are required to deposit in advance to cover expenses.

D. Doing Your Own Research

There is often a viable alternative to hiring a lawyer to resolve legal questions that affect your will: You can do your own legal research. This can provide some real benefits for those willing to learn how to do it. Not only will you save some money, you will gain a sense of mastery over an area of law, generating confidence that will stand you in good stead should you have other legal problems.

Fortunately, researching wills and related issues is an area generally well-suited to doing your own legal research. Most problems do not involve massive or abstruse legal questions. Often you need only check the statutes of your state to find one particular provision.

 Getting More Help

Legal Research: How to Find and Understand the Law, by Elias and Levinkind (Nolo Press), gives instructions and examples explaining how to conduct legal research.

First, locate a law library or a public library with a good law collection. There is usually one in your principal county courthouse that is open to the public. The librarians in county law libraries are generally helpful and courteous to nonlawyers who wish to learn to do their own legal research. Ask them how you can locate the state's laws—called codes, laws or statutes. Usually what you want is called the annotated version, which contains both your state's written laws and excerpts from any relevant case decisions and cross references to related articles and commentaries.

Once you have found your state's statutes, check the index for provisions dealing with wills or a specific subject that concerns you. Generally, you will find what you want in the volume of statutes dealing with your state's basic civil or probate laws. These are usually called a name such as Civil Code or Probate Laws. These codes are numbered sequentially, and once you get the correct number in the index, it is easy to find the statute you need.

Once you have looked at the basic statutes in the hardcover volume, and checked the pocket part at the back of the book for any amendments, you should skim the summaries of recent court decisions contained in the Annotation section immediately following the statute. If a summary looks like it might help answer your question, read the full court opinion cited.

■

Index

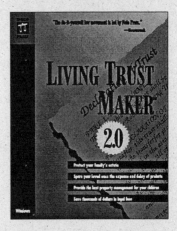